D1611628

Penguin Books
New Writing in Yugoslavia
Edited by Bernard Johnson

NEW
WRITING IN
YUGOSLAVIA

EDITED BY
BERNARD JOHNSON

PENGUIN BOOKS

60162

Penguin Books Ltd, Harmondsworth,
Middlesex, England
Penguin Books Inc., 7110 Ambassador Road,
Baltimore, Maryland 21207, U.S.A.
Penguin Books Australia Ltd, Ringwood,
Victoria, Australia

First published 1970
Copyright © Bernard Johnson, 1970

Made and printed in Great Britain by
Hazell Watson & Viney Ltd,
Aylesbury, Bucks
Set in Linotype Juliana

Contents

6 Contents

3. Kad kuća gori, barem da se čoek ogrije.
   When a house burns down at least someone should be warmed.

4. Ne možeš ti svet ramenon ispraviti.
   You can't straighten out the world with your shoulder.

5. Ko vetar seje, žanje oluju.
 Who sows the wind, reaps the storm.

6. Nebo visoko, a zemlja tvrda.
 The sky is high but the earth is firm.

7. Niko ne zna šta nosi dan, sta li noć.
   No one knows what the day brings, nor what the night.

10. Čega se čovek najviše boji, ovo če mu na glavu doči.
    Whatever a man most fears, it is that which will find him out.

11. Ko za svijetom plače, bez očiju ostaje.
    Who cries for the world is left without eyes.

Foreword

The system of orthography for Yugoslav names used in this book is that of the Croatian Latin alphabet. This is basically a one symbol=one sound system but some letters are used two or three times, with different notation marks above them, to indicate that they are used for differing sounds. Several letters have sounds that are different from their English counterparts. The following are the approximate sounds in English of these letters.

c=ts	j=y (consonant)	dj ⎫ =very approximately j
ć=tsh	š=sh	dž ⎭ as in English 'jam'
č=ch	ž=zh	h =ch as in 'loch'

In addition, in Slovene, Serbo-Croat and Macedonian, all letters are pronounced and all vowels are syllabic: an 'r' in a syllable where there is no other vowel is of vowel quality and is hence syllabic.

Acknowledgements

I should like to express thanks to all my Yugoslav friends who have helped in the compilation of this book; Michael Scammell and Dr E. D. Goy have also been unending sources of help and information. My thanks go out to all the translators who have supplied material. Needless to say, any shortcomings are purely my own responsibility and none of theirs.

B.J.

For poems, acknowledgement is made to: Matija Bečković, Bogomil Djuzel, Danijel Dragojević, Vlado Gotovac, Jovan Hristić, Jure Kaštelan, Kajetan Kovič, Ivan V. Lalić, Slavko Mihalić, Branko Miljković, Miodrag Pavlović, Radovan Pavlovski, Vasko Popa, Stevan Raičković, Tomaž Šalamun, Ljubomir Simović, Ivan Slamnig, Antun Šoljan, Gregor Strniša, Veno Taufer, Dane Zajc.
Acknowledgement is also made to : Miodrag Bulatović, for an extract from the novel *Vuk i Zvono*.
Živko Čingo, for the story *Fromova K'erka*.
Bora Ćosić, for an extract from the novel *Priča o zanatima*.
Dobrica Ćosić, for an extract from the novel *Bajka*.
Vladan Desnica, for the story *Pravda*.
Antonije Isaković, for the story *U znaku aprila*.
Danilo Kiš, for an extract from the novel *Bašta, pepeo*.
Erih Koš, for the story *Čovek koji je znao gde je sever i gde jug*.
Mirko Kovač, for an extract from the novel *Moja sestra Elida*.
Lojze Kovačič, for the sketch *Sporočila v spanju: Bog*.
Ranko Marinković, for the story *Koščene zvijezde*.
Dragoslav Mihajllović, for an extract from the novel *Kad su cvetale tikve*.
Živojin Pavlović, for the story *Prva ljubav*.
Borislav Pekić, for an extract from the novel *Vreme, čuda*.
Meša Selimović, for an extract from the novel *Derviš i smrt*.
Antun Šoljan, for the story *Kiša*.
Aleksandar Tišma, for the story *Ličnost*.

Introduction

This book has been compiled with the intention of presenting a cross-section of artistic prose and poetry which has appeared in Yugoslavia since the war. The responsibility for the choice of its contents is a personal one, but in general the title 'New Writing in Yugoslavia' has been interpreted as referring to the newer currents which have come to the fore in the post-war period. A number of well-known writers have not been included: The Yugoslav Nobel Prize winner Ivo Andrić, Miroslav Krleža, Blaže Koneski, Miloš Crnjanski, Edvard Kocbek, Oskar Davičo, Novak Simić, Dušan Matić, Vesna Perun, Branko Čopić, Desanka Maksimovič, Mihajlo Lalić and Petar Šegedin, to mention but a few. This is because the work of these and some other prominent authors seemed to come partially outside the terms of reference set by 'New Writing', but it should be emphasized that their exclusion was governed by the thematic composition of the book as a whole and by the amount of space available; no disparagement was intended and the reader who is troubled by the absence of such names will find that the majority of these writers have appeared in full-length translations or in earlier anthologies in the United States or this country. On the other hand, a number of older generation writers have been included, notably Meša Selimović, since they are integrally part of the modern current.

In the Yugoslav context, the problem of selection is complex because the areas to be covered are so varied. Yugoslavia has three Slavonic literary languages: Slovene, Macedonian, and the several regional varieties of the main one, Serbo-Croat, which some linguists consider to be the separate, unhappily married languages of the Serbs and the Croats (although the problem is more a historico-cultural than a linguistic one); two widely differing areas of cultural involvement and external influence: Byzantine Greek, Slavonic and Turkish in the south and east, and Latin, Germanic and Italian in the north and along the western seaboard; three major branches of religion, Orthodox, Catholic and Mohammedan, with all that this implies in terms of cultural background, spiritual concepts and material development – all of which has given rise to widely differing regional centres of literary activity which in the past have often functioned for long periods almost independently. So at first sight the anthologist's task is not easy and an attempt at a traditionally 'representative' form seemed unacceptable. The alternative was to group authors together according to the various currents of theme and style predominant in the post-war period, with the result that regional groupings, although not entirely ignored, have been given only secondary importance. The most satisfying feature of this non-regional presentation has been the emergence of clear affinities between writers in each section belonging to completely different regional backgrounds and the resulting whole would seem to be comprehensive and balanced. But perhaps these affinities are not entirely unexpected. Despite immensely different regional backgrounds and tendencies, it would be untrue to say that cultural activities in Yugoslavia today are dispersed. On the contrary, intensive cultural life in the modern setting is in the main restricted to the capital centres of Skopje, Sarajevo, Llubljana, Novi Sad, Zagreb and Belgrade, with the two latter by far the most important. Almost all writers work in these towns, whatever their background or that of their writing. And there is considerable contact between the different centres, even if sometimes only at a personal level, so that although it is still difficult to speak of a 'Yugoslav literature', it is very apparent that literary groupings in the different centres often coincide sufficiently in orientation, theories and aims as to be able to make common cause. So it can be that earlier regional and historical differences are often exaggerated in the face of converging literary trends which cut across the traditional dividing lines.

The second principle of compilation has been to include a sufficient quantity of each author's work to give a fair picture of his writing. Extracts which are too short are often meaningless, but again for reasons of space, the selection of authors has had to be correspondingly severe. The decision also had to be taken to include only literature of the Slave peoples of Yugoslavia; that of important

Hungarian, Rumanian and Albanian minorities could not be given consideration. A balance between writing in Serbo-Croat and that in Slovene and Macedonian was an aim which could also only be achieved arbitrarily, but it seemed indisputable that the major part of the translations should be from the major medium of literature in Yugoslavia, the Serbo-Croat language.

The Yugoslavs themselves consider their own political experiment to be significant, not only in their own country, but also for both Eastern and Western Europe. In the West, considerable publicity has been given to those occasions when political or semi-political figures, such as Djilas and Mihajlov, have come to grief because they published material which went beyond the limits which Yugoslav officialdom at a given moment in the involved game of diplomatic poker with Moscow and Washington was prepared to regard as permissible. Yet such harsh decisions were clearly geared to the external political situation rather than to developments on the literary scene, and in contrast, the position of literature and the writer vis-à-vis the authorities and censorship in Yugoslavia is viewed with envy and admiration by the majority of writers in the Eastern bloc countries, who regard the situation as it has evolved in the Yugoslav environment as a model of the optimum of what they themselves could hope to achieve in their own societies. And since the process of de-Stalinization started early in Yugoslavia, well before Stalin's death, subsequent developments in both political and literary spheres were of enormous significance to writers in Poland, and more directly, in Rumania, Czechoslovakia and Hungary.

Like many intellectuals in the Soviet Union and probably the majority in the other countries of the Eastern bloc covertly, writers in Yugoslavia openly require freedom of expression in print as the prime condition of their creative activity. At the present time they seem to have gone a long way towards achieving this and the atmosphere is to all appearances liberal, with only a few reservations and an occasional contradictory incident; but this, in Eastern Europe exceptional, position was hard won and by no means arrived at overnight. Immediately after the war, post-revolutionary Yugoslavia followed very much the dictates of Moscow and literature went through a period of Zhdanovism which only began to end with the political break with Stalin. The disappearance of the 'informbureauists' and the break with Stalinist policies at home meant that strict Party control of literature was gradually relaxed and direct interference from on high became the exception rather than the rule. But the literary dogmatists did not give up without a stubborn fight and the early fifties saw the battle between them and the liberal modernists at its height; it was fought out on the surface in the literary journals in Belgrade, although this was probably only the visible tip of the iceberg. Politically, the outcome was for a time uncertain since there were elements in both camps who were important in Party and Government, but from the literary merit of the pre-war generation, and it was they who in-modernists were to be found almost all the surviving writers of any literary merit of the pre-war generation, and it was they who influenced the first young, post-war generation of writers which was to prove to be of such high quality. Moreover, the Zhdanovist doctrine of socialist realism showed itself to be artificial and sterile, and, as elsewhere, produced little of any literary value. The point of no return from the political aspect was probably Kardelj's speech at the end of 1954, which closely echoed Miroslav Krleža's exposé to the Third Writers' Congress at Bled in 1952, and which confirmed the principle of freedom of creative activity and of the non-interference of the Party in questions of form and expression. The direct result was that the conflict was taken out of the political arena and became a purely literary one. In general terms it was all over by the mid fifties and from then on the earlier imposed doctrine of socialist realism was no longer given serious attention, although in some of the regional centres there was a considerable time-lag as compared with developments in Belgrade, and, most notably in Slovenia, the atmosphere remained rigidly doctrinaire for rather longer.

Clearly there are still some political taboos and limitations, many of which are unwritten and acknowledged instinctively rather than decreed, and occasionally individuals still fall foul of them. The most important areas of risk are direct criticism of Party and

Government rather than of individuals, unsympathetic treatment of the partisan and Party role in the struggle for liberation from the Germans and Italians, and direct attacks upon the Soviet Union as distinct from on Stalin and the personality cult. These last two have at various times been partially eroded, although recent events seem to some extent to have brought them forward once more.

The fact that there is no official censor and that the lines which must not be crossed are not clearly defined can at times result in troublesome situations. The Public Prosecutor's office must receive copies of everything published and it will institute proceedings if it is decided that a particular text can be considered to have infringed some article of the Constitution. But this can be only after the text has appeared in print so that it is in fact the newspaper-man and the publishing house editor (a position which, incidentally, is occupied by a large proportion of the modern generation of writers!) who in fact control what can and what cannot be published. It is the editor jointly with the writer of a work who is held responsible for publication should something subsequently go wrong. Given such a situation, it is perhaps surprising that editors are not more cautious than is the case, but it is by a process of pushing hard against the accepted limiting and conventional restrictions that authors and editors have gradually succeeded in moving them back and wearing them away to give the present day atmosphere of liberalization.

Another factor in this progression towards wider horizons can be seen in the scope and volume of literature in translation which has appeared in the post-war period. Since the early fifties a well-selected cross-section of modern European literature has found its way into print. By the sixties it was possible to translate such controversial material as the political satire of Zamyatin's *We* and George Orwell's *1984*, Pasternak's *Dr Zhivago*, and Solzhenitsyn's *Cancer Ward* and *First Circle*, among other works which would still be inconceivable in the Soviet Union or the Eastern bloc.

So the most basic and positive literary development in post-war, post-revolutionary Yugoslavia has been the extent of the move towards that concept of artistic literature where writers are judged by the aesthetic and literary merits of their writings and not for their political involvement or lack of it. And even if progress in this direction has at times been slow and arduous, it would seem that the process has now reached a stage where, short of some new cataclysmic upheaval, it is no longer reversible.

Second only to this primary attainment of freedom of expression has been the resultant rise in stature and overall quality of artistic writing in Yugoslavia since the war. The two predominating features of earlier periods of literature, traditional regionalism and naïve lyricism, have been reduced to a subsidiary role; they are no longer ends in themselves but subordinated to the development of wider and more universal themes in which the effects of the country's traumatic experiences during the war have been rarely far below the surface. Only in Macedonia, probably because of the very recent general development of the area, is regionalism in literature still dominant.

The post-war years have also shown that the majority of writers have ceased to be purely imitative of European models although they continue to learn greatly from them and adapt their lessons to their own requirements. No small part here has been played by the emergence of Serbo-Croat as a modern literary language in its own right. The last fifty years, and especially the last thirty, have shown that it has finally freed itself from the straitjacket imposed on it by Vuk Karadžić's peasant, colloquial and basically agricultural norms. During this time it has become a modern literary medium, capable of expressing high-level concepts and enriched by abstract vocabulary and syntax, not necessarily always from external sources. Much the same can be said of Slovene, and even Macedonian seems to have begun to move in a similar direction.

Finally, much of the enormous broadening of literary horizons has been brought about by the large increase in the number of solid craftsmen of the writer's trade who have appeared in print since the war. If at the beginning of the period there were two or three outstanding authors, amongst them, let it not be forgotten, a Nobel Prize winner, it is fairly clear that at the end of the sixties this number has not fundamentally increased. But it is equally evident that there is a very much larger spread of good, newly established writers, and not a few outstanding works of literature. It is above all this breadth of literary talent that is characteristic of the post-war period and it is this situation which is in the main responsible for the raising of the overall qualitative value of Yugoslav literature to a European level. For a small, multi-language land which has scarcely outgrown its disastrous historical destiny as the cockpit of Europe, this, in itself, is no mean exploit.

Antonije Isaković

APRIL FOOL'S DAY

The train had only five carriages. The officers were in the first two, behind the engine, and they all had the same insignia on their shoulders – violet epaulettes. There were boats on the carriages' tin roofs and the oars had been fastened down with their ends stuck out of the windows like short sticks. There was a continual hum from the crowd which had assembled in the small area between the station and the iron barrier, and people were all the time craning forward to look inside the forbidden military train.

The Engineer Corps, where are they going? Up to the front or to the rear?

Will there be another train, will there be one for us?

How the hell do I know.

You're polite, aren't you? ...

Shut up, old man, what are you doing here with your withered legs. Your throat's much too wrinkled and your tie's choking you. Just take a look at that nose of yours, go on, don't be shy.

There's not enough room, you'll crush that woman.

What a way to speak to an old man. ... Times are really hard.

Stop whining, old man, this is a station, there's no ikons here and there's a war on!

Let me through, I've got some beads, some fresh popcorn, Mr Sergeant, sir, some coloured beads for your girl, are you going to the front?

Listen, do you know for certain where the Germans are?

Does anyone know that; the Engineers are always the last to leave. They blow up the bridges.

Take it easy, you stuck your elbow in my ribs.

What's that, they've already blown the bridge, who says so?

Them over there ...

The crowd was leaning on the wall of the building and on the station barrier. There were close-cropped heads, caps, straw hats, and ordinary grey-black ones with greasy ribbons; a few light and dark coloured scarves and an occasional felt hat. Those who had been fortunate enough to get past the barrier walked aimlessly up and down the platform. A boy in a blue overall was trying to walk along one of the rails.

A policeman was strolling up and down in front of the barrier trying to keep the crowd calm, important in his clean, white cap like a crisp meringue, gleaming in the weak April sunlight.

At the window over the big clock stood the stationmaster's wife. She was thin, and strands of her wavy hair were grey and singed by her perm. The grey background of the pitted station façade was only broken by the green of the cushion under her elbows.

A group of peasants were sitting next to the black lavatories where a few blades of rye-grass stuck up out of the ground. Uncertain what to do, half-drunk and excited, they had settled themselves down on the gravelled space in front of the station. And since they had lost all patience and any hope of going anywhere, they had begun to unpack their soldiers' boxes. Scattered around at their feet lay gnawed chicken-bones, bottle tops, crumpled, greasy newspapers, bits of string and bulky sacks. The station cats and mangy dogs scratched around among these scraps until the peasants started singing a folk song in two-part harmony.

At last the train moved off. The officers shook their heads, none of them looked towards the platform. The crowd noticed this and began to move about and shout.

The Engineers are going.

They're leaving us behind, all of us as if we were a load of rubbish. So they're going without us, all on their own, there's treachery for you.

Shhh ... you mustn't say things like that about the army.

Somebody's got to give an explanation.

Ask that cop!

I can't see him.

In the last war the army and the people were one, I can tell you that, I fought on the Salonika front. But those officers, white gloves ...

The stationmaster's wife was still at the window over the big clock; she had a sad look about her and no one knew what she was thinking about.

Under the wooden porch in front of the depot, the first refugees had taken up residence : three families. Scattered around them in disorder lay their household effects : bundles, suitcases fastened with straps, a mirror, a sewing machine, boxes from which jug and pot handles, soup-spoons, cushions, feathers and the base of an iron candlestick were sticking out. They had stood the mirror upright between two boxes and it showed a length of track, the branch of a lime tree and the better part of a petrol-tanker truck. Children were whimpering, sitting on a mattress spread out on the ground. A tall man gave them a handful of dried plums as he went past. And very soon the children were all sticky as if they had been eating jam.

At last the stationmaster came out and announced that there would be one more train. This reassured everyone, somebody even heard a whistle; they asked if it was a civilian or a military train and in the general confusion decided that it must be a civilian one. The stationmaster banged the glass doors behind him and the crowd were left in the belief that they would not have to wait beside the deserted rails for ever. Almost immediately a young clerk appeared and wrote in chalk on the board : the last train from ... will probably arrive in an hour's time.

The people in the crowd began to move about again, to get angry and to lose hope, many of them were alarmed by that 'probably'. The clerk stood in the doorway and hesitatingly tried to explain that all this had been arranged by the stationmaster, but since the crowd seemed to want to put the blame on him, he fled back into the office. Once agitated and aroused, it was not easy to calm them down again. And in any case, it seemed that there was no one with the authority to do so. ... Many of them went right up to the glass doors, and those behind wanted to break them down. Someone reminded them that it was official property, but that even further inflamed the ones who were on the concrete apron between the station and the barrier. And just when the iron barrier was be-

ginning to creak and the plaster to flake away from the pockmarked
façade, the signal bell suddenly started to ring, sharp and strident,
at regular intervals; its bell, like the pulse of an enormous official
heart, brought the crowd to a halt. Stopped in its tracks, it was as
if it were dazed for a moment. No one bothered to climb over the
barrier, although it was no longer forbidden since the policeman
had disappeared at the same time as the military train.

The stationmaster's wife was still leaning on her elbows at the
window. She looked down at them as if from some balcony shelter,
set high above them. Her face had become even more washed-out
and greyed from watching them, like a plaster cast beneath the
window.

Near the black lavatories, the peasants were insistently repeating
the same song.

The station began to smell of petrol. A group of people were
wandering about beside the tanker. And then a lot of others
climbed over the barrier with a varied assortment of containers in
their hands, whatever they had managed to get hold of, and rushed
towards the truck.

The ground beneath the petrol tanker had already begun to stink
of petrol.

Take it easy, don't shove!

Watch it or we'll all go up in flames. Put your cigarette out.

It's aviation fuel.

High octane, high octane ...

Where's our air force got to?

Move over, you don't want to wash in it, do you, let someone
else in.

He wants to drink it.

They say the Russians drink crude alcohol.

Come on then, let me fill my can up too. I'm as dry as a bone.

Isn't anyone in charge here? Where's that cop?

Shut up, what do you want the law here for; the country's done
for so we might as well knock this truck off as well. I've paid for
my bit of it too, you know, friend.

Me too, me too ...!

Three armed soldiers suddenly appeared on the platform. They were in full battle order. They were young, powerfully built and had new, yellow boots, and one of them had a black, pointed moustache. The other two were smart and clean-shaven. They roughly broke up the crowd around the tanker and re-established order and at that very moment the policeman reappeared. The crowd began to get heated.

Who do you think you are?

If you're the army, you belong to us . . .

I bet you wore peasant shoes too, before you put those yellow clod-hoppers on.

What have you got to be so grand about?

Put things right at the front, not here !

That's right !

The soldier with the moustache sized up the crowd, and in a hoarse voice said the first thing that came into his head.

— We're a military patrol. This section of territory is under martial law. Stand back. Stand back when I tell you !

The crowd began to retreat towards the iron barrier. The boldest of them shouted out :

— Then the Germans'll capture it.

— What Germans !

Somehow it got through to the soldiers that there were not going to be any more trains, and that they were already, perhaps, in no-man's-land. At this, the one with the moustache straightened himself up, hitched up his cartridge belt and shouted :

— What the hell ! The High Command's gone off somewhere. The front's right here. That's accurate information, any other news is fifth column.

This convinced the crowd, they basked in their good fortune, they wanted to believe in it.

Down with the fifth column !

Fifth columnists, I say, the army knows.

It must be the uniform, that's quick work.

Give us some weapons.

What does a fifth columnist look like?
And why do they call it the *fifth* column?

All three soldiers were standing by the barrier, the crowd, full of curiosity, could not take their eyes off them, and one of them began to tell, in a formal, self-important voice, how they had caught a fifth columnist by a telephone line, in a field, in the middle of a field in broad daylight; he had plugged in on a line from the High Command.

– And?
– And nothing. We dealt with him summarily, on the spot . . .

The soldier with the moustache spat eloquently, then he came right up to the barrier and began asking to see identity cards. The crowd squeezed up a bit closer, unprotestingly pulled out their identity cards and went on with the tale of the fifth columnist who had been caught.

Where was he caught, here?
No, of course not. In a field.
And what did they do to him?
He was shot.
Yes, well, you can't fool around with the army.
In which field?
Here somewhere or other, the telephone wires pass through a field.
Field telephones, they're military ones, I know that, I was in communications.
I always said that peasant children should go to school; shepherds could stop all that. Keep away from the telephone wires, it's a Serbian shepherd who's guarding them.
What's that, some shepherds caught him?
Fancy that, our peasant's nobody's fool.
Just think of our folk songs, what was he wearing?
He had a check coat. You could see at once he was a foreigner.
Could you really, how?
Those people at the back say he had a little chain round his neck.
Of course, it's only girls who wear chains round their necks here.

He said his mother had given it to him.

It's always like that, everybody talks of his mother when he dies.

The soldier breathed in through his moustache; he examined the identity cards patiently but sternly and most of all the photographs since that was the only thing he really understood in those crumpled little books. Then he asked:

– Name?

– It's written down there.

– I know, I'm just making sure.

The stationmaster's wife was still looking down from her peaceful little island, as if from some kind of nest, at the whole platform beneath her. A hen brooding over her chickens. She looked somehow lost against the dark window.

The crowd was again getting restless, a hundred lips were being bitten, feet had got hot and legs were sweaty from standing, the crowd could feel itself breathing; the rumour had got round that the promised train would not arrive and that the town had already fallen to the Germans.

– That's fifth column! – barked the soldier with the moustache. And the crowd became alarmed yet again and began to swear.

The fifth column's here, amongst us!

Let's catch him, this fifth columnist, he's given us enough trouble.

Let's get him, tear his throat out, smash his legs, son of a dirty Austrian bitch!

Where's the fifth columnist, where?

They're looking for him.

Why's the army standing around doing nothing?

A slightly-built man was leaning against a lime tree, he had been there for a long time, he was tired and was trying to get away from the noise. On his head he was wearing a beret and he had a camera slung across his coat. The soldierly trio went up to him and demanded to see his papers. The man looked at them absently, he straightened himself up and the gravel crackled under his feet as he moved; he looked at them again and said:

– I haven't any papers.

– What's that, no papers?

– Everything got burnt, the house was bombed, I escaped from Belgrade.

– Hmmm. Everyone has his own little story, you're one of those . . . a fifth columnist.

The man's face contorted with laughter, he could not grasp the seriousness of it all; word was passed through the crowd behind the barriers that the fifth columnist had been caught. Many of them leant forward over the barrier to get a better look at him.

Where is he, what does he look like?

Let me have a look at him.

Him over there by the lime tree.

A beret, you can see he's a foreigner.

I noticed him a long while ago.

Me too, he was walking around all the time over there, by the barrier.

That's it, lads, get the evidence together.

Look how brazen he is, he's trying to confuse the army.

What will they do to him?

I don't know, see for yourself.

It was as if the man had only now come to his senses; resentful and angry, he began to explain himself. But the soldiers remained unconvinced. The peasants who had been sitting beside the lavatories stood up behind the military patrol. One of them said :

– Do you hear how he says his 'r's'? Serbs don't speak like that.

The man explained that he had talked like that from birth and he wanted to add something else, but the soldier interrupted him :

– We were all born with two legs and one head, but who are you? That's the question.

The weak April sun began to go down. The horizon over towards the mountain had taken on a pink glow. A grey darkness was coming up from the west and the station had begun to smell even more strongly of petrol and people. The young clerk lit the station lamp. And then the soldier with the moustache settled his rifle more comfortably on his shoulder, hitched up his cartridge belt importantly; the crowd broke through the barrier and the policeman's hat rolled away across the gravel.

They all surrounded the soldiers and the man. It was difficult to breathe, and no one could understand anything.

Let me through, I want to see him.

We ought to twist his nose off.

Move over a bit, at least tell me what he's saying.

He's trying to wriggle out of it. It's people like him who have destroyed this country.

They sent jam in the boxes instead of hand-grenades.

And pearl-barley !

And macaroni.

I'd like to stuff him full of macaroni.

It's because of them that the trains aren't running as they ought to.

And what'll happen now?

They'll hang him.

How?

They'll hang him by his legs from that tree.

The soldiers, the man and the crowd were all sweating profusely. The man wanted to convince the soldiers, the soldiers wanted to convince the man and calm the crowd. But the crowd wanted only one thing: to see its enemy. The man made use of a short silence to say :

– I'm a newspaper reporter.

– He's lying, he's got a camera.

The man looked sadly at his camera and said :

– That's my profession.

The crowd moved back a little and became even angrier than before. Everyone was leaning on someone else, they could feel people's legs, other people's words, the crowd's words belonged to everyone.

Did you hear?

His profession.

He admitted it's his profession.
Of course, that's what he's paid for.
Money!
Spies are better paid than anyone else.
He ought to be dealt with summarily.

The first soldier grabbed the man by the sleeve. The man struggled and shouted:
  – But listen everybody, I've got a wife and child here.
  – Where are they? – the soldier asked him.
The man called to his wife, the crowd laughed. They laughed uproariously.
  – Hey, be quiet – the soldier warned them – let's make certain, go on, call her again.
The man stood there anxiously, it looked as though he did not want to shout any more, but nevertheless he stretched up on tiptoes and again called out to his wife.
  – Does anyone know this man?
They all kept silent, someone in the crowd said:
  – No one.
  – Where's your wife? repeated the soldier.
  – She's here somewhere – the man said weakly.
He's having us on.
He's lying, they always lie!
He'll have to be dealt with summarily.
Death . . .
That's it, but where?
At once, here, now. The army's not soft-hearted.

The soldiers seized hold of the man and dragged him towards the station wall. The crowd followed them and its step was hollow and ragged, as if they were walking over sloughed skins. They stood the man up against the wall and a buzz of something like terror came from the crowd. The soldiers stepped back, the man turned his head dazedly towards the drain pipe and when he again straightened up, he saw the rifles pointing straight at him. He gave a terrified scream and with outstretched arms, took a step or two towards the muzzles. It looked as though he wanted to stop them up. And at that moment the weak April sun sank down behind the mountain and was hidden. Down by the wall the man was bowled over by a volley; he fell into the sparse rye-grass. Then the soldiers went up to him and one of them took off his camera. The other two dragged the corpse across to the other side of the track.

The crowd quietly went back to the platform. The bell announced the arrival of the train. And then someone pointed to the woman and the child. A lot of them went off after her. At first she moved towards the carriages, and then went back towards the station barrier. The crowd followed the same short path. The woman stopped and at last she realized that everyone was looking at her. This was unpleasant for her, she was frightened, and she drew the child towards her. She looked at the dense circle of people around her. Then she asked :

– Where's my husband?

The crowd was silent, many of them bowed their heads, someone began to cry but he was at once whisked away. The crowd was afraid of being guilty and each one thought that he was not to blame. The woman, as if defending herself said :

– I was making some tea in the buffet, for the little girl . . .

And here she stopped. But the silence gave her courage and she asked loudly :

– Where's my husband? Do you know . . .

No one moved, only the sound of breathing could be heard. Then a man pushed through the crowd.

– Look lady, your husband has already left.

The woman did not believe him, and the man went on hurriedly :

– Yes, ma'am, he said I was to tell you, he went on the train before. He wanted to be sure of finding somewhere for you and the little girl to stay the night.

The crowd confirmed this with nods and grunts. The woman seemed not to want to move from the spot. But the crowd pushed her gently, almost carried her – her and the child, towards the train. Everyone wanted to help and they found them a comfortable compartment. Somebody even brought some beads for the child.

The people standing on the platform asked where those three soldiers had got to. But they were nowhere to be found, like the policeman. The train moved off, taking with it the woman, the child and the crowd. The station became empty.

All around there was a stench of petrol. On the mattress, a little boy was playing with the policeman's hat. The refugees lit a small fire, two of them crossed over the track. They carried spades on their shoulders. Then the stationmaster put out the light. And at long last, his wife closed the window.

Translated by Bernard Johnson

Erih Koš

THE MAN WHO KNEW WHERE THE NORTH WAS AND WHERE THE SOUTH

Jefto Stojanov Čokorilo, a contractual policeman, served his five-year term in various police-stations round Višegrad, then took off his policeman's uniform and donned once more his peasant clothes and returned to his village of Pale above Sarajevo. There he married a certain Joka, who was already four or five months pregnant, with whom he had had relations while serving at the police-station at Sjeversko; armed with the recommendation of the village priest, he went down to see the chief magistrate of the district court at Sarajevo, and was taken on as warder of the court-house jail with a wage of six hundred dinars a month. He at once put on his new uniform – greyish green, with purple insignia on the cap, collar and shoulder-straps – second-hand, it's true, and too tight for him, stout, tall and broad as he was. And hearing that at No. 14 in the street leading to the hospital and cemetery the lodging and post of caretaker were vacant, Čokorilo brought his wife from Pale, came to terms, and settled in at once – the two of them to live there, and she to clean and look after the building.

The lodging could not have been worse. A damp, dark den of a place on the ground floor of a huge block of flats, which overshadowed and completely buried it. A single room, with one tiny window looking out on to a light-shaft full of refuse and filth, and a stinking W.C., which also served two shops, and was always leaking and making the wall of Čokorilo's lodging damp. The neighbourhood was dull – brickworks, military bakeries, garages, warehouses and a furniture factory – the street was unpaved, dusty in summer and muddy in winter; the building itself was dilapidated, the plaster peeling from its walls, the tenants all had crowds of children, and the caretaker's job brought in nothing – only a few tips for opening the street-door at night and meagre New Year gifts from the not very generous tenants. Previous caretakers had not lasted long. One died of tuberculosis, two drank themselves to death; the last had found a better job and escaped in time. The tenants said the new caretaker wouldn't last long either, but they were wrong. Jefto Čokorilo settled in with his wife Joka and began to arrange his life in that miserable lodging.

He was a strong fellow, with broad shoulders and powerful limbs. Since he had been a policeman, he knew how to wear a uniform: he held himself well, with a straight back and his chest thrust out; his shining leather leggings made his steps seem firmer; he kept his left arm pressed against his side so that it shouldn't swing as he walked, and his stiff collar made him hold his head up and look straight in front of him. His face was square, and rosy as a child's, but serious and grim in expression; he never meddled in any disputes or quarrels in the house, or made friends with anybody in it; he minded his own business and his own duties and, for more than a year, nobody even heard his voice.

His wife was short and fat. When she came from the country to live in the town, she laid aside her peasant dress for the first time and put on town clothes which, being clumsily made, hung from her shoulders over her large flabby breasts and swelling stomach like a shift, so that, as she was unwashed and unkempt, she always looked as though she had just got out of bed. At the police-station at Sjeversko her work had been to scrub floors, so here she passed a wet rag over the passages and stairs three times a week, and any-one entering the house as she was doing so would come on her bending over her pail, with her sleeves turned back and her skirt hitched up, her fat legs showing up to the buttocks, which were embarrassing to look at, yet impossible not to see. She was slow and lazy. The miserable hole in which she cooked and slept was always dirty and blackened with smoke; like her husband, she didn't meddle in quarrels in the house either, but she was capable of standing for hours on the staircase listening to the conversations and disputes of the tenants and their servants.

Soon after they moved in, a son was born to Čokorilo. A year and a half later he sewed on a white bone star above the purple chevron at his throat and got a rise of two hundred dinars. Two years

later, he sewed on a second star, and his wife had a second child,
another boy, and then stopped bearing, although, being so fat, with
her protruding stomach, she always looked as if she were pregnant.
And Čokorilo continued to advance in the service; one year, in his
own street, he killed a prisoner who tried to run away while he was
being taken to hospital; for this he was commended. The children,
and the grown-up tenants too, began to fight shy of him, but in
his ninth year in the service Jefto received his third star and a
sword and belt, so that in a short time he had caught up with and
passed many who had entered the service before him. And so he
climbed the whole ladder of promotion and there only remained
for him to receive periodic increases of pay and yellow stripes on
his sleeves, until he reached the stage of waiting for his pension,
with the rank of chief warder of the court-house jail.

During all these years, Čokorilo had very rarely called at a
tavern, although he had plenty of opportunity, and he had never
got drunk, although on Saturday nights and holidays the street
was full of drunks. As a representative of law and order, he was
careful what he did, took a drink or two only on the family saint's
day and at Christmas, and that in moderation and at home, between his own four walls. He thought that his duties and his uniform called for the cold, severe and measured bearing which people
would consider appropriate to the law and the paragraph of the law
under which he served. And that indeed was how he conducted
himself : coldly, with measure and restraint, more like the military,
whom he admired, than the civilians whom he might at any time
be called upon to clap in jail. He spoke little, slowly and deliberately, went to and came from his work punctually by the clock,
quarrelled regularly with his wife and handed over his pay to her
on the first of every month – all except what he kept back for
tobacco and coffee, which he hadn't been able to give up.

He continued to live in the same miserable lodging, which now
that he had two children seemed smaller than ever. In the eighth
year after he came there, the grocer's shop to the right of the street-
door was put up for sale and as several months passed without
anybody offering to buy it, Čokorilo got it for a low rent and in
his spare time broke down the wall between it and his lodging,

nailed up the outer door, painted the shop-window white and stretched a sheet across it. Then he brought the beds into what had been the shop and so acquired a bedroom and a kitchen; on the wall above the beds he hung two enormous pictures which he had found thrown away in the courthouse yard, and had framed and brought home; one was of the late Prime Minister Pasić, an old man with a great white beard, and the other of the Crown Prince in his Guards' uniform, wearing a tall fur hat with a tassel. Then, giving up tobacco and coffee for more than a month, he went to the photographer's and had himself photographed, head and shoulders, in his uniform and got the picture enlarged and coloured and hung it between the two already on the wall.

And he didn't stop at that. He still felt he owed something to himself, to his position and reputation, and, seeing himself every day hanging so stiffly and correctly between the other two portraits, he began to carry himself more rigidly than ever. He strode along the street like a soldier on parade, with his neck as stiff as a poker and his body tense, as though he were leaning back against the wind. From his previous habits as a policeman, he retained a love of smartness, and from his peasant upbringing a respect for clean, shining, complicated things he didn't rightly know the use of. So he wore a broad leather belt, and at one time spurs on his boots and even a pistol at his belt, until his superiors told him to take all that off; in his breeches-pocket he always kept an enormous whistle on a red plaited cord, and a large watch, bought out of his pay while he was still a policeman, which he took out and wound up and adjusted in front of every watchmaker's shop and every public clock. He bought and took home a leather pouch such as only officers wore, and although his wife reproached him for spending so much, he then purchased several special military maps of the town and surroundings, although in fact he hardly ever went beyond the street leading from the jail to his house, and that road he could have found blindfold. He began to use expressions from legal documents and archives when he talked, so that neither his superiors nor the prisoners could understand him properly, and for some time he had been greeting the better-class tenants with an ingratiating smile. When he met them in the passage, he exchanged a few casual words with them in a high thin voice, bending his tall figure towards them and, not knowing what to do with himself to show his great civility and gentility, he bowed and twisted and turned his hips like a peasant bride and in doing so scraped the wall behind him with the waving end of his sword.

His wife bobbed her hair and gave herself the airs of a lady. On Sundays she wore a red dress, which differed from her everyday shifts in colour only. Round her neck she wore a glass necklace bought at the fair in the churchyard, and thrust her feet into black, low-heeled shoes which, although they were the largest size, looked like black-beetles on her great swollen feet. Then, fat and heavy-breasted, she would sit with her two stupid-looking children one on each side of her, on a short bench she brought out into the street beside the front-door. When he was not on duty, Čokorilo would join them and all four – the wife and two children on the bench, Jefto standing on the left, bending slightly over them, with one hand on his sword-hilt – all as stiff as in a fairground photograph, would sit gazing at everything that went on before them in the street: the funerals which passed every day, even on Sundays, on their way to the cemetery, the great closed bus which took the town prostitutes to the hospital for inspection, the people going to visit their sick relatives and friends, the town water-cart with the huge barrel behind which Gipsy, the dustman, wielded the canvas pipe which he waved right and left, sprinkling the dusty street. For the two children clinging to their mother's skirt, there was no money left and little could be done for them. Half naked or in little shirts, or in short pants as they grew older, they were always tousle-headed, snotty-nosed and dirty and, however much Jefto worked, struggled and contorted himself, advanced in the service, polished his boots and his leggings, minced his words and thrust out his chest, decorated his lodging with pictures and did it up – he still remained the chief warder of the court-house jail who himself spent his life in the jail, while his wife was a peasant, fat and dirty, his children puny and stupid-looking, and his lodging a miserable hole beside the stinking W.C., dark and damp, in an ugly surburban street which led to the hospital and the cemetery.

The day when Čokorilo sewed the third stripe on his sleeve and received his last rise, he went out of the jail where he had been on duty ever since the previous morning, and as though he himself had been unexpectedly released, he felt a bit dazed at first, hardly knowing which way to turn and what to do.

It was perhaps about five o'clock – a pleasant, warm, lazy Saturday afternoon between springtime and summer, when cats doze in the sun alongside the house-walls, when coats are unbuttoned and then taken off, strained muscles are relaxed and throats begin to feel dry with the dust already filling the air. He didn't like going home, to the darkness of his wretched lodging – it would be like going back into the prison, he thought – and his mood was mixed; he was pleased about the new stripe on his sleeve and his full wallet seemed to warm him through the pocket of his tunic, but he was tired after his night on duty and felt somehow listless, empty, missing something, aimless and dissatisfied. He would have liked to rest in some garden and drink a glass of beer, or to drop into the nearest tavern for a nip of brandy but – today being Saturday, and the first of the month – everywhere was crowded with drunks and it wasn't seemly for a representative of law and order to mix with such as they – so, not knowing what else to do, he turned out of the dim, dank, foul-smelling street which wound between the high walls of the government buildings, and took an alley he knew which led out to the main street and there he mixed with the passing throng.

For some time he took pleasure in greeting officers and soldiers out on their Saturday afternoon furlough, he watched the young people walking slowly in twos and threes, swaying as they strolled along the pavements, he listened to the news-vendors shouting the evening news, and as he passed, without stopping, he glanced at the shop-windows: shoes, haberdashery, books, clothing, shirts and caps. At the corner he stopped, took out his large heavy watch, compared it with the clock above the watchmaker's shop, assured himself that they agreed to the fraction of a second, then he stopped to look in the shop-window which, as usual, held his attention, fascinating and exciting him.

Among the watches and clocks, large and small, which he recognized as having seen before, his gaze was arrested by a largish unusual dial on which instead of hands there lay a long dark-blue and silver needle, which quivered slightly in the sunlight that slanted into the window. Čokorilo bent down to read the signs on the dial, remembered that he had seen a similar instrument a long time before, in the police training-school, and only once since, when he was on military service, and it struck him as strange that the dark, northern end of the needle was pointing just in the direction of his house. A passer-by happening to catch on the projecting tip of his sword, he moved aside and apologized, and turning again to the window, he noticed a beautiful black pair of field-glasses on the shelf above the clocks, and remembered that he hadn't had a pair in his hands since he left the police-school – in the prison, where he only had to peep through the spy-holes in the cell-doors, he had certainly had no need of any – and he felt a great desire just to touch them and raise them to his eyes, so without stopping to think, almost involuntarily, taking care that nobody saw him, he quickly slipped into the shop.

Inside all was orderly, clean, dark and mysterious as in a church, and full of little ticking and humming sounds. Čokorilo timidly approached the counter. The watchmaker, an elderly man in a black apron, took a magnifying glass from his eye, pulled out several cases, added two or three pairs of field-glasses, and set them all before him.

'Take your choice!' he said. 'Have a look at them! No obligation!' and he leaned back against the shelf behind him.

Čokorilo wiped his perspiring palms and felt he was trembling. As he moved the objects set before him, the lid of one of the cases sprang open and showed the round dial of a compass, but the needle was stationary – its darker end pointing somewhere to the side, beyond the watchmaker, to the back of the shop, where an electric light bulb burned even in the daytime. Čokorilo looked sideways at the shopkeeper, who smiled slightly and released the needle, which sprang to life, began to revolve and oscillate and finally came to a standstill, quivering like quicksilver, and the astonished customer saw through the window that the north was where it had been before – just in the direction of his house.

Then he turned to the field-glasses; they were beautiful, with their hard, shiny black flanks and curves. The shopkeeper almost thrust a pair into his hands: 'Take a look!' he said. 'Adjust them to your sight!' And Jefto removed his cap, laid it carefully on the counter, took out his handkerchief and wiped the perspiration from his forehead. At first he could only see a haze which dazzled his eyes, then with trembling hands he pointed the glasses at a distant hill, and houses began to reel about on it, and tall red rocks, and he could see a road winding up the hill.

'There's a car ... it's going up!' he exclaimed, putting down the glasses; the hill at once shrank in size, disappearing in the distance, and Jefto could hardly see the houses, whose very windows he had just been able to count.

He turned back to the counter, picked up his cap and put it on, straightened his tunic and stood up, ready to leave.

'Well?' asked the shopkeeper, serious and businesslike. 'Shall I wrap it up?'

Čokorilo was confused. 'What's the price?' he asked, pointing to the compass, and to gain time began untwisting the cord on the hilt of his sword.

The watchmaker told him the price. Then he added: 'I'll let you have twenty per cent off as it's you!' Čokorilo was amazed: he had thought the compass would be much dearer; he reckoned quickly that the price was just equal to three months' rise and he thought he would be able to keep it quiet from his wife for as long as that. 'All right, let me have the compass' – the words escaped his lips and the shopkeeper at once began to initiate him into all its secrets, to show him how to release the needle, to open and close the case, and then offered the bewildered customer, who felt beads of perspiration starting out on his forehead and his cheeks flaming with excitement, to sell him the field-glasses as well.

'There,' he said, 'that pair's one of the best. It goes with the compass, and it'd be a pity to separate them.'

Čokorilo was dumbfounded; the price of the field-glasses was more than he had dared to think of. 'That's because of the Zeiss lenses! I'll let you have them on the instalment-plan; you'll have paid for them in a year's time,' explained the shopkeeper, beginning to wrap them up and, seeing that his customer still hesitated, he re-opened the parcel and put in two cases. 'See, I'll throw you these in too,' he said and wrapped them all in rustling tissue-paper and held them out to the dazed Čokorilo across the glass counter. 'Pay at the desk, please !' he said. 'You know, you've made a good buy. You won't regret it !'

Ten minutes later Jefto Čokorilo came out of the shop with the precious parcel in his hand, as hurriedly as though he had stolen it and was afraid of having to return it. He felt he wanted to be alone, to hide himself and his booty from the eyes of the world, so he crossed to the other side of the street where it was quieter, and set off for home, excited and trembling as if with a fever.

On the way, he kept feeling a longing to open the packet and look at his purchases, and when he got into the park he couldn't resist any longer, but with trembling fingers undid one end of the wrapping and raised the parcel to his nose. He could smell the odour of the dressed leather, mingled with the exciting, indefinable smell of new, clean, shining varnished goods, and he sniffed it again and again, filling his lungs with it.

Slowly, a step at a time, he reached the street leading to his house and had not repented. But when he turned into it, his excitement began to evaporate and the parcel to feel cold. He remembered that he would have to explain to his wife what was in it, what he had done with his pay and his rise, and in order to think of an excuse he turned into the nearest tavern, pushed his way through the customers to the counter and, leaning on it, drank at one draught two noggins of brandy. But he didn't manage to think of anything, and the parcel on the counter beside him began to seem somehow superfluous, unnecessary, a nuisance. He decided to wait till it was dark and to take the thing into the house unnoticed, and as the waiter, without asking, kept filling up his glass, Jefto Čokorilo, before dark, had put away a fair amount and set off for home already several over the eight and with trembling knees.

He slipped sheepishly in at the front door, reeled along the dark passage where the stench of the W.C. assailed his nostrils and the mouldy smell of the walls stuck in his throat, groped for his own door and opening it, holding the parcel behind him, entered the kitchen. The two children were already asleep on the settee; his wife was not there. Čokorilo slipped into the bedroom, hid the compass and field-glasses under the pillow on the bed, and when he came out again, he found Joka in the kitchen busy at the stove.

'Where've you been all this time?' she said.

Čokorilo didn't hurry to answer. He put his sword down in the corner by the door, sat down and began to unfasten his leggings. His wife was warming up his supper on the stove.

'Did you get your rise?' she asked.

Čokorilo took off his tunic and hung it on the back of his chair and placed his leggings beside his sword.

'No,' he said and bent down to untie his shoe-laces.

'And why not?' asked his wife, and as Jefto still didn't answer, she moved closer to him and smelt the brandy.

'My God, you've been drinking!' she cried and was going to add something more when she saw that he was looking at her in a queer way, so she refrained, went into the bedroom and remained there some time; when she came out she had the parcel in her hands.

'What's this?' she shouted from the doorway.

'You can see,' returned Čokorilo. 'A compass and a pair of field-glasses, that's all.'

The woman didn't understand and the answer didn't satisfy her.

'Where did you get them?' she wanted to know, and Čokorilo went on untying his shoe-laces.

'What did you pay for them?' was Joka's next question, and she approached the chair where his tunic was hanging and put out her hand to take the wallet.

'Leave that alone!' shouted Čokorilo and, as his wife took no notice, he seized her by the arm and pushed her aside more roughly than he need have done, so she realized what had become of the money, shook herself free, and again approached the tunic and the wallet.

'That's where your pay and your rise have gone!' she said, and they wrestled with each other dumbly until Čokorilo swung out his arm with full force and struck his wife with his fist on the side of her neck just under the ear. She fell back against the table: the

plate, dish and spoon, and the compass and field-glasses all crashed
to the floor, and Jefto completely lost control of himself and began
to beat his wife furiously.

For some time his blows rained down on her, then she began to
try to defend herself and Čokorilo started swearing and shouting.
The children woke up and cowered against the wall, whimpering.

He continued to strike at her blindly, with fists and feet and
even with a chair. The woman, who had at first tried to defend
herself, snatching at his arms, then began to draw away, and after
she got a few heavy blows on her belly and sides, realized it was
serious, and taking fright, started throwing herself against the
walls, stumbling on the overturned chairs, at last flinging herself
to the floor and lying still, as though she were dead. Čokorilo
seized his tunic and without dressing properly, his collar unfastened and without his leggings, ran out of the house, banging
the door behind him, and went off to the tavern. He drank and
drank until closing time, then returned home, found the lights on
in the kitchen and his wife sitting at the table crying, so he locked
the door and began beating her again.

Midnight passed, all was quiet in the building, most of the
tenants in bed and asleep, but the noise in Čokorilo's lodging woke
up those on the lower floors. They banged on the floor above, and
as it sounded as though somebody down below was being murdered,
the professor on the first floor came down, began knocking at the
door and tried to open it, but nobody took any notice of him and
he had to go back. And Čokorilo continued to beat his wife: for
the sake of the money he'd spent, for the compass and field-glasses,
which he'd lost all heart for, because of the children who were so
puny and stupid at their lessons, for the many years he'd lived in
that den of a place, for a hundred other reasons which he couldn't
remember. And he beat and beat her till he was wearied; dawn
found him stretched out on the settee, his wife, half dead, on the
floor among the broken, trampled pots and glasses, the overturned
table and chairs.

Next day he didn't go on duty — it was Sunday, and he'd been on
duty all the previous day. In the caretaker's lodging all was quiet,
the door remained closed all day, even the children didn't appear

in the street, nor was the bench brought out in the afternoon as usual, although it was a warm, sunny day. The tenants wondered what had happened during the night, but concluded that it was no good meddling in such matters and with such people, for only unpleasantness and inconvenience could come of it. And the professor on the first floor, the oldest tenant in the building, remarked: 'You see, even this one hasn't lasted. He's taken to drink and now he'll start beating his wife every Saturday, and soon it'll be every day!'

But that, however, was the last of it. The whole week the staircase remained unwashed. For several days the 'caretaker' didn't come out of her lodging, and when she appeared for the first time her face was swollen and there were purple rings under her eyes. Čokorilo went gloomily and moodily to his duties; he thought of returning the compass and field-glasses to the shop, but in the fight he had trodden on the case and scratched the varnish on the glasses, so he had to give up the idea. As he had spent practically all his pay on drink that wretched Saturday, he borrowed a few hundred dinars from his juniors for once, and calculated that it would take him two years to pay the instalments on the things and make up for the damage done. The next Sunday, which was sunny and warm, so that the town was full of people walking out, he dressed himself carefully again, cleaned his shoes, leggings and sword; his wife put on her red dress and the necklace, combed the children's hair and wiped their noses, and in the next-door garden, from which they had a good view of the street and the hill opposite, they spread a rug and sat there on the grass, among the nettles, thistles, hemlock and thorn-apples, as though they were having a picnic. They were silent all the time until Jefto Čokorilo, solemnly measuring his words, asked his wife sternly, as though it were an examination, while she still bore beneath her eyes the traces of the previous week's blows:

'Joka, do you know where the north is now?'

Joka started, turned towards the sun, and pointed her hand in one direction, while Jefto took the compass, carefully opened the case, set it in front of him on his knee, moved the clasp which held the needle and the latter began to jerk, to swing backwards and forwards, and finally stood still. Then Čokorilo, bending over the compass as though it were he who controlled its movements, carefully read the signs on the dial and said to his wife who, with her mouth open and a vacant expression, was gazing into the street: 'No, it isn't there; it's more to the left. .... By that poplar-tree. .... So now you know where the north is!'

Then they all sat silent again for a time, till Čokorilo asked where the south was, and showed Joka all four points of the compass. Then he closed the compass and took out the field-glasses and began to inspect the hill opposite.

'I see,' he said to his wife, 'somebody driving a horse up Gorica. Can you see them, Joka?' he asked, and as she lazily muttered a negative 'nnnn' through her closed teeth, he, who could see things she couldn't, things invisible to the ordinary human eye, began to tell her, although she was weary and jaded with sitting so long: 'There! I can see two people at a window – a man and a woman. ... Now there's a dog running across a field. ... There's somebody clipping trees in that garden ...' and then he turned the glasses on the passers-by in the street, a score of steps below them.

So they all sat until the sun started to go down and the street emptied. Then Joka picked up the rug and the children, who all the time had been quietly sitting at her feet, and Jefto Čokorilo, crossing the straps of the compass and glasses across his chest, stood up straight and stiff, went down again to his miserable lodging, and hung up the compass and glasses on a nail under his portrait, like a lamp under an icon.

From now on, they went out every Sunday and sat in the garden as long as the fine weather lasted, taking no notice of the tenants, who watched them from the windows and balconies, or of the passers-by in the street, who looked at them with astonishment and made fun of them. Čokorilo would hold the compass in his hand, as though all the laws of the universe were under his control, regularly showing Joka the north, south, east and west, as though he had fixed them there, one week in the direction of the poplar-tree, the next in that of the brickworks chimney or the lightning-conductor of the nearest building – depending on where they sat in the garden – and then, like a staff-officer on the battlefield, he would inspect the hill opposite through his glasses and see that it was getting half swallowed up with brickworks, pigsties and dusty lime-trees drying up by the roadside, where the dog-catcher's cart was passing, with children running behind, and folk were carrying flowers and wreaths to the cemetery. Then he would turn back into his wretched lodging, ready to go on duty again next day.

Translated by Mary Stansfield-Popović

Ranko Marinković

BADGES OF RANK

Against the background of the awesome strategic designs of the Second World War, some account should be given of the exploit of Torquato Coa, an undersized lieutenant in the Bergamo division of the occupying forces. During the very first days of hostilities against our country, he, a detail of some importance, sprang out of a small motor-boat on to the shore of our little island, a pistol in each hand, pointing at the Town Hall, and roared fearsomely 'Zurr-rr-rendere!' so that the astonished Town Hall was hard put not to gasp out on the spot: 'We surrender, without more ado.'

But nobody answered Torquato's call to surrender, for there was no one anywhere about. Even the emaciated dog, a cynic, who chanced to be absent-mindedly loafing along the beach, deep in his own thoughts like a philosopher of antiquity, would not have barked at the invader, who, from his dog's viewpoint, he considered a quite unimportant phenomenon, had not Torquato attracted his attention by his strange behaviour, such as no dog had ever seen before on our island. But even then this dog-cynic, with the wisdom of philosophy, did not utter a sound, but only cast his eye over Torquato – very superficially and so casually as to be almost offensive – then raised his hind leg against the corner of the Town Hall as if saying, 'Here you are. I surrender it to you,' and continued on his way.

Being very sensitive about anything concerning his honour, Torquato without difficulty concluded that the dog's gesture was very offensive indeed, and even – if you will – that such an encounter with one's enemy was most unfortunate; it aroused his anger so greatly that all of a sudden it seemed to him that the dog was not a dog at all, but a reasoning being, intent at parodying his military exploit. Torquato felt himself spurred on by the Duce's fiery slogan 'chi non è con noi, avrà del piombo', and entered the

Second World War with his first bullets, sensing the full importance of his contribution. On the receiving end of the lead from both Torquato's pistols, the four-footed satirist realized too late that the enemy had got the joke and, revolving drunkenly several times about the spot where he would lie down for the last time, he howled lugubriously as though cursing his murderer, so that Torquato's heart contracted with some vague fear.

Surrounded by the detachment of his men of the Bergamo division, Torquato felt very uneasy on land. Around him there were some hundred forty-year-olds, all of them reservists of the 1901 class, and they immediately, without waiting for his orders, had taken to walls, gates and corners, and every possible cover, even to the barrels and the two or three stunted palm-trees on the quay which were sadly waving their withered fans as if in sympathy, offering some miserable sort of peace to these frightened humans.

Torquato had a lot of trouble with the unhappy and very personal cautiousness of these men dressed in identical clothes, with rifles thrust into their hands, sent as soldiers to land on foreign shores, climb up foreign cliffs, and clamber about foreign rocks, and told that if anybody asked them what they were doing there, they were to consider him an enemy and where possible kill him. Such extremely personal cautiousness cannot be called fear when men are dressed in identical clothes and carry rifles in their hands; that pitiful human feeling is named fear only in enemy propaganda inclined to exaggeration, whereas later on men-of-letters, truth-loving chroniclers of human feelings, try to understand all such emotions and make stories out of them in which they do not mock at human fear, but at its false name.

When – not too loudly – Torquato cried 'Avanti', the forty-year-olds sluggishly moved forward and took up 'new positions' and the 'front' again became stabilized. Torquato's offensive could not advance from the quayside into the narrow inner streets, where still not a single living soul was to be seen, which only increased the Bergamians' cautiousness.

The torpedo-boat *San Marco* stood protectively still in the middle of the bay with her guns trained on the town. But that could only be a guarantee of the successful issue of the operation as a whole.

If we take a closer look at the pale, unshaven face of the old clothes dealer from Bergamo, pressed against the Harbour Master's door, while he fervently prayed from his very soul that the inhabitants of the island would forgive him for being there through no fault of his own, what protection could the torpedo-boat *San Marco* with all her guns offer him, if a rifle could at any moment be fired from some window and a bullet come whistling through the air into his head?

'Oh, mamma mia,' sighed the rag-and-bone man from Bergamo, and Torquato cried 'Avanti, evviva il Duce !' Torquato shouted this order so as to earn promotion and praise, and for all the advantages this exploit of his could bring him, but he himself kept his back hard against the wall as if glued there. And the rag-and-bone man sighed again because it had become unbearably serious to think that he might die there, the moment he left the shelter of the Harbour Master's door to go into the narrow little street, where one could be finished off with just a stone. And still Torquato shouted 'Avanti'.

'Antonio,' whispered the rag-and-bone man to his neighbour, wiping his eyes with his thumb and forefinger.

'Francesco,' answered Antonio and turned pale as if he had seen death.

'Avanti, ragazzi !' shouted Torquato, waving his hand in a brisk and commanding manner, so that the Colonel on the torpedo-boat could see that it was not just a stroll about the town, but entailed all sorts of difficulties, 'porco can !'

But everything went wrong; from the military point of view it even became serious.

'Ma ragazzi ...' Torquato was no longer ordering them – he sounded as if he were asking a favour of them : 'This way, please, to the right, for God's sake ...' but the forty-year-olds, having civilian occupations of their own at home, knew how to understand Torquato's care for them differently too – though the touching word 'ragazzi' reminded them of their mothers, those old women dressed in black, with their vows and their rosaries, and every man felt the gentle protective pressure of the holy medallion on his breast, steeped in his mother's tears and prayers. Torquato was only a little student in whom those GUF people had developed an enthusiasm for fighting and for forcing others to take castor oil. His ancestors were Scipio and Caesar; he was one of the She-Wolf's sons and, when he left for the war, it was not a Loretto medallion that his mother hung round his neck but the Duce's words: 'Chi non è con noi, avrà del piombo'. He had been given lead soldiers, and now the boy had difficulty in moving them forward: fear is heavier than lead. But Torquato believed in the strength of the wall: otto milioni di baionette, and his army stuck firmly to this belief: stone is more impenetrable than mothers' tears, after all. There is some strength in every faith, and those forty-year-olds, being honest and never supplying their own country with poor goods as the war racketeers did, zealously offered Torquato what they had.

But indeed, had it depended on the strength needed to throw a stone from one's shoulder – the strength that comes from the heart and flows along one's veins – those mothers' sons would not have been walking around that island of Ilija's! But such a simple device as a sling once brought down Goliath and made a king out of a stunted little shepherd, and here the guns of an enemy torpedo-boat were trained on Sergeant Ilija, the commander of the Gendarmerie Post and of all armed forces on the island, and those guns required Ilija to capitulate.

Six gendarmes – six rifles headed by Ilija with his sergeant's sword at his thigh – and over them the cowardly *San Marco*, with her big calibre guns pointed this way as if saying, 'Surrender, you poor wretches, there is no escape.' 'Eh, me boys, if it weren't for all that hardware . . .' mumbled Ilija angrily, looking out of the small garret window and seeing the *San Marco* moving her fingers about, there in the bay, as if poking into the town to find him, Ilija, and crush him like a bed-bug. 'Just you wait a bit! We didn't get this bit of our country for nothing,' said Ilija, touching his sword and straightening himself up there in the garret and spitting over the roof down into the street.

Oh, God! how long Ilija had waited for that sword! There had been corporals butting in like rams; ready to do a bit of fiddling and to trip him up so as to make him fall down flat on his nose, while

they went on and took his place. It is only the third star that en-
titles you to a sword, and with a sword – my word ! – you've really
become somebody. Your arms no longer hang down unoccupied as
with ordinary gendarmes : you stick your thumbs importantly in
your uniform belt; your sword negligently rattles along the pavement, and you lift it up under your right elbow as if it were a
crying child so as not to trouble you, or you throw it behind you
and stand talking to somebody as if you were sitting on it, while
you are aware all the time that you are standing on your feet like
a man – a sergeant. And as a sergeant Ilija understood a lot of
things about high-level politics, and at the barber's he contributed
his opinions, and could even judge between Hitler and Mussolini –
an authority well acquainted with all the subterfuges of other
authorities. Ilija used to bang his sword on the floor, and express
his thoughts soundly and decidedly; there was nothing to be afraid
of; make no mistake : 'There's no soft soap about me, no "kiss your
hand", as those Zagreb folk say. Where I step, no grass grows
again. Ever !' And the barber's shop would go deathly silent : you
would only hear the click of the scissors cutting short both hair
and thoughts : of course, there must be some order in every state.
Ilija's sword zealously banged on the floor and the scissors clicked
on.

'Sergeant, sir' sounded attractive to Ilija when a soldier addressed
him; and it was fine to hear 'Signor Ilija', too, the way the shopkeeper who sold him hair-lotion said it; that sort of familiarity
brought some respect into their relations. And after all once you
entered a shop as a customer, you were expected to exchange a
couple of words with the shop-keeper, it was the thing to do among
the better sort of people.

'And I think so too, Signor Ilija; Hitler is stronger than Mussolini !'

But Ilija realized now that Mussolini had driven him into that
garret, that mouse-hole, and that the *San Marco* was watching him
from the bay like a cat, pretending to be quiet and all the time
pointing her guns at him as if she'd already sniffed the mouse there
in the garret of the gendarmie and said 'All right, we'll just see
how he gets out of there.'

As if Ilija himself had not thought about getting out, as if Ilija needed that macaroni brain of theirs to think about it! It won't be the way you want it, not likely it won't; I wasn't born yesterday! Oh-ho! go out on to the quay and be blown sky-high by your guns? Not on your life! Parade all the garrison out into the open for them to carve us up nice and neat like a butcher? Not a chance, mate, I'm staying here. Come over and get me if you're not too yellow!

'Sergeant, sir! Sergeant, sir!' It was a gendarme with a face that was pale, sallow and unshaven like a sick man.

'Don't bother me! What is it?' Ilija did not like such faces. (And how many times had he told them to shave, imbeciles! It's a disgrace to face the enemy unshaven like that.) 'Tighten your belt unless you want to drop down into your pants! What is it then?'

'They've landed, sir.'

'So what? Have you welcomed them with bread and salt, you joy of my life?'

That was the way Ilija spoke, but even so something stabbed him in the pit of his stomach: 'What? God almighty; already!' It seemed to Ilija that this landing had come too soon and was somehow against regulations. He had expected first a bombardment by the ship's artillery and only then the advance of the infantry. Well, thought Ilija, you've landed all right, but you won't get back on board ship. I'll teach you how to fight a war, cowards! You'll soon see my tactics. Let your Roman God help you then!

'What are we to do, sergeant?' He had forgotten the gendarme, who was looking at him with imploring eyes.

'What are you to do? What are you asking me for? Look at him! What's he to do! And don't you know what the duty of a soldier in wartime is? To fight and to die, my lad! That's it. That's what to do!'

The gendarme took it seriously.

'Does that mean we're to open fire, sergeant?'

'Open fire at who?' Ilija was losing patience. 'At who, you trigger-happy maniac?'

'Well ... at the enemy. ...' The gendarme was almost sick with his own stupidity: he just couldn't grasp the sergeant's train of thought.

'And where is this enemy of yours? Can you see him?'

'My God, what next!' thought the gendarme in his misery. 'You can't get any sense out of this madman, and the enemy's already down on the quay!'

'Well, I haven't seen him yet, sergeant,' he ventured to raise his voice towards the sergeant's star-studded shoulders, 'but we shall be seeing him soon ...'

Ilija heard his own discarded idea coming out of that unshaven mouth and felt somehow plundered of his wisdom. As if the gendarme had forced his way into the HQ's secret archives and stolen the war plans; he looked closely at him like a lion-tamer and asked him sternly as if he had him in front of a court-martial: 'And where did you find that out?'

'What, sergeant?' the gendarme looked as innocent as a virgin being questioned about unspeakable things.

'That we're going to see the enemy soon?'

'Well ... they've already started shooting, sergeant!' The gendarme's amazement was the result of his not unnatural fear that the sergeant had gone off his head. He had run off into this garret and was going mad ...

'What, and you've actually heard it! You know too much my lad! ...' He put his two fingers between the buttons on the gendarme's blouse, and drew him gently towards him as if he wanted to whisper something very confidential into his ear; the gendarme meekly stretched out his neck and offered his ear, and Ilija hissed right into his ear-drum: 'Traitor!'

First the gendarme's ear itched with the sergeant's hot breath, and then the word struck him like a thunderbolt. He tried to smile like a man who can take a joke, but his smile remained stupidly etched around the corners of his mouth; the sergeant with a gesture of disgust pushed him away, and, sighing disappointedly, looked out of the garret window at the sky.

The sergeant himself had become afraid of his own strange inability to take action and had found treason as his ally: it is easier when two people share a lack of loyalty. The gendarme did him a service with his readiness to fight, and he would have loved him for it, had he not begun to believe that he himself had indeed been betrayed. He even tasted the sadness of loneliness in his mouth and swallowed it down bitterly together with his saliva, like a great man awaiting his destiny with appropriate dignity ...

Only the place itself was not adequate for destiny. There were some chests standing around in the garret and upon one of them sat a fat tomcat, Dioko, the gendarmes' pet, who all this time had inquiringly been watching first Ilija, then the gendarme, and who, when the word 'treason' was followed by silence, miaowed impatiently: 'What sort of men are you ...'

Dioko's voice gave the gendarme courage; he could not swallow the word 'traitor'.

'Sergeant, sir,' he began in the solemn tone of a civilian, but the words stuck in his throat when he heard that strange alien voice issuing unexpectedly from it as if from a gramophone.

Ilija turned on his heels, and his sword slapped conspiratorially against his hip as if to remind the gendarme who Ilija was.

'You're still there! Get out of my sight! Don't let me see you any more!' Dioko jumped down from the chest, threw himself in front of Ilija's feet, and began to rub against them ingratiatingly as if seeing injustice being done and begging for pardon. Ilija did not like anybody fawning around his feet where official matters were concerned, and he kicked Dioko with his heavy number 46 box-calf boot, so that the self-sacrificing cat took off among the chests wailing and stupefied with surprise. Such a thing had never happened to him in that house before.

Ilija remained alone in the garret. He remembered that he was there to keep a watch on the situation and began to survey the neighbouring roofs with a strange absentmindedness, pretending that the *San Marco* with her guns was of no importance, but never letting her out of his sight. The *San Marco* was moving her horns like a snail ...

'Snail, snail, put out your horns . . .' said little Ilija in the meadow, his fingers touching the feelers of the yellow snail that with some effort was creeping across the stone carrying its little house on its shoulders. The snail drew in its horns, and Ilija lisped with pleasure: 'Snail, snail, put out your horns or I will sell your house. ...' Ilija lifted his fingers to his eyes and, in his imagination, touched the guns of the snail – *San Marco*. He was playing. The sheep were grazing on the stony Zagora meadowland and Ilija was building a bridge of leaves between the two stones for his snail to cross, and he enjoyed watching it move along the bridge ...

Something rustled and ran across the garret on bare feet. Ilija started.

'Dioko!' but the tomcat gave no answer. Ilija was sorry now for Dioko, and began calling him pet names: 'Diokins, look! a little mouse! Come here then. ...' But the indignant Dioko only purred somewhere behind the chests and would not move.

'What a shame, Diokins, you could make a feast of the little beast ...'

In his Croatian highland school-days there had been some such nursery rhyme about a little mouse which had always seemed funny to Ilija: 'Where she smells a morsel, either cold or hot, she at once of course'll gobble up the lot!' and now he wanted to encourage Dioko, but the cat did not respond. Ilija felt the bitterness of loneliness, and sighed. Those six men, down there, and all those cowards on the island, as well as those across the sea on the mainland, all of them had deserted him! There in those towns, at HQs and garrisons, who would now be thinking about him, commander Ilija, sitting there helplessly on this mousetrap of an island: 'Go to the left – there's no way through; go to the right, the wire's there too ...'

Ilija listened like a mouse, and heard some voices, quite new to his ears.

From the narrow streets there came unintelligible shouts as if people were calling to each other in the dark. And darkness fell before Ilija's eyes: 'It's them!'

'Sergeant, sir!' and Mile's head appeared in the garret; he was a big eater but, notwithstanding, his trousers hung over his behind like a deflated balloon and the gendarmes used to tease him about it. 'I blow it up but it doesn't hold, not my fault,' Mile used to say.

'Sergeant, sir!' repeated Mile, trying to make out the sergeant in the dark corners of the garret behind the chests.

'Here I am! Where do you think you're looking for me? I'm not a cat!' shouted Ilija angrily; 'It's that filthy traitor down there who has told them ...'

'Well, what is it, Mile?' he asked calmly, like an army leader in retreat. 'What's the situation?'

'They've broken through, they're holding the corners!'

'Which corners? Be clear, blast you!'

'Well ... you might say ... from the public conveniences to the chemist's. ... And then from the lawyer's to Bata's boot-shop.'

'And now they're laughing at us, the devils ...' and Ilija added loudly: 'It means the enemy has properly cut us off, huh?'

'Yes, sir.' Mile was waiting for further orders, gun in hand, and standing at attention: this was war. 'I reckon there are two platoons of 'em, with some reserves.'

'It means they knew where to find the gendarmerie,' continued the sergeant, analysing the position. 'And what does that mean? It means ...' there he stopped and bent his nose back with his fore-finger, meditating ... 'that somebody gave away our position to them ... and they came straight towards us. If they'd advanced on the Town Hall. ... It's clear – if there'd been no treachery, they'd have gone towards the Town Hall! ... I had a plan in that case; attack from the rear and then strike at their left flank from the Post Office ... and drive them straight into the sea. But now ...' Ilija waved his hand resignedly, and fell into thought.

'Er, yes,' sighed Mile, and stood at ease, with his rifle in front of him.

The war was over.

And he went down from the garret, stooping, using his gun instead of a stick.

Ilija heard the butt of Mile's rifle knocking against the steps like the drum in the funeral march the military band had played last year at the gendarmerie commander's funeral. The regimental commander who had opposed his promotion: 'Well, I'm still alive!' At that time – God forgive me – the drum echoed sweetly in my heart, like a waltz. A select company of bold gendarmes had marched with sad steps in the funeral procession, and Ilija had been ready to dance to the music. The old man had died. At last he would embrace his beloved, his long-desired sword. And, indeed, not long after, he kissed it and belted it at his hip in the firm belief that he would never again part with it.

'God damn it! It's not six months since!'

Ilija took his sword like a dead infant into his arms, and gave it a long last tender kiss, parting from it as the living part from their dead. Then he unhooked it from his belt and put it at the bottom of the chest as at the bottom of a grave.

'It's all over,' he said, his heart wrung. 'Less than six months ...'

'Sergeant,' Mile was calling from the steps in a strange voice but without showing himself. 'Sergeant, they're looking for you ...'

Nothing mattered to Ilija at all any more ...

Torquato was as excited as a boy arriving first at the winning-post.

Ilija saluted him. Torquato smiled contemptuously and raised his hand negligently to his eyes. With his little yellow boots and his little alpine feather he was very much like a small bird hopping about on a twig. Though so small in front of Ilija, he felt a personal satisfaction in the victory. He kept putting his hands, first one and then the other, on his hips, walking about Ilija's room as if it were a conquered country, kicking the submissive chairs about, and halting in front of a map of Europe on the wall to measure it with his open hand as if he were walking over a continent with immense, stamping steps, up to his neck in victory.

'You could make a feast of the little beast ...' Ilija remembered the nursery rhyme and felt a bit more at ease for thus revenging himself.

Torquato put his finger over a spot on the map (our island was under his finger) and looked up at Ilija inquiringly.

'Yes,' confirmed Ilija darkly, as if by saying that he was surrendering the island to the enemy.

And indeed, after that, Torquato made him a sign to get out. 'So that's it – get lost,' Ilija said to himself and went out.

In such moments one thinks only of sleep. Ilija wanted to lie on his back with his legs wide apart and his arms under his head and sleep like a man, and let everything else go to the devil! It had come and gone!

In the corridor, leaning against the wall, there stood six rifles like six orphans with no mothers or fathers; and on the bench were bayonets, pistols, belts, like a dead girl's dowry. Not a gendarme to be seen! 'Cowards,' said Ilija and felt the pathos of his own fate swelling up in his chest. Holding his head high, he walked proudly along the corridor so that even the Bergamians made way for him respectfully and whispered that this was 'quel caporione'. This whispering about his own person so pleased Ilija that he did not even deign to look down at his wretched enemies.

On his bed was a straw-mattress, good unbleached linen sheets and some brand-new blankets smelling of naphthaline. He quickly rolled it all up, fastened the bundle with a leather strap and hitched it on to his back.

The rag-and-bone man, Francesco, who knew the value of materials, came up to him inquisitively and felt the quality of the blankets and sheets. Ilija, of course, misunderstood this gesture.

'Get away! Or perhaps you think it's your father's?'

By the very tone, Francesco understood what he was being told to do and, almost ashamed, stepped aside. 'Sissignore, scusi!'

Ilija went out into the street. But where was he to go with this burden now? As if trying to save the last bit of the country, he briskly turned the corner and set out towards the shore. As he was walking with his head bent under the burden, at the Town Hall corner he stumbled over the dead dog and stopped for a moment to give it a superficial inspection. 'He did for you, old chap, eh? Bloody coward!' 'It's no joke!' thought Ilija, and realized his burden might be understood as a theft, and might cost him his head. He remembered the guns of the *San Marco* and peered in that direction from under his straw-mattress; they were pointing right at him! He experienced that unpleasant feeling which – for lack of a more adequate term – could be called fear. But even if it wasn't, Ilija was looking for some shelter. In the chain of unhappy events that were taking place that day, Ilija found himself (excuse the trivial detail) in front of the public lavatory and he enthusiastically kissed the hand of Providence which had so mercifully brought him there. Once inside the tiled cubicle, he felt in an atmosphere of safety, as if under a hospital roof protected by the international sign of the Red Cross.

'Ooph,' uttered somebody on the other side of the partition, and Ilija's heart sank. 'Ooph, ooph!'

Ilija coughed in response.

As if it had been a password, from behind the wall appeared Manzo, the old attendant of that establishment, and looked wonderingly at Ilija.

'Manzo ...' whispered Ilija hurriedly, 'don't stand staring at me like a calf, but. ... Hold on, are we alone? Well, listen then, store these things for me. You'll get a blanket.'

Manzo scratched behind his ear, then settled his cap further on to his head as if not wishing his thoughts to be seen.

'Humph,' he continued as if he had understood something. 'A blanket?'

'Have a look at it, it's new. I've only used it twice. It still smells of the store.'

Ilija pushed the blanket under Manzo's nose to tempt him with the naphthaline smell. But Manzo did not like it, it made him feel sick; he preferred the odour of leather.

'Give me your boots ...'

'Boots? Am I to walk around barefoot? You good for nothing! Here, take the blanket!'

'I don't want it. ... Give me your tunic, and put all those things over here.' Manzo showed him a small compartment where he kept his lavatory-cleaning equipment.

It was hot. The April sun was scorching down so that the sweat was trickling down Ilija's body under the thick serge of his winter uniform.

'I'll have to take it off anyway,' thought Ilija, trying to reconcile himself to the situation; but then there rose before him, somehow officially, the severe word 'uniform', all buttoned up to the neck, and with his left hand he felt like punching Manzo's lavatory snout.

'You want to strip me naked, you bandit! I'll bust your teeth in.' But his rage was somewhat eclipsed by the straw-mattress, and thundered pitifully and harmlessly away.

'I'm real scared, Ilija,' said Manzo, looking for him under the straw-mattress. 'Where's your sword?'

'Hmm!' sighed Ilija, martyr-like, but decided to swallow the insult; at the same time it was a sign that he would accept this rogue's conditions. He knew the rules of war: he had taken a bit of spoil out of the very beak of his enemy, and who knows by what laws 'they' would judge him.

'Well, you old bastard,' said Ilija in a conciliatory way. 'Where's this hen-coop of yours, then?'

'And what about the tunic?' Manzo did not believe a down and out with no power and no salary. 'You'll get it when I put my civvies on.' Ilija was trying to convince him by shouting at him.

'Not likely! Just like you used to say, not bloody likely, my lad!' and Manzo barred the way with his arms. 'Give me the tunic at once, or take the whole lot away with you. I'm not going to swing for you.'

'Hmm,' muttered Ilija once more, and bent his head under the burden of fate. He put the things in the little cubby-hole among the brooms and pails, then he wiped the sweat from his face with a crumpled handkerchief and stopped in front of Manzo with all his former authority. With the burden taken off his shoulders, the white bone stars of his rank showed up again, and Ilija straightened himself up and thrust out his chest; in his breast he again felt the dignity of a sergeant, and even in his legs and arms. For a moment he allowed himself once again to be deluded by the past so that he almost succeeded in blurring even Manzo's sense of reality. But from this momentary happy dream, Ilija was rudely awakened by loud steps in the street, and strange voices brought him back to the reality of the tiled communal establishment and Manzo's impatient physiognomy in front of him.

He began bemusedly to unbutton his tunic almost solemnly, as if at every button he had to say a special little prayer, then out of his pockets he took his purse, a propelling pencil, a comb and the small round mirror with the picture of a naked woman on its smooth rubber back. He drew his arms out of his sleeves, with his eyes closed, as if taking the skin off his back and then, for a moment, held his tunic in his hands, as if bidding it farewell.

'Not so fast!' shouted Ilija to the savager of this dramatic moment; then he took out his pen-knife and cut off the six bone stars, and after counting them once more in his palm, he put them carefully into a special compartment of his purse.

'Take it, Shylock!'

Manzo looked the tunic over twice, on both sides, and held it up to the light to see that the moths had not made holes in it ...

'And when will you come for these other things? Because they may give this job to one of their own people. ... And me ... you know, if they find them, well, I won't ...'

'Don't be afraid. I'll get them as soon as I find a lodging.' Ilija moved towards the door, tucking his shirt into his trousers.

'Take your cap off, Ilija,' Manzo reminded him in a friendly way. 'How can you go about with a cap on without your tunic?'

Of course! He felt sick at the thought that he would now have to walk through the town like a beggar, in only his shirt and breeches; but he still had his gendarme's boots on; he didn't know himself how to walk, for the question was: what was he now? It occurred to him to have a smoke as a minor aid to reassessing the situation. From his pocket he produced a crumpled orphan-like Ibar cigarette that almost aroused pity with its poor white crumpled cigarette paper. He put it gently to his lips as if to kiss it – and did not light it.

For some time Ilija hesitated at the door of the said public establishment; he would put one foot forward ready to step out, but drew it back immediately as if he had stepped into cold water. At last he made up his mind, and taking off his cap with both hands as if it had been a crown, he blew away the cobwebs that it had collected in the garret, unfastened the cockade and put it into the same part of his purse where his stars already were. With his handkerchief he wiped his sweating forehead and the leather band inside his cap (this he did simply out of habit, not giving it any deeper symbolic meaning), then he handed his cap to Manzo to keep for him ...

Well, now the State was done for. ... That was what Ilija felt at the touch of the cool air on his bare head; and a melancholy sense of irresponsibility began to console him more and more insistently as if he had been looking forward to just that. An immoral feeling of liberation started to bother him, so that he even felt sorry for the State, as if for some dignified old person with moustaches and the rank of general. He felt relieved in an uneasy way, like having been sick after a night's carousing. Soon some new hopes began to be born; they were pink and plump and had rosy cheeks and swelling bosoms, and stout, rounded legs. A sense of warmth came over Ilija, a carefree, idyllic dream of a soft bed with fresh white sheets, and soft round arms naked to the armpits. Something naked and soft stirred his desires like a breeze that slightly ruffles the surface of the water.

He hadn't the courage to step out into his new state, and so he hesitated there at the door as if plucking the petals off a forget-me-not : yes – no.

Ilija had become good; he felt an urge to entreat somebody for forgiveness or to save a child from drowning. He wanted people to love him, or, at least, to pity him, if they found it easier. In a word, he wanted to carry the burden of his martyrdom in public, passing through the warm whispers of the onlookers, and then to vanish round the corner into oblivion ... leaving behind him only wonder and appreciation. ... He sought some modest dignity to cloak his indefinite personality before stepping out into the road ... almost naked, with only his shirt and gendarme's breeches on, and the boots on his feet that couldn't walk in a gendarme-like way any more. His legs wouldn't move like sharp scissors any more (and justice-loving scissors at that; Ilija used to say : I'm a strict commander, but a just one), they could no longer decisively, as of old, chop up those streets of the State, up and down, to and fro, and chop you up too if you happened to cross their path; chop you down to size so that you would remember me ! I am strict but just !

And now. ... As if newly born that very day, he felt all of a sudden, everywhere around him, a big unknown world full of tricks and ambushes.

The people at the barber's were our own folk, homely, you knew them through and through; they would say something they shouldn't, jokingly, it's true, but you had only to raise your eyebrows to have them tiny and good again upon your very palm, and could put them in your pocket. If they wanted to steal away round the corner you only had to step on their toes and say, 'Don't go away, my lad, don't grow where you haven't been sown; go back and stay where I can see you. Get a haircut and a shave like a man and if you've anything to say, the barber's is the right place, and not braying around in the dark how you would do this and that if only. ...' Well, 'this' and 'that' were just what was in store for him now! Didn't I tell you nicely, sonny? ... But you just called me 'basher' and 'copper'. Just you try anything against that little cock with his feather now. And here he is, look, right here.

And Ilija wanted to move away, to go inside, not to be in Torquato's way as he came round the corner with – what can we call it? – an historical gait, looking up at the windows to see if flowers would be strewn on him, though the feather on his hat was trembling anxiously over his head, since he could really expect nothing good to come from above. But Torquato was confidently walking on soil that had just been conquered and that was now peacefully and submissively spread under his feet. Rome – Home.

Ilija felt the soaked tip of his cigarette in his mouth and bit it off, but it was too late now to spit it out; it might be misunderstood – 'I'll teach you to spit at me, you wretch!' And it wasn't in order : the man was passing by decently – so to speak – as if someone you knew were walking along the street; well, you can't simply spit in front of him. ... Eh, how like cattle we are sometimes! ... And a smart, peaceful officer at that. ... The hen's feathers on the officer's hat somehow tickled Ilija; but he winked discreetly and sensibly, ignored the untimely joke, trying instead to strike a cultured pose to attract the officer's attention. Ilija eagerly showed himself at the door. One soldier facing another, or – no help for it – a non-commissioned officer facing an officer of the army that has won the war; that had to be admitted. He might approach me – we already know each other – and speak a few words, inquire what the people are like here. It's not easy for him, he's taking over authority, and who could better inform him than myself who is a peaceful citizen, and who is that good-for-nothing who brays in

the darkness. .:. And surely he'd say: 'Thank you, sergeant; if
you need anything, don't hesitate, I'm here.' And I'd answer:
'Thank you, captain sir, I shan't be in need of anything for myself,
but I might happen to need something for these people here and
they'll have a glass of primissima wine and some good fish for you;
I was like a father to them. ...' 'That's why I'm here,' Ilija seemed
to hear the officer say as he passed by.

Ilija clicked his heels smartly and thankfully lifted his hand
above his ear, but he only touched his bare head and that made
him leer confusedly at the officer so that one might have thought
him one of those homeless idiots that spend their time hanging
round the cauldrons of military kitchens with a tin-kettle in their
hands, who are paid for doing some small job with pieces of old
army clothing out of the stores, and who salute everyone in uniform, believing themselves also to be military persons. It seems that
Torquato took Ilija for such a creature, for he first looked at him
with a protective, sympathetic smile, and then beckoned him
forward.

'Ohè, tu lazzarone! Vien qua!'

'Sir!' replied Ilija readily. (You see, he's a real man, just as I
thought.)

'Guarda,' with two fingers Torquato turned Ilija's head towards
the murdered dog. 'Quel cane, hè, butta via: Capito? Butta giù,'
and he pointed at the dog and at the sea.

'Oh, yes, it's unhealthy to have carrion lying around in the
street,' said Ilija, making conversation. ... 'And this sun is really
scorching ...'

'Eh?' asked Torquato with mild authority.

'I say it's hot, eh? It's just too hot to keep your tunic on,' and
he began to roll up his shirt sleeves to show ...

It seemed as if Ilija was rolling his sleeves up to get down to
work, and Torquato liked this ready obedience and offered Ilija a
thick fine-smelling cigarette which he took out of a packet wrapped
in cellophane ...

'Oh, thank you!' Ilija stuck the cigarette behind his ear, and unbuttoned his shirt at the breast as if suffocating from the heat, and
said 'oogh!' to prove that he was.

Torquato thought Ilija was fooling about there in front of him in gratitude for the cigarette, so he gave him another, but then he felt he had to go away quickly to save his reputation. 'Fa, presto, hè?' said he, departing and pointing at the dead dog.

'I'll do it at once, signor. ...' Ilija was surprised to hear himself use this last word; it came to him all of a sudden and he seized upon it as on an old acquaintance. Like some sturdy but green country boy with curly hair and hairy chest who had just done his military service and come down into town in his army trousers and white peasant's shirt to look for a job, Ilija stayed in the street with his long arms hanging down unoccupied, addressing everyone as 'signor'. And he moved about humbly and obediently like a verger in church as though he had rubber heels on his boots so as not to disturb the town's solemn procession. Ilija went up to the dead dog and bent over it as over a dead man responsible for his own death.

'Well, old chap, so you barked, did you? and now you've had it,' Ilija kept saying to the dead dog, picking it up gently in his arms like a poor dead orphan; he was sorry for the animal and reproached it for dying. 'Oh, oh, there's nothing to carry, just a few bones. ... Why did you have to stick your nose in, poor old dog? Wanted to argue with an officer, eh? Eh, old chap, you shouldn't have barked out of turn ...' and Ilija stroked its ears and its back, and tears came into his eyes.

'No, no, he didn't bark at all, it was the man who was in a dog's temper,' mumbled Manzo from the lavatory, busily clattering his pails about.

Ilija didn't listen to Manzo, but went on crooning to the dog as he carried it down to the sea: 'Eh, poor old chap. ...' All of a sudden he heard Dioko miaow somewhere near and looked round for him. But there round the corner stood Mile the Eater in a short civilian jacket and on his head he had a cap with a hard cardboard peak that was broken in the middle and made him look even drier and sterner; and Dioko came to Ilija and miaowed and rubbed himself around Ilija's feet.

'Leave it alone, sergeant,' said Mile to him seriously, and Ilija seemed to hear a tone of command in his voice.

'But why should I, Mile?' He was looking at Mile now as if in a dream, not believing his eyes. 'Sergeant' came to him as from afar, sounding like some vague memory. He had the impression of being again drawn back into some painful, indefinite status, into something very difficult and rigorous, full of obligations and responsibilities. ... They wanted him to put on a uniform again, to be what he no longer was, since everything was over now and dead, and his tears were shed over that death ...

'Let it alone!' repeated Mile, his voice trembling with fury.

'What for, Mile?' asked Ilija subserviently, as though his junior.

'Leave that dog!' shouted Mile, his voice getting more and more angry. 'Have you become the enemy's refuse-collector?'

'What do you mean – refuse-collector?' (The word aroused him.) 'Imbecile. It's got to be done; it might spread disease.'

'So what! Is it any business of yours? Let them see to it.'

'Ah, so it's order that bothers you, eh, Eater? So that's it! I suspected what you were even before. You were with those who brayed in the dark! Traitor!'

'Hee, hee, hee,' laughed Manzo from inside, among his pails like some evil lavatory demon.

Mile went pale, and his hand shook in his pocket, but he turned abruptly on his heel and disappeared round the corner.

Dioko, the cat, stayed there on the corner and miaowed helplessly like an orphan.

'Come on, Diokins, come here ...'

Dioko started at his voice, which reminded him of something unpleasant, and ran away after Mile, calling him along the empty streets and miaowing unhappily.

Ilija put the dog down on the ground, and tied a big stone round its neck, and without tears or any comforting words, hurled it high into the air and well out to sea from the shore.

Manzo watched him from the lavatory, turning his back and spitting at the thought of such a job.

The water swallowed the dead dog, and Ilija gazed at the circles on the surface of the water.

'Well, that's the end of you, old chap ...'

And he rubbed his palms together as if washing them, like Pilate ...

Translated by Svetozar Brkić

Jure Kaštelan

MASTS

No roots nor noise-filled branches,
no nests nor birdsong.
Mast, tree stripped naked.
Mast, tree of love.
Mast, tree of restlessness.
Tall masts in seas amidst the stars,
in sounding bells, in whistling hawsers,
in storm-winds' splendour, in the sun's own valour.
Masts. Masts.
Your wood-grown memory forgets the lakeside stillness.
Laughter for you is sobbing, your repose a fitful dance.
You put forth no squirrels nor stag's love-call
when sailors hum their sad nostalgic songs
of home beneath you.
At anchor in the bay you cannot see your image
in the salt water.
The shoreline knows you by your flags,
the hatchet by your hardness,
and I who learnt from you to breathe,
alone amongst travellers,
know your soul:
erectness.
Straight masts.
Tall masts.
Tree remembered.

STONE'S LAMENT

Return me to the bedrock, to the fissure, to the mountains' weft.
My virginity to the laws of eternity.
Cast me into the seas, the oceans, give me up to thunder.
Lords of earth, give me peace and sleep.
May your armies' hoofs not ring out above me.
May no tears flow.
Tear me out of pavement and street, from doorways of gaols and
    cathedrals.
Let lightning and storm beat upon me. And the stars
be my crown.
                    And you, hand which raises the chisel,
give me no human life.
Nor heart, nor reasons, nor eyes
to see.
Give me back to the marble seas, to dreams, to mists.
Lords of earth, give me peace and sleep.
            You, hand which raises the chisel, do not wake me.
Nor give me eyes to look upon evil.

THINGS

Your body remained immobile
and the blood of a love.
Your hairpins were left behind and a ray of your hair,
the band of white with which you bound your breasts.
A doll and a shoe
which moved mountains.
A sketch book, a wooden flute, a seashell,
a little stone, a button and a chain
and a box of all precious colours

creating the wonder of life.
Making
the world an endless rose
of non-existence.
I take the thread of your unrest for the sake of happiness.
And, when dreams are no more
things remain.
The wind's axe on the brows of the river
remains outside time.

SHEPHERDESS

She knows each sheep by name
but does not know her love.

She is drunk with dreaming
Like a river with its own rustling.

She summons all by name
but her love is nameless.

The sheep return to the fold
but her love has no shelter.

LULLABY OF KNIVES

Move off without looking back ! You go at the head of the dead.
Look down the sights at the first violets. Sleep in your boots.

     Dark knives are seeking out your throat.

Don't drink at the springs, they are poisoned
For the mountains have split with snakes' venom.

     Dark knives are seeking out your eyes.

There's no sleep in which lovers' anguish may dream
Nor a scream which rings out in cleft and crevasse.

     Dark knives are seeking out your hearts.

Dark knives sound your lullaby,
    They cut the dawn which you glimpse
into two halves
       of dreaming and blood.

Translated by Bernard Johnson

Slavko Mihalić

METAMORPHOSIS

I want to know from where
comes this emptiness so that
I change into a glassy lake in which
the bottom can be clearly seen, but without fish.

But without crabs, without shells, without
water weed, which at least
bears some name, for I today
am nameless. Almost without entity.

And so speaking of emptiness I move
water within the lake, it scatters
sand and some small particles settle
down to the bottom. My stomach is sickened.

I go through the streets, my head bowed, alongside
some other lake mainly sombre
and poisonous; we don't speak of those
foul beings which crawl in our depths, so that
now I breathe in my own stench.

DON'T HOPE

Don't hope that you can escape, friend.
There's hunters enough on your trail for you to be caught some
    day;
So handsome your scream that the woods around will blossom.
Your pain has a beauty existing with no care for you.

No point in hoping or hiding, just keep going forward,
Fear neither arrow nor bullet – they'll finish you off just the same
    in the end;

But at least be great in your gracious submission
Which is not for their plundering gaze nor their ravens' eyes.

LOVERS' FLIGHT

I tell you, we must leave now at once
Where to – we can always decide that later
The important thing is to go right now
I can feel my innards beginning to rot.

My eyes have dried up and are more like burnt leaves
My heart's clock is stopping, it can scarcely be heard
Must I really be sorry to leave my grave empty
What can I do if for someone it's pleasant to lie there.

Come, let's not tarry, love,
A plague on the coffins, they're surely already infected;
But not by the highroad.
Maybe an ambush awaits us –
We'll follow an aerial way alongside the stars.

'I'M TRYING TO STOP TIME'

I'm trying to stop time,

In between those who are trampling
And those who are trying to hide

Confused before a pompous triumphal arch
Derided, with all the things that I've spoiled

By a hand's gentle movements, a hand to which blows are
 abhorrent
By eyes made beautiful by the pain within them.

I'm trying to stop time
For an impatient driver, for a frightened deer

To give form to an extraordinary happening in the street
Which only half-happened.

Translated by Bernard Johnson

Stevan Raičković

STONE LULLABY

Sleep now
Wherever you may be –
With kindly hearts
Or bitter thoughts
Or bloodstained hands;
Impassioned
Enraptured,
Hands moving in the grass,
Lips murmuring in the hay,
Sleep now.

Grow now
Into a blue-stone sleep –
You who are now alive,
You who will be dead tomorrow
Black waters, edged with white foam,
Bridges bending over the void,
Sleep now.

Sleep now, plant, without withering;
Sleep now, marigolds, turned to stone;
Sleep now, you sad and you weary –
Sleep together.

The last bird lingers in the sky,
Turn towards my face
And breathe that name once more, bird,
then turn to stone in air.

EPITAPH FOR BRANKO MILJKOVIĆ

Not a path to be seen in the frozen waste;
Only the wild geese move in the sky,
And dusk falls early. I go to my bronze friend,
Watching the geese as they fly southward.

Can you hear how they drown us with cries?
(Almost like you I have nothing to say.)
Above us they drift in slow, steady flight.
Shall I wipe the snow away from your head?

Do I see (or perhaps foretell)
My own death and that of our comrades?
What a strange, magnetic silence I hear
In the breast of your statue.

INSCRIPTION FOR THE MONUMENT
AT PRKOS*

Amidst the war we never touched a gun
But we all fell by the executioner's hand.
Once we were living people, women, children,
Now we are nothing, neither dust nor shade.

And none of us will ever come again
We lie here in the night of no return.
Appearing only now and then in Prkos
Transmuted into dew or into grass.

Translated by Muriel Heppel

*The village of Prkos was the scene of a particularly bloody massacre during the occupation. On 21 December 1941, out of 608 inhabitants, 470 were put to death.

Danijel Dragojević

ON THE DECK

I often think of how
Tobias journeyed with the unseen three.
They were with him while he broke bread
When he was angry and in wearied sleep,
So his dwelling place was named.

We have full knowledge only of the illustrated
Sight, hearing and the sweetened story,
A litte more perhaps, but
There's room for everything within the camera's eye.

In that company Tobias (it is said)
Lived in agreement with his hands,
Whilst ours rely only upon themselves;
The left one browbeaten, the right one wild,
Hardly a recommended accord for the body.

But we'll explain it all.
We know both where and when. Why.
Swiftness and beauty's concord sing in us.
Just keep on going onwards, music.
Sober and well-rested faces.

What do we say? Where did we live?
In a whitewashed, historical,
Fine clear room for night time
We'll fill in all the details, change them
Somehow or other, any way. A wondrous apparatus!
Where, in what district did Tobias disappear?

Behind a curtain and inside a well
We are not summoned up by demons,
We stayed outside the unseen swallows.
Tomorrow, please, a ticket to go on further!

Hands on the rail and a firm horizon.
Needed hand, voice of another dawn
Which knows our weakness and our own misfortune,
We might have pitied that we were so young
With strength but not humility. We know.
But still we didn't push away the cup, the bitter wall.
Please don't allow this blindness, arrogance.
Thy Will be done.

UNDER THE UMBRELLA

Perhaps we shouldn't have come out.
Immediate darkness, deafening thunder, wet feet,
Desire for the warmth of home,
The thought that we are powerless and dead
Under the big drops.
We could have waited just a while
Others are peacefully asleep, we here
Huddle around our wooden staff,
The one firm place round which our room is breaking.
We were never closer than now
While that black rag protects us from the sky,
Never so simple, never so together.
Two bare branches in the night.
Where now the wish to build, the arrogance,
The arrested gesture, the body's transport?
Perhaps the seed is already alive in the furrow
And there are good thoughts in bright windows
For us after death.

But the water takes our land away from us,
Not letting us look upwards,
And all is moisture, loaded with emptiness
In two abandoned bodies
A dog somewhere gnaws at a lonely bone.
While a lover strives to create a mirror
Amongst the scattered bedrugs.
There's no despair here, nor feeling for the future,
Pictures and thoughts to lean upon –
There's no such dust now.
All is so simple, uncomplicated !
The rain falls, holes fill up, darkness and wind,
Slowly we move away.

AUTUMN, WHEN SOWERS FAIL TO RECOGNIZE THE WAYS OF THEIR SEED

LOVE IS THE OPPOSITE OF ALL REVOLUTION
(from another book)

You see, the gesture with which you directed thousands of souls has
    withered.

It's here in the elation of cars on an outing,
It's here in your room at the piano keyboard.
How easily we used to go out of the home !
The darkness waiting for us so inhospitably,
But we flushed with laughter, happy, it didn't deter us.
The very first morning the thud of a body falling.
Afterwards silence. Later it multiplied, multiplied,
Perhaps it was something to do with origin, treason, defence
It's a splendid thing lined up in front of a wall.
That's how the road to the longed for freedom began.
Nowadays you part your hair in the middle almost unthinking.

Neither those who sent the reports nor those who received them
Knew how to read from their contents the vision of change
Which on our marriage bed will rise up like a hairy shadow.
We answered hatred with hatred, suffering with longer suffering,
And now our children's faces are those of the victims.

FISHING IN AN OLD PICTURE

Now is the thought of God
Come among men who pull in their nets
Tranquil, with no thought of shipwreck
Away from the leaden sun
Which paces beside us.

What rare splendour.
The hand – a sign of brotherhood,
Strength is turned into deed
An ordinary day into piety.

Is this remembering
Or a foresight of what is to come?

On all sides, from the open sea
Amongst those faces,
In colours and in the hands,
From the watery crests behind,
Something tells us
That all things perhaps
Could culminate in good,
Both thought and deed,
That we could live
In all simplicity,

With simple speech
And just a little hope,
To take our bread
From the depths of sadness.

Translated by Jovan Hristić and Bernard Johnson

Vladan Desnica

JUSTICE

One Sunday afternoon a few years ago, returning to town after a long walk, a revolting sight met my eyes. In the middle of the road a man was mercilessly beating a woman. His face wore an expression of sheer, animal fury. He'd grabbed the poor creature by her hair and dragged her till she fell on to her face and then begun to beat her on the mouth, the eyes, heedless of where his blows were falling. Sickened with disgust, my first impulse was to hurl myself at him. Had I done so, my attack, impelled as it was by motives of mercy, would have equalled the strength of my moral indignation and my moral indignation was such that, without doubt, I too would have attacked with blind fury, striking him on the eyes and mouth, heedless of where my blows were falling. It is also probable that, had I done so, my face too would have taken on an expression of sheer, animal fury and, certainly, no one would have been able to read in it the nobility of my purpose.

As, however, I recalled the countless occasions in the past when I had acted too hastily, a drop of icy doubt fell on my fury and cooled my ardour for humane intervention. It is possible that this was due to a short, middle-aged man with chubby cheeks and fair, straw-coloured hair who was calmly looking on, with an uncertain smile. I remember that, at first, his comfortable indifference roused in me a feeling of disgust. But immediately afterwards I did just what he was doing; stuck my hands in my pockets and proceeded to watch. Example, as is well known, is irresistible. In the majority of cases (let us be frank) we consider others more stupid than ourselves. On the other hand, however, we usually redeem this in practice by following their example. And so I controlled my indignation.

No sooner had I done so than that well-known 'other self', the one that reasons and doubts, began to speak.

I have long been convinced that a sense of justice largely depends on the imagination. In order to be an impartial judge, we must be acquainted with the background of motives and causes, with the relation and interdependence of the matters we are judging. We must not be led astray by first impressions, by superficial appearances. On the contrary, we must seek out the hidden causes, the conditioning factors, the long chain of wrongs committed and wrongs suffered, we must probe our way to the very depths of the people we judge so as to discover the end of the tangled skein. It is our duty to do all this before we have a right to pronounce judgement.

I began to think: who knows what offences this woman may have committed against this man? Who knows what he may have done for her, what sacrifices he may have made, how much he may have borne, how often he may have forgiven her, enduring his own suffering in silence? Who knows to what depths of shamelessness and cynicism he may have sunk in her wickedness? Perhaps she's a heartless mother who's left her child to suffocate with the croup, while she went out with a lover? If this is so, then would it not be true that she's also guilty of driving her husband to act in this disgraceful way, of reducing him to the state of a savage beast? Would it not then also be true to say that his action, however ugly, was at least understandable in human terms? And, if this were the case, would he not consider our intervention on his wife's behalf an act of extreme injustice? – Yes, perhaps it was a good thing I hadn't interfered.

But, while I was thinking along these lines, and the blows continued to rain down, a third passer-by appeared. He was an athletic young man with long, wavy hair, dressed in a blue sweater and carrying a tennis racket under his arm. He took in the situation at a glance and, casting a look of scorn at us two passive spectators, flung himself on the man without further hesitation – just as I had wanted to do a few moments before – and began hitting and punching wildly, careless of where his blows fell. Taken by surprise, the man immediately let go of the woman and began to defend himself against his attacker. In the meantime, the woman, with an alacrity scarcely to be expected after such a beating, squirmed out of the way, rose to her knees and got up. Dusting her elbows and knees and tidying her dishevelled hair (seeing this concern for her hair, her stature as the innocent victim rapidly diminished in my eyes) she slipped away unnoticed.

At this moment, across the street, there appeared an elderly man leading a small boy by the hand. He looked like a grandfather taking his little grandson for a walk, looking after him with typical grandfatherly solicitude. He was just engaged in pointing out something in the branches of one of the poplars lining the avenue, probably a bird or a nest, when he caught sight of the struggle and halted, amazed. But he too quickly summed up the situation. He saw a young man, a hefty brute, attacking a man much older than himself, beating him mercilessly and, clearly, without justification (for we instinctively consider the weaker to have justice on his side). He also saw two selfish, unworthy wretches who were calmly looking on – and in an instant his mind was made up. Leading the child to one side, he drew himself up and leapt upon the aggressor (for we instinctively identify the stronger with the aggressor) and began to punch him with all his might.

Faced with a new complication, it occurred to me that, but for the prudence I had shown a moment ago, I should have been the recipient of those blows and would have been returning them with bitterness and deep conviction, striking back at the man who had intervened for exactly the same motives as I had myself and who was, in fact, therefore my ally and fellow champion of fair play.

Thus, all for the sake of justice and in the name of humanity, three human beings were beating the life out of one another in the defence of the innocent while, a few steps away, two unworthy egoists refused to lift a little finger for the sake of their fellow man. Two egoists, three aggressors, four bruised and battered victims. Thus the five or six of us were guilty of several kinds of offence. There were those guilty of taking part in a brawl, those guilty of passive non-intervention, those guilty of interfering in other people's affairs without knowing the rights and wrongs of the matter and those who were guilty of not doing so, faint-hearted egoists and furious philanthropists; those guilty of meting out arbitrary justice and those who were guilty of preventing that justice, however arbitrary, from being put into effect. When I first came on the scene I'd looked with contempt on the chubby-faced man and then immediately followed his example. From then on, I'd sided with each participant in the fray, only, a moment later, to condemn him in favour of the newcomer whom, also seconds later, I began to see as the aggressor and wish him defeat in his turn at the hands of his new assailant. The affair had taken its course and the interventions had taken place exactly as I had wished – almost as if I had invisibly controlled them. And now, after all this, I was still far from sure as to who was in the right and what I desired the outcome to be. Of one thing I was certain, I wanted defeat for the aggressor and victory for each of the victims, success for the weaker and failure for the stronger. I wanted the weaker to become the stronger and the stronger the weaker, the aggressor to become the victim and the victim the aggressor. But the difficulty was that all the participants had passed, successively, through the roles of stronger and weaker, aggressor and victim, champion of justice and offender against justice. How could I un- ravel such a tangle or give an impartial judgement now? Was it possible that injustice was identical with strength? That justice lay in weakness? Did the title of righteousness have to be pur- chased at the price of defeat?

At the end of the avenue, still a long way off, there appeared the silhouette of a policeman. The mere appearance of official justice had an amazingly rapid effect. All the militant zeal went out of the combatants and the fighting ceased. The elderly man remem- bered the little boy and rushed off to find him. The husband tried to restore some shape into his crumpled hat while the young man pressed a handkerchief to a swollen eye and shook back his wavy hair. His surplus of accumulated energy had evaporated into the warm, Sunday afternoon.

JUSTICE WAS SATISFIED!

Translated by E. D. Goy

Dobrica Ćosić

FREEDOM

The freest people of my generation become spectators and witnesses at trials. The Satanoid world, infuriated by its lack of freedom and happiness, is preparing for Total War against our freedom and happiness. By means of the sad, the stupid, the shy, the timid, the feeble and the naïve, and by means of fanatics, misanthropes, homosexuals, pessimists, lyricists, metaphysicians, Utopians, ascetics, masochists, all enemies of civilization and high technical standards, and other subnormal types, the Satanoid states are organizing a network of spies to ferret out all kinds of dissatisfaction and discontent with happiness and freedom; they are organizing acts of sabotage against our happiness, conspiracies against Him and Kamonia. Newspapers and books, radio and television, psychovision and somnovision, cinemas and theatres, music and painting, architecture and technology, restaurants and churches, museums and beaches, sports-grounds and shops – everywhere and without ceasing men are taught how to be happy and how to enjoy freedom, and warned against Satanoid aims and ideas and against Antiistic actions and methods. And yet there are more and more Antiists; they keep turning up everywhere.

The Forum of the Creators of the Future has told us that this is in fact a clear sign of the death agony of the Satanoid world, which is making a last desperate effort to destroy our happiness and freedom which are, of course, indestructible. In addition, they say, the appearance of so many Antiists is evidence that Kamonia, together with Him, is marching invincibly forward into a perfect future; and that this is the final, great purification of the Kamonian people of all kinds of weaklings, paranoids, cowards, unbelievers and malefactors. In this last, sacred reckoning we shall commit to the flames the last remnants of doubt in our happiness; we shall confess all unfree actions, ideas and intentions, and we shall punish once and for all every criminal and wrong-doer.

Our science and our art have shown us that in fact we are none of us entirely free from guilt in this respect; if we are not Antiists ourselves, we have certainly heard or seen an Antiist, and we can be sure that on that occasion he did not let slip the opportunity cunningly and skilfully to implant his seeds in our souls; if we are not guilty now, there is a strong possibility that we will be; if we have not yet seen, heard or met a Satanoid or an Antiist, there is every likelihood that we will do so. We are beginning to believe that every Kamonian is guilty, or that he could be or will be; if we have not yet participated in Antiist activities, we can be certain that we are present and future participants; to put it plainly, no one can be certain that one day he will not begin to have doubts about his happiness for one reason or another. So it is absolutely necessary for Him to continue to convince us of our Happiness and Freedom, that we should study His Principles more and more thoroughly, that we should love Him still more and convince ourselves of the fact that we could be even happier.

Every day and from all parts of the country we write messages of love and devotion. A movement is developing for the writing of such messages at the end of each day's work, after performances in theatres and cinemas, after concerts and football matches, after every joyful experience – such as the awakening of spring in the countryside, walks by the river, delight in the first snow, weddings, nights of love, the birth of a child, and, of course, after funerals. We must be continually expressing our love for Him, affirming the strength of our happiness and expressing gratitude for it, and bearing witness to our faith. To ensure the prompt dispatch of telegrams, the Post Office is opening special counters in shops, in all public institutions, in restaurants, factories, offices and cemeteries, and we are promised that in the near future every house will have a special post and telegraph centre for sending letters and telegrams to Him. In addition, teams of special advisers are being organized, consisting for the most part of poets, who provide those citizens with less literary ability and philosophic vision with new, pithy metaphors, lofty phrases, and eloquent epithets; this service is free. We are the creators of Total Love for Him : never in the history of the world has any people so greatly loved someone as we love Him.

We know by heart everything He has ever said; we study His Dreams, we speak with His Accent, we have all practised His Gestures to perfection, we tell only His Jokes. Everything that He thinks, we all think too; what He wishes we all wish; we all eat whatever He eats. Beetrage and Chocoroon, His favourite dishes, are always to be found in all restaurants; the Mariblack, His favourite flower, can be seen in every house in Kamonia; Pline, His favourite tree, has the place of honour in parks and gardens, and special care and attention is given to it; all citizens of Kamonia carry reproductions of His favourite fishes in their pockets and handbags; if we feel like having a good laugh, we listen to gramophone records of His Jokes. At those times when He likes pornographic pictures, all the existing text-books and readers are replaced by new ones with the appropriate pornographic pictures, and grown-ups devote themselves in their free time to the philosophy and aesthetics of sex. The songs which He likes have become our hymns; in fact, we always recognize as a hymn a song or singer which He likes best. Since He is, perhaps, a man of small or short stature, or will be such, or has been, or so it seems to us – for we see Him only in photographs – we must, just in case, be shorter than Him; indeed, the harmony and unity of Kamonia is being perfected according to this truth : we elect to the Electory people of shorter stature than Him, as short as possible, in fact, so that in all photographs where He appears with the Creators of Total Victory and other appropriate persons, He is not only a head taller, but unequivocally a giant among dwarfs. Our film stars, model girls, famous sportsmen and all other prominent people are shorter than He is; thus the Kamonian type of masculine beauty is a short man. The Cult of the Short Man is supported by fables and other historical literature. The Academy of Memoristics has published several scientific works, with lavish illustrations and exhaustive documentation, which confirm the fact that all great men and geniuses in the past were people of small or short stature. The Academy of Memoristics has also published an Anthology of Faults and Imperfections, which shows unmistakably that tall people in Kamonia are suspected of being Satanoids; from their early childhood tall people are subject to scorn and rigid control so that there is no possibility of them falling into Antiism.

In our total identification with Him, our freedom is conditioned by His allergy to meat. How to abstain from meat is one of Kamonia's major problems. The movement against eating meat has achieved massive dimensions and resulted in a general emasculation which is acquiring an increasing aesthetic significance although it is not reflected so favourably in sporting results especially in boxing and field athletics – not that anyone doubts for a moment that the spirit is stronger than the flesh. Another national problem is His short period of sleep and His most original dodecaphonic wheezing and snoring during His sleep. Although the Mass Non-Sleep Movement has yielded exceptional results – the national record-breakers sleep for only ten minutes – the snoring contests broadcast by the Central Somnovision Authorities have not proved so satisfactory : the whole of Kamonia is convinced that His snoring is musically unique and inimitable.

In addition to our Universal Happiness Contests organized at the beginning of each season of the year, and the election of the Happiest Kamonian, our greatest glory is the Day of the Future. No one knows exactly when this day will be, nor why it is that particular day; the date is kept as a great state secret. I suppose this is to prevent the Satanoids and Antiists from attempting anything that might spoil our Happiness. Of course, weather conditions also play an important part in the determination of the Day of the Future. It is always a fine day, with a gentle breeze. Indeed, as we never know which day is going to be the Day of the Future, not only are we always psychologically prepared for this celebration; we have even abolished the usual seasons of the year, and divided it up into Preparations for the Day of the Future and Analysis of our Happiness after the Day of the Future.

The general discontent with our lot in Kamonia is exclusively concerned with the inadequacy of our means for expressing our Balance of Happiness. The numerical indications of our National Contests for Happiness and the Enjoyment of Freedom have long ceased to satisfy anyone in Kamonia. The Academy of Joy has been asked to find a new and better method of calculating happiness, and the corresponding measures and equivalents in which we could at least approximately define our condition. Attempts to express tears of joy in tones, to measure laughter on the dials of an anemometer, pleasurable excitement in terms of gravitational pull and pure happiness in time units whose basic and lowest unit is the decens, have not according to general opinion so far yielded appropriate results. Moreover, the election of the Happiest Kamonian and the solemn proclamation of the victor have found many critics who have no doubt influenced his reputation. The imperfections of our criteria for selecting the Happiest Kamonian are well known to those of us who are volunteer Joysters who, together with the professional Protectors, go round the whole town and all its houses in turn for twenty-four hours on the Day of the Future; wherever the singing is dying down, the laughter becoming uncertain or hollow, or the party spirit losing its boisterous tempo, we supply appropriate remedies to revive the mood of festivity and rejoicing, which lasts for the time necessary for the earth to turn round on its axis. And so that the victors of happiness and enjoyment may not doubt the possibility of being even happier, that those who are Happiest of All may not become demoralized, He has proclaimed the Two Silent Principles: Happiness is eternal, subject only to one condition; and Light cannot exist without darkness, which exists from time immemorial.

After the Day of the Future we are happy that it has been and begin to prepare for the next one, continuing to vie with one another in our visions of Absolute Happiness after Total Victory. The rewards for an absolute vision not only ensure the glorious winners a place in history, but also give them the right to indulge in a brief mood of lyrical sadness when the autumn days come along. This liberty makes them exceptional among our free citizens.

But there are always more and more Antiists, and in places where no one would dream of finding them. Announcements of new Antiist conspiracies are published in the newspaper; one such serious plot was revealed in the Forum of the Creators of the

Future itself, among the people closest to Him, people whom we had adored because they had become famous in happiness by loving Him and by freedom in the struggle against the Satanoids and Antiists. Experience continually confirms His revelation that we are all actual or potential Antiists. This has called forth a new wave of gratitude and admiration for Him.

Day and night the Protectors indefatigably seize and arrest Antiists; columns of Protectors' cars and ubimobiles from all parts of Kamonia rush to the Defensories and fill them with criminals. Actually, the Protectors only fulfil certain technical functions, since all citizens are in fact Protectors; every free and happy Kamonian is a Protector as a matter of course, keeping a constant watch over happiness for the sake of happiness. From midnight onwards, in front of the Protectors' offices, there are queues of free citizens who have come to report Antiists and all those who do not believe in or who doubt their Freedom; innumerable telephone lines have been made available for reporting to the Protectors: in addition a special corps of volunteer Protector-Investigators is being formed, and they attend a short course of evening classes on the recognition of Antiism and Methods of Overcoming Silence. The gramophone-record industry has made recordings of the General Principles of the Theory and Practice of Suspicious Persons. These records are in very great demand; every family wishes to possess them. In every house people listen to and study the Science of Discovering Plots and the Recognition of Antiist agents. For two hours each day the radio broadcasts instructions and practical advice for the discovery of Antiism; television and psycho-vision are also utilized for this purpose, while the Guilty Men Quiz arouses such widespread interest that all trade and communications are brought to a standstill.

The country suffers from the lack of a sufficient number of courts and buildings where Antiists can be prepared for trial. Schools, hospitals and warehouses are converted into temporary detention centres, while restaurants, bookshops, fashion salons, art galleries, cinema and similar buildings are adapted for use as courts. But even these measures are inadequate to meet the growing needs. The Forum of the Creators of History has given orders that prefabricated courts, designated by serial numbers like railway wagons and ships of the river networks, are to be erected day and night in all markets, parks and public squares. The complex numbers of these courts do not represent any technical trick, nor any attempt to conceal Kamonian secrets from foreign, Satanoid spies; these numbers, which include all the letters of the alphabet and six-figure combinations simply reflect the true situation with regard to the growing shortage of court premises.

My brigade of spectators and witnesses works in two shifts; and soon every court will pass sentence in three shifts. I attend the hearings from one o'clock in the morning until midday ! I have no time for breakfast. In the short pauses while the criminals are led in and out we are given instructions as to how we should give evidence and how we should behave towards the criminal. Moreover, even we ordinary spectators and witnesses put forward creative suggestions for the rationalization of sentencing. While working on the night shift, which is mainly devoted to passing judgement on dead offenders who have been denounced and vilified by living Antiists, I, as a free citizen, feel some uneasiness that the triumph of liberty and right is not absolutely complete; so I wrote a letter to the newspaper *Tatata* suggesting that in the cases concerning dead Antiists the usual bureaucratic formalities for sentences *in absentia* should be dispensed with and the sentencing of volunteer criminals be introduced. These would be happy citizens of Kamonia who would volunteer to represent the dead men, i.e. to play the part of the guilty men and receive their punishment. Such volunteers should be chosen at special and illustrious assemblies from among the freest and happiest citizens; lists of these honorary criminals should be at the courts' disposal and as soon as required, they could be summoned by telephone and sentenced just like guilty men. Naturally, it would be better if they received their accusations in good time, so that they could prepare exhaustive confessions, but as this would present technical difficulties, and much time would be lost in summoning and bringing them to court, the simplest thing would be to have a certain number of volunteer criminals in reserve in the Defensories prepared for all crimes.

My proposal was received with enthusiastic approval by the free public, and one of the Creators of the Future greeted my initiative in His name, paying full tribute to it. There began to develop a movement of 'Voluntary Criminals' whose numbers, and readiness to accept all punishments, especially the death penalty, amazed even our most loyal subjects.

I became famous overnight. Both the daily papers and the illustrated weeklies were full of my photographs, my biography, my achievements and anecdotes about me. I have been elected Rector of the Corps of Spectators. I have been proposed for the Electory since in addition to my services to the cause of Liberty I fulfil all the other conditions required for the highest legislative and political body of the land. I have a strong voice, which is essential for the prolonged and loud chanting in the Electory whenever we look at His photograph, or at someone who is thought to have seen Him at some time, or who is likely to see Him before he dies. As well as a strong voice, I have remarkably large and muscular hands, which are essential for applause in the Electory, and also an excellent nervous system and the inborn patience required for sitting without moving day and night while listening to His programme for the Perfect Future and the Plan for Total Victory, which members of the Forum of the Creators of History take it in turn to read. But I have begged to be excused from election, because as a young spectator at the courts I feel I have not yet acquired the experience necessary for a politician. This modesty of mine has caused some of my colleagues to have doubts about my Freedom. I just set my teeth and say nothing, convinced that I am so happy that everybody else will soon be convinced of it. So I just get on with my work, freer than ever before, but just in case, whenever I have a little time to spare I call in at the Centre for Righteous Feeling Design or the Self-service for Accepted Facts.

Meanwhile the criminals confess their crimes, and make some contribution to the accusation according to their intelligence and feeling for historical perspective. Many of them beg for the death penalty, and these we spectators greet with free and prolonged applause. The court carefully defends the criminals, diminishes the weight of their confession and gently announces the penalty, which is always milder than the criminals themselves wish, or than they ask for.

The cases concerning the suicide of parents, children, neighbours and acquaintances are even more interesting than these classic ones. In this former type, in addition to establishing the fact of the suicide of happy people in a happy land, it is essential to spare no effort to discover and admit the reasons for suicide and to provide concrete factual evidence. The second part of these hearings is devoted directly to the crimes of the accused : why did he fail to notice in time the suicidal intention of his father, brother, daughter, neighbour, acquaintance, or compatriot, and why did he fail to prevent this Antiist act. At these trials there are often very moving scenes : unforgettable proofs of people's insight, psychological penetration and accurate premonitions. From the point of view of Freedom, it is most important to train and develop the imagination, which becomes both the confirmation and the defence of Freedom in our life. It is particularly valuable that the untrammelled visionary quality of this imagination cannot easily be inherited or stolen; for every suicide has his own unique method of behaving and concealing his intentions and the means of their achievement.

Psychological trials can also be associated with those just mentioned as regards beauty and interest. These are trials where children give evidence against parents, parents against children, sisters against brothers, husbands against wives, wives against husbands, brother against brother, and so on. In trials of this kind, the duties of the spectators are usually performed by writers – in my opinion with indifferent success. In fact the practical aim of such trials is to enable writers to study the general application of psychology. They are mainly quiet hearings, and the public, that is the writers, sit with their notebooks on their knees and write down every word, without raising their heads. Only at the end, when the members of the court and the criminals have left the room, belated or purely intellectual applause can be heard.

Recently, psychological trials have been enriched by the acquisition of new subject matter – criminals of love and friendship. It would seem that love and friendship represent basic Satanoid methods; it would also appear that even free and happy people can never have enough of love and friendship, and our enemies know this very well. And so doubts have arisen as to whether we should renounce love for the sake of happiness, and friendship for the sake of freedom. Most people are prepared to do this, the more readily since a harmless method of loving is available: we can love babies, children who can't yet speak, and incurable invalids. It is also permissible to love parents and persons close to us in general when they are at the point of death. However, since we can never be completely sure that the dying person is not a deeply concealed Antiist, who is using his last hour of life to inflict a poisonous wound, we prefer to concentrate all our feelings of love on babies and small children. Never in the history of the world has so much love been lavished on children as in Kamonia. Babies and children are half-crazy with happiness. The birth-rate is very high; every woman is either pushing a pram, or pregnant. As for our natural inclination and tendency to friendship, we do not renounce it; only we transfer it to other objects; instead of making friends with people, we do so with animals, things and machines. Cats and dogs, birds and fishes, wild-life and rabbits, mice, tortoises and snakes have acquired an enormous significance in our lives, which they enrich emotionally and spiritually. In them and with them we find the fulfilment of our whole integrated human personality. In the animal world man finally becomes a real and sincere bearer of love, friendship and mutual understanding. The movement for taming and breeding animals has become nation-wide, and is leading to new and exciting economic expansion. Almost overnight the land has become covered with farms for the selection and care of animals; and shops for the purchase and exchange of animals have become as common as food-shops. Capital is being redirected to the production and distribution of the 'true friends of man', as this propaganda describes animals. Special institutes have sprung up for particular kinds of animals, and soon they begin to specialize in particular breeds and varieties; and there is now a vast literature dealing with the taming, training, cross-breeding and rearing of animals. The entire morning television programme is devoted to the selection and care of animals and the buying or selling of them.

The owners of farms for red and yellow snakes have become millionaires and national figures, and the Forum of the Creators of History have enrolled them for life as honorary Supremely Happy. The price of red and yellow snakes is fantastic; if they are more than a yard long, they are not much cheaper than a two-seater aeroplane or one of the smaller ubimobiles. In the general pattern of our economic life, the constant rise in the value of shares in enterprises for the production of Super-Mice is outstanding. For His propaganda has no difficulty in convincing people that of all animals, mice can satisfy our human need for the expression of tenderness and loving-kindness with the minimum expenditure of money, time and space. Mice are the cheapest friends – we hear whenever we switch on the radio or the television; mice keep us company, smiling at us from tunnel walls and hoardings, when we travel along any motorway in Kamonia. Our houses and gardens are full of all sorts of animals. We are always doing something with them – washing them, stroking them, playing with them. Our love and devotion to animals was quickly reflected in the rapid fall in the number of marriages and in the increased incidence of divorce; and also in the fall in the birth-rate and the volume of tourist traffic.

But as a result our Happiness Balances are in a more favourable state than ever before.

Our love for animals has been accompanied by a passion for things, objects or machines of all kinds. Despite a massive propaganda campaign in trade and industry, backed by scientists and in particular by psychologists, to try and convince us that material objects are really the best and most devoted friends, and despite the seductive advertisements of flower-shops and market gardens for plants which show us Friends who are alive and beautiful, yet dumb and motionless, the position and importance of animals in Kamonia remains as basic as ever.

But even so, in spite of this general re-direction of our natural feelings of tenderness, our need to love and be loved, the number of offences in connexion with passionate love and romantic friendship continually increases. The more we fear love and friendship, the more criminals and Antiists there are. It is generally agreed that love is the internal destructive force for our happiness. I have therefore decided not to marry, since all the girls that attract me show such strong and passionate feelings of love that I cannot but doubt the purity of their incitement and intentions. Some of them, whose feelings were most extreme and who clearly wished to destroy my peace and happiness, I reported as *agents provocateurs* or future Antiists, and the court punished them accordingly. Attacks of romantic friendship have come to light even among the Protectors, the Happiest Citizens, the spectators at court, the Judges and other equally happy people. Every morning, in front of the relevant institutions, you can see long queues of people who have come to report provocative acts of love and friendship; and the queues are even longer after working hours. These crimes create new problems. The existing courts and Defensories are already being used beyond their capacity, and temporary Defensories and judicial premises have been set up in all our larger institutions.

From the scientific point of view, the most valuable trials are those connected with children on the verge of puberty and other potential Antiist material. The exciting and far-reaching nature of these trials lies in the choice of potential and future Antiist material. Here everything depends on the power of human foresight; unfortunately this is a very rare, indeed exceptional gift. Good will, the accustomed freedom and current happiness achieve relatively little in this aspect of the struggle for Total Victory. We are all convinced that the greatest scientific and artistic problem of our freedom is to discover and disarm our potential future enemies.

The general spread of Antiism gives rise to all sorts of dissonant ideas in the minds of the free. Some people believe that Antiism is a pathological phenomenon, and that it should be regarded like any other illness and treated in the appropriate way. The Forum of the Creators of History has reacted promptly and decisively to this attitude, which it regards as naïve, stupid and in the last resort a form of sabotage.

Antiism is not a virus, as the Forum of the Creators of History tells us, from which we could defend ourselves by permanent immunization; it is in itself a sure sign that we are free and happy. Without Antiism it would be difficult for us to know how happy we are, and to continue the struggle for Total Victory and the Perfect Future. In addition, Antiism provides us with the objective conditions for the fulfilment of our free, many-sided and creative personality, and confirms the absolute superiority of our Kamonian way of life over the wretched existence of the Satanoids. Hence Antiism brings us the excitement, surprise and joys of victory – the most lasting joys there are.

The people of Kamonia have greeted these new directives with enormous enthusiasm, and the Palace of the Forums has been flooded with telegrams and messages of devotion, while the adherents of the idea that Antiism is a pathological phenomenon are being denounced and condemned.

All this has added fuel to the flames of the struggle against Satanoid influence from abroad. The frontiers of Kamonia are completely closed. As we have an abundance of everything we need, trade with foreign countries is unnecessary; it is true we lack certain spices and diamonds, but our Kamonian technology has succeeded in producing these artificially, and of a higher quality than the natural products, so that we have freed ourselves from the last trace of dependence on the Satanoid world. The Satanoids can still exercise their hostile influence only by way of our rivers, even though we have not bathed in rivers flowing from foreign countries for a long time now, nor eaten fish from them, or even used their water for industrial purposes or irrigation. In accordance with their 'Catonic Strategy' our General Staff has asked the Forum of the Creators of History to construct special filters at the frontiers to purify every drop of water coming from the Satanoid world, and special budgetary funds have been set aside for this purpose. In addition to this inspired measure, His Secret Order to the Space Academy to prevent winds from coming to our country from abroad – an order which has somehow trickled through to the public, probably as a result of the free enthusiasm of the scientists, has further confirmed in us our feeling of unlimited power and invincibility. To this conviction has also contributed His Pronouncement concerning Antiism, that the view expressed by the

Forum of the Creators of History that: 'the joys of victory are those that last longest' is the work of provocateurs and perfidious saboteurs; for this reason all those Creators of History who believed this and spoke in this way have been put on trial and shot. We are infinitely grateful to Him for convincing us that Antiism cannot bring joy in any shape or form, and so we have undertaken a final reckoning with all those who thought otherwise.

In addition to the conspiracies which are revealed nearly every month in the Forum of the Creators of the Future, the General Staff, the Academics and Kamonia's other highest institutions, the wave of unmaskings of concealed Antiists has also affected the Protectory, its investigators, courts and other judicial, state and freedom organs. Because of the nature of the crime these trials last a long time and enable us to give full play to our temperament. At these trials we can harangue, shout and swear to our hearts' content; we can even lynch the accused. These Antiists and conspirators from the highest places, the freest and the happiest, those whom we loved and trusted most after Him, convince us that there is no limit to human naïvety – otherwise there would have been an end of wickedness, unhappiness and slavery. He has also taught us that the roots of Antiism are to be found in the remote past. We must uncover them as well.

And so we are beset by a feeling of sacred duty as we are setting out in search of errors and criminals among our dead and distant ancestors. We study the past, biographies, chronicles, literature – we bring to light documents concerning the ideas and nature of our ancestors, and we begin to try and condemn them. All our schools are being turned into courtrooms. The sentences bring us peace and alleviation. Nearly ninety per cent of our well-known ancestors against whom accusations have been levelled have been declared guilty and condemned to perpetual contempt and oblivion.

The Administration and members of the Bureaux of Analysts, who have strikingly increased in numbers in recent years, have shown in their pronouncements under the slogan 'Truth is a number' that there has been an increase in the number of malcontents among traditional intellectuals, especially philosophers, historians and poets. This gives confirmation to lengthy human experience : knowledge is not to be found in books and cannot be learnt with the mind; true knowledge is found in everyday life, and is achieved by the work of hands and body. Nation-wide anger against the intellectuals, the Forum of the Creators of the Future, is becoming more and more inflamed.

A new and, it is generally thought, protectionist policy is trying to shift the weight of responsibility in the task of uncovering concealed Antiists in the family circle; we all watch each other conscientiously, seizing upon every word and intonation, every movement, every crumb of thought, all shades and changes of mood. Before and after dinner we discuss our observations and suspicions and accuse each other, giving evidence and judgement and proclaiming each other criminals even before the offenders are brought before the Protectors and the court. In fact, our homes have become courts – our dining-rooms, beds, bathrooms, kitchens and the rest – and courts of high judicial instance at that. Some authorities assert that these family courts outdo the customary classical ones as regards the severity of the accusations, the plausibility of the evidence and the harshness of the punishments. Certain problems of a formal nature arise in families consisting of only a husband and wife, or a mother and daughter, since their sentences do not fulfil the required legal conditions; the accused have no one to defend them. Some complementary procedure is therefore necessary. The weekly illustrated magazines are full of descriptions of lyrical and romantic judgements between old married couples, who only after fifty years of bed and board together have discovered that their partner is an Antiist, without happiness and freedom. The accounts of the unmasking of future Antiists among young married couples are no less moving and interesting. Many exploits in the defence of freedom are carried out even during the honeymoon.

The customary and natural manner of expression for a free and happy man is to speak everything out aloud, even the most intimate and shameful matters; no one whispers any more, even when embracing, or in bed, or in the performance of their marital duties: so that no suspicions may be aroused, everything must be audible; even children must hear the truth, even the neighbours know what we feel and think. This free behaviour has had a radical effect on all customs, habits and relationships. For instance, few people want to live alone in a house, a flat or a room : people offer flats to live in, invite guests, and visit each other constantly; they entreat, give money or bribes and go to all lengths in order to live in the largest possible units, and never to sleep with only one other person. These needs and desires are revolutionizing the architecture and the interior arrangements of houses and flats; nearly all the traditional forms of furniture and fittings are being abandoned; doors and windows are being removed, and only put in position if the weather is very bad, and then only by timid persons or those in poor health. Houses and flats of transparent material fetch a high price. Whole streets and estates are being built of completely transparent houses with total audiovigil sets. Whereas at first the Protectors used to install total audiovigilators secretly in houses and public places, we now do this openly and freely and voluntarily. The installation of total audiovigilators is regarded as evidence of our high standard of living, and we are happy that our citizens of Kamonia are the only people in the world who can freely install total audiovigil sets which are linked up with the Kamonian Central Information Service.

The Forum of the Creators of the Future is bringing in a Five Year Plan for Total Audiovigilation, according to which it is proposed to install audiovigilators not only in all public places and highways, but in all picnic areas, woods, river banks, lake-shores and at the sea-side. In addition to this State Plan, there is a powerful private industry for producing devices to secure intimate information. The National Corporation for the exchange of personal facts and the Verification Bureau for them have become, as it were, overnight, large concerns, with big profits. Psychology, particularly psychosynthesis, is now the leading science in Kamonia. But Industry and Commerce, Science and the Skilled Trades are closely followed in this respect by the Arts, particularly by the Seven-Dimensional Film and Somnovision which by their thematic structure are primarily and universally informative.

For we cannot be free and happy if we are unaware of what the people around us are thinking about us, and if we have no knowledge of the thoughts and feelings of the people with whom we live and work, and whom we meet and see regularly. To be really free, we must know everything, without exception : dreams, food-menus, sex and family relationships, quarrels, intentions, wishes, passions, jokes. For this purpose we have to equip ourselves with the appropriate technical devices. We buy, sell and exchange information and facts. Curiosity about intimate secrets, and their revelation and documentation is becoming a universal and national passion, which has made many Kamonian citizens millionaires and extremely powerful figures; in fact there is no longer any doubt that the richest and most powerful people in Kamonia are those who know most about others. Also working total audiovigilators has become our favourite pastime. They have reached such a stage of technical perfection that by merely twiddling a knob we can see and hear what is being said, whispered and done in any house in any part of Kamonia, together with the corresponding colours and smells. We usually spend our evenings in this way, and this has resulted in an abrupt decline of interest in the theatre, cinema, television, somnovision and concerts. The foundation of a Somno-centre where, one by one in order of our arrival, we relate and discuss our dreams before a large public, has brought us new joys, and increased our Freedom even more. Attempts are being made to meet the need, which is growing exceptionally rapidly, for such centres, by organizing circles for the narration and discussion of dreams in groups of houses and blocks of flats. But nobody is satis-fied by these improvised arrangements, above all because of the inadequacies of the audience, so the Forum of the Creators of the Future is being asked to make increased investment in the building of somnocentres.

The unmasking this year of the sixth conspiracy against Him in the Forum of the Creators of History and of the Future, in the General Staff and in His personal bodyguard of the Protectory, and the third conspiracy running of the Silent Left has convinced us that the Satanoids are stubbornly resolved to destroy our Happi-ness. But He has made public his Salvationary Thesis and his Prophetic Message to us : It is widely known what conditions are like in the Satanoid world. No less well known are the conditions in those countries where the people believe that they have the best of everything. To recapitulate:

Firstly, THE SINGLE STATE.

Its people are only numbers. They have a number for both surname and Christian name, because they have no individual characteristics. They all wear the same uniform. Love is forbidden. Sex is rationed and distributed by coupons. The use of coffee, alcohol and tobacco is forbidden. The people are deprived of all emotional life. Imagination is forbidden and people are treated for it like any other disease. Love for the Benefactor is instilled by mechanical means. All aspects of life are under police control.

This order of things requires no comment.

Secondly, OCEANIA.

Although the standard of living is relatively high, poverty and inequality are the rule. A man need not be poor and unhappy, but he is because this is Big Brother's wish. And Big Brother has a compulsive need to do only evil. In this society sadism and efficiently organized tyranny prevail.

Again, no comment on this order of things is required.

Thirdly, THE WORLD STATE.

Technology has annihilated man. He no longer knows anything of mother-love, family life, morals, or natural emotions. No one knows what spontaneous passion is. People are produced in laboratories, according to a well-ordained plan. They are all alike, and everyone belongs to everyone else. Their only games are with machines. Joy and excitement are bought at the drug store.

Again, no comment is required on this technocratic order of things.

What do the best among the Satanoids believe? They believe that Happiness and Freedom are irreconcilable. Their naïve folly is to be pitied.

What do we believe? We believe that Freedom and Happiness are indivisible. Only Antiism is irreconcilable with them.

What do the best among the Satanoids assert? They hold that power is an end in itself and that power only exists for the sake of one man's power over another. This is clearly an abomination.

What do we hold?
We say that power is neither a means nor an end.
What is the general conclusion? It is clearly self-evident.

We were so delighted by the depth of His thought and the elegance of His style that we decorated all our buildings – factories, churches, offices, and block of flats – with the slogans : This order of things requires no comment. Their naïve folly is pitiful. This is clearly an abomination. It is clearly self-evident. These last words of wisdom have particularly impressed us, and we have begun to greet each other with them. They have also furnished both the title and the subject matter for many poems, and doctoral theses; and we have been promised an opera and a number of cantatas based on the same words – it is clearly self-evident – in the near future.

In his Prophetic Work concerning Us, He has condensed into two sentences the content of a multitude of books, and said everything that any man needs to know, so as never to err in any way.

Everybody can be Happy, but everybody can be an Antiist. Anyone who is not Happy is an Antiist.

All of us have studied these supreme truths, which form the hub of our scientific, intellectual and artistic life, and the basis of a new industry of ideas and morals. This spirit inspires scenarios and dramas, the production of films and plays, and the composition of symphonies and songs.

A New Era has begun – the universal liquidation of the unhappy. All those who for any reason are not happy, or whose happiness is in any way dubious, are denounced to the Protector and brought to trial and judgment. Accusations of crimes of the following type are particularly numerous: he didn't laugh at my joke; he wept too much at his child's funeral; he breathes heavily, or yawns, or moans in his sleep.

Since the existing capacity of the courts is inadequate to deal with the new offenders and Antiists, the Forum of the Creators of History have announced their decision that a number of trains, tramcars and buses should be turned into courts. The advantage of these new types of courts is that they are mobile, and can be concentrated in the places where the number of criminals is greatest. Trains have a special technical advantage; they can stand in sidings in the stations, and each coach can be labelled with a special category of crime, lapse or error, whilst the individual compartments, which makes very intimate courts, are used when specifically required for the narrower fields of responsibility in any offence. Sometimes these courts – as soon as they contain the requisite number of people and carry the optimum weight, are used to transport Antiists to their prescribed destination.

While the Satanoid world, we are convinced, is in the grip of universal poverty, hunger and epidemic disease, and is torn by strikes, revolts and terror, we in Kamonia live in plenty. We have everything we need. The official organ of the Forum of the Creators of History, the radio, the television and the psychovision repeat the Forum's proclamation every morning:

At all times and in all places, say what you want. Ask that all your wishes should be fulfilled. Invent things that will make you even happier. Buy more than you have money for. Buy everything that is for sale. Spend more than you earn. Whatever and however much you have, want to have something else, and more. Keep on buying everything and spending continuously.

In the Forum's Reform Associations and Observations, from waking to the beginning of work, when a considerable number of people are morose, ill-inclined and even anxious, Two Optimistic Instructions are given: Think what you will buy today; and Record both what is ugly and what is beautiful.

And we buy, spend or record. We don't know what to do with all the food and clothes, furniture and machines, cars and gadgets; but we buy them, because every day something new and different appears; because: other people are buying things, everybody is buying things; because: if we are not always spending money, we are not happy. Today we are eating purple bread, because it has been advertised as the bread eaten by happy people; we drink 'heliojuice' because it is said to strengthen sexual powers and to maintain them all one's life; we use 'Chloromol' soap because it is said to arouse lyrical dreams. And when the next day we hear that red bread is the bread eaten by outstanding people, we buy it; that the cosmic boxing champion's favourite drink is 'Python's Blood', we buy that too; that 'Sturgeon's Eye' soap was used by Cleopatra and St Augustine, we buy that soap. In fact, the general belief is that anyone who does not spend much or buys little, who does not buy a new psychovision, a new ubimobile, new gadgets, new machines and methods of amusement, anyone who thinks he has enough money, is not a true Kamonian. Such people are universally regarded with suspicion, and publicly branded, derided, boycotted and condemned.

As well as buying things, at the same time we follow the Forum's Second Optimistic Instruction, and uninterruptedly record all that we see and hear. Already sixty-eight per cent of our average life is recorded; according to the plan of the Forum of the Creator of the Future, in the course of the next ten years there will be a publicly and privately produced audiovisual record of ninety-six per cent of human life so that, for all practical purposes, nothing will be left unrecorded. In addition to giving us amusement while we look at photographs and films of scenes and places we have seen, and listen to the noise of the streets, conversations in shops, concerts, masses, private conversations, jokes and laughter, our films and tapes will be at the disposal of analysts, psychosynthetists, and the Protectory for them to study and establish the corresponding facts and conclusions. The results are incalculable. In all probability traditional witnesses, judges and courts will be abolished. On the basis of photographs, films and material provided by total audiovigilators everything will be scientifically analysed in the laboratories, all our needs, habits and wishes will become known, and it will be possible to establish exactly our convictions, moods and behaviour, to know where we have been, and with whom, what we did and said. In short, there will be an accurate factual and permanent record of who we are and what we are. And that will have, and indeed already has, inestimably progressive results, as well as influencing our economy, arts, science, law and religion.

Translated by Muriel Heppel

Borislav Pekić

THE MIRACLE IN CANA

Jesus saith unto them, Fill the waterpots with water, And
they filled them up to the brim. And he saith unto them,
Draw out now, and bear unto the governor of the feast. And
they bare it. When the ruler of the feast had tasted the
water that was made wine, and knew not whence it was:
(but the servants which drew the water knew:) the
governor of the feast called the bridegroom, And saith unto
him, Every man at the beginning doth set forth good wine;
and when men have well drunk, then that which is worse:
but thou hast kept the good wine until now. This beginning
of miracles did Jesus in Cana of Galilee and manifested forth
his glory; and his disciples believed on him.

John, 2

Simon, son of Jona, by God's will Peter, apostle and servant of our
Lord Jesus Christ, this Epistle General to Bishops, Archdeacons,
Priests, Elders, and all those who with us have received the one
true and only faith, Hebrews, Romans, Corinthians, Ephesians,
Galatians, Philippians, Colossians and Thessalonians, and to all
newcomers: Grace and Peace be unto you from God our Father and
the Lord Jesus Christ.

2. And may this instruction find you wherever you are, with
charitable and not wooden hearts, and with thirsting and not with
sated souls, and with ears opened wide to the word of truth.

3. This missive, therefore, to the Elders of Christian communities
is from the son of Jona, Simon Peter from Bethsaida of Gennesaret,
whom the Saviour called Cephas and turned into a firm rock on
which to build His Church. To the Glory of the Father, the Son
and the Holy Ghost, Amen.

4. You ask me to come among you, you cry out for me since I am

necessary to you; necessary to Corinth, necessary to Thessalonica, most needed by Jerusalem, irreplaceable for Athens, and even idolatrous Rome cannot do without me.

5. Dissemblers! Blasphemers! Hypocrites! Have you not yet learnt that nothing is indispensable save faith, and nothing is irreplaceable save faith. Not doctrines, nor their teachers, nor the Creed, nor the faithful. Only faith.

6. And do you tell me that you do not know where I am, that you do not know that I am rotting in a Roman prison, and that to-morrow at dawn I shall be crucified on the cross from which for a long time now has been hanging the flesh of your brethren in Christ? Dissemblers! Blasphemers! Hypocrites!

7. And what has Peter to do with you when you have nothing to do with faith; when you can hardly wait for my third death rattle to be proclaimed Urbi et Orbi to fall like the pestilence on the Lord's heritage, dividing up that which was made indivisible, rending asunder that which was given as indissoluble, casting apart that which was presented as unseverable.

8. When not one of the faithful nor any leader of a pious community of Christians is convinced that only Peter's sacrifice – I call it thus being an offence that was pleasing to God in its courage – in that night of betrayal, pierced with a kiss and the three sharp cries of the first priest-cockerel, preserved our faith, and that only Peter, that foundation stone of the Church, capable of destroying all people, was able to, and in continuo does, preserve all that which is of merit and faith in them, and that they, in order to live longer, ceaselessly divest themselves of merit and give up their faith.

9. What have I to do with you, dearest brethren in Christ, when I can no longer enjoy your devotion, even though it still calls to me in some still loyal heart, which cannot beat freely, for I am not there to record that beauty forever and ever as the days go by. I am not there like a sacred, saintly bell with its giant-like tolling of the uncertain beating of your hesitant hearts on the doors of true life, there is no one who knows how to arrest nature, saying: enough now, enough, stop, go back into your inhuman limitations, to your soulless insignificance.

10. But all that incessant beating, because it will have come to an

end, spreading amongst you and your dearest ones fear, suffering, and a martyr's ending, will be like to the nails of curses hammered into my back.

11. What have I to do with you, my brethren in Christ, when the time has come for me to ask selfishly was I right, and in my cell into which the daylight throws the arrow-shaped shadow of the cross, there is no one to answer me.

12. When I am uncertain whether I shall be a saint or an outcast in dreams, books and on the lips of people who come (whither, for after us no one will come!) to break, defile, dishonour their dead idols, and their sons to gather together the broken pieces for their hearths, that in front of their renewed glow they may again worship.

13. What have I to do with you, my brethren in Christ, when my master – never mind your praises and curses, apotheosis and anathema – has built a world in which I would like to live, not as a builder but as a user; a subject, not a lord; a fisherman of Gennesaret, not a Roman saint.

14. And when, since death has wiped away all the ugly details, smoothed out all His inelegant coarseness and uneven contours, I stand before the colossal magnitude of His work.

15. The Church and its architect, one dependent upon the other, one for the other, and one in the other.

16. And you, I hear, lament that many of our virtuous brethren have suffered because of the zealous haste with which Peter has carried out the instructions of his God; are a few thousand Christians more important to you than Christianity, a few dozen haphazard churchminders of more value than the Holy Church?

17. Verily I say unto you, when praises are sung to the Lord under the protective vaults of the Church, not one of you will remember the masons, the carpenters, the icon-carvers and the engravers who perished in the building of it.

18. And not one of those Zacharias who were consumed by the flames, or those Nahors, who were broken on the wheel, or those Jonases, who rotted in prison, or those Joshuas, who were torn asunder, or those Japhets, who were hung up by the testicles in front of the town guardhouse will summon me to answer for their

torments. Which one of those Christians, offered up as a contribution to God, will hold me to account for his sufferings? Can we accuse the dead at the last judgement? Can we now?

19. And could the children of Israel have been delivered out of Egypt had not God sent hunger, thirst and pestilence to help them; and hunger, thirst and pestilence, are these things blessings?

20. And how would the Moabites and the Ammonites have come about if Lot's daughters had not lain down with their father? Is incest then a virtue?

21. And would the most revered patriarch Jacob have been the forefather of Israel had he not, swathed in a goatskin to seem like Esau, deceived the blind Isaac into giving him his blessing, which was intended for his hairy, but firstborn brother? And is a lie then truthful?

22. How could the guilty and the innocent in Sodom and Gomorrah have been separated if the sinners had been burnt and the righteous blessed with the cool of paradise? Is injustice then good?

23. And was it not from original sin that this world began, from a drop of bitterness squeezed from the apple of Eden which is now most sweet to all living beings? Is sin then innocent?

24. And who today blames Moses, Lot's daughters, Jacob, Adam, or our God, because they made use of the weapons of sin so that sin should be vanquished?

25. So then, must you revile Peter?

26. For lo, besides the Church, Peter leaves you a sharpened sword with which to defend it against unbelief, heresy, schism and faint-heartedness. And just as our most blessed Saviour left us his bequest to spread the gospel amongst all peoples, so I too, the heir to his power on earth, bequeath to all the heads of churches, and foremost to the Bishop of Rome and those who after him will sit upon Peter's throne, this message.

27. And this will not be one of the Saviour's sermons, for the effect of words is dependent upon their speaker and upon those who listen, and what am I before the golden-tongued Son of God, and you compared to his golden-eared followers?

28. And it will not be one of the miracles which he worked, loosening the tongue of the dumb, returning madmen to their

senses, or resurrecting the dead; for in unravelling entangled tongues you will only obtain a crowd of babblers, that is to say betrayers; by raising cripples to their feet you will only obtain a crowd of swift runners, that is pursuers; by giving the blind their sight, you will obtain nothing but a crowd of seekers after knowledge, that is spies; by bringing corpses back to life you will only obtain still more sinners, that is enemies. Leave off from such miracles, my brethren in Christ!

29. For such miracles transformed only those upon whom they were worked, and they left the onlookers afraid of God instead of trusting in Him.

30. So your good shepherd Peter bequeaths to you one particular miracle, which, while it was happening before our very eyes, did not promise anything of greatness, but doubt swiftly gave place to the certainty that there was no defence against His spells, and that before Him every belief was powerless.

31. And that was the miracle of Cana of Galilee. And this miracle came about thus:

32. On the third day after my coming to the Lord, there was a great heat, and we were cooling our heels in Gennesaret in the vague expectation that something might happen to shorten the time dedicated to the study and interpretation of his sermons.

33. For we were His first disciples, and although up to that afternoon we had not learnt anything in particular except to keep out of the way of unbridled Herodites, Pharisees and Sadducees, we felt honoured that we, who were so lowly, had been chosen from amongst so many exemplary Israelites to preach the gospel of the kingdom of God.

34. In addition to myself and my brother Andrew were chosen Philip, whose trade was washing dead bodies, from Bethsaida, Zebedee's twin sons from Capernaum, whom the Teacher called Boanerges (which means sons of lightning), from respect for the likeness of their fists to summer thunder, and a certain Nathanael from Kirbet Cana, of Galilee.

35. And this latter joined up with us out of pure curiosity: thinking simply, that nothing good could come out of the Saviour's

Nazareth, which was known mainly for its brothels, and he came along to make sure.

36. But thus spake Nathanael himself, but others less surprised at his care over public morals, said that he was looking for new company, since his old friends had been nailed out on crosses from Rama to the Hebron.

37. Now Nathanael was a robber.

38. But I say to you, noble elders of communities, that those crosses, as far as their shape, composition and the way they are set up is concerned, are the same Roman crosses from which the bloody remains of our brethren hang. For the crosses are old, but the martyrs are new: and the sinners have been replaced by the righteous.

39. And so, unified in pain, separated in the remembrance they leave behind, unified in outcome, but separated in the reasons for their torments, the righteous hang on the crosses alongside sinners, robbers amidst saints, and evil-doers between the good.

40. And no words pass between them, for the guilty will not beseech the innocent to intercede for them, nor will the innocent think to defend the guilty.

41. For never again will it come to pass that the guilty will say to the innocent: remember me when you come to the heavenly kingdom !

42. Nor will it ever again come to pass that the innocent answer the guilty : verily I say unto you, this day you will be with me in paradise !

43. And I tell you of this so that you may see who Nathanael was, and so that you may see to it that there are no such men amongst you that you may pluck them out as a poppy from the harvest of the true faith.

44. And this Nathanael saw us when we were passing by the fig tree under which he was resting, and waited for us to come back from the solitude of worshipping in which we got to know God, and he went up to Philip and enquired about the Teacher and his teaching.

45. Philip could not tell him much about the teaching since the brilliance of the sermons had not yet illuminated the darkness of

his very simple soul, but concerning the Teacher, he informed him that he was indeed the one of whose coming the prophets had foretold, the Son of God who by suffering would redeem the world from the sins of our forefathers.

46. And he told him also that his name was Jesus, and that he was one of the sons of the carpenter Joseph of Nazareth, and some woman by the name of Mary, but that these apparently simple facts seemed quite different when they were considered in their higher significance.

47. For Jesus Christ, our Lord and Teacher, was begot by Jehovah by means of a short angelic annunciation, before Mary was espoused to Joseph, so that the Saviour's being can be accounted half God and half Man, God in the half which was seminated by God, Man in the half which was conceived by woman.

48. And the dual nature of his origin made his birth ambiguous, neither God nor Man but something in between the two, and there can be no doubt that he looked like a man and was God, and that sometimes he had the qualities of God, although he was only Man.

49. Nathanael wondered greatly at this and said: take me to this man that I too may serve him. For if the union of heaven and earth has found in him its most perfect model, why should I go on seeking someone who will disappoint me with his shortcomings? And Philip took him.

50. And when the two met, when the most righteous and the most guilty came together, the Messiah proclaimed Nathanael a true Israelite in whom there was no guile, and Nathanael without hesitation acknowledged Him as the Son of God, and his Lord. And no one was present at the conclusion of their agreement.

51. What advantages have flowed from this exchange of favours cannot be understood unless the Rabbi was aiming at confirming the Pharisees' accusations that he surrounded himself with publicans, sinners, harlots and criminals, by the choice of an outlaw as an apostle and Nathanael (who remained with us under the false name of Bartholomew) mistakenly thought that by associating himself with the Christians, he was joining a promising robber band.

52. And I tell you of this so that you may see who Nathanael

was, and so that you may see to it that there are no such men amongst you that you may smash them like earthenware vessels.

53. For they are a misfortune for the Church, the sowers of doubt and the reapers of unbelief, and they have pillage in their hearts, desiring to seduce you away from God, you will see.

54. And so we were close to Gennesaret, seven of us with the Teacher, and we were waiting for Him to relate something to us, but the Son of God remained silent, and was not at all like that so blessed-tongued prophet from the Mountain.

55. And Andrew took it upon himself to divert us by retelling the miracle in the wilderness of Bethsaida when the Teacher fed the five thousand with five small loaves, but we remained silent, we had become too hungry to listen to such sermons.

56. Then Nathanael said that Halilieh, a rich man of Kirbet Cana of Galilee, was marrying his son to a girl from Jericho and that we could go along if we had nothing better to do than to yawn and to prepare ourselves for the blissful state of God's kingdom by exercising our jaws.

57. And when we told the Messiah of the wedding, Philip rebuked us, saying: How can we go when we are not invited, and is it the custom in Israel to go along uninvited on that day?

58. And Jesus said to him: behold, the lamb goes hungry and thirsty and whosoever will leave him to bleat before the closed gate of the fold, will he not merit my Father's anger? But let us go and work the miracle in Cana, for our time is come.

59. And when we set off, we did not yet know that Cana of Galilee would be the beginning of the miracles to which the Saviour would be guided in the service of his adopted father, because after Cana He began to go in uninvited, to answer without being asked, to teach without being sought, and to save without being entreated.

60. And all this, dearest brethren in Christ, because saddened and angry, he saw that the world which He was trying to save had no notion of His awesome pain, and that it felt no need at all for healing.

61. For the yoke of Rome was even heavier than the intangible yoke of sins and it was grievous for Israel to greet the arrogant manifestations of Pagan might, to pay tribute to the insatiable

Caesar and to toil on his conqueror's highways, which crossed
David's kingdom in quest of new provinces and slave mines, but it
was even more difficult for Israel to recognize that hidden disease
of the spirit which was eating away at individuals and the nation
and which only sporadically took on the ugly forms of paralysis,
leprosy or madness.

62. And how could our Saviour wait for His mission from God
to begin only when those through whose transformation that
mission was to be accomplished, should invite Him? And when
would those who had been swallowed up by Satan's company have
summoned Him? And would Satan have let them?

63. Could He have knocked gently where He had to burst in, to
have earnestly entreated where He had to make use of a command-
ment, to have hesitated where Salvation depended on the utmost
urgency.

64. For God ordained a time for the world to be delivered from
sin, and gave the world to the Saviour for his lifetime that that
which was joined together on earth should also be linked in
Heaven, and that which was resolved on earth should be resolved
in Heaven also.

65. And with the assurance of this highest summons, we could
neglect the absence of the lower one; uninvited by Halilieh the
host, but guided by the Lord, we arrived at Cana, and found ourselves before the rich man's home.

66. For the sake of truth I must admit that even then no one invited us into the house, but amongst so many guests it was not
possible to see that all those who went in were invited or not, and
still less those who went out, although there were none of these
latter.

67. But since it was God's purpose that had brought us there,
the Lord's and our business and not men's, let it not be known that
we were not invited either individually or as a group, but let it be
thought of us that we were invited. Moreover, I, Simon, son of
Jona, the first keeper of the keys of the Church, affirm that honest
Halilieh invited us and any other interpretation of our presence
in Cana is from Satan !

68. And we spent some time chewing goats' flesh and swilling

wine, since we were exceedingly hungry, for not one of us seven
was working to earn anything, but we lived like the birds of the
air, who sow not neither do they reap, but they still live.

69. And thus He whom we followed taught us, saying: consider the ravens, they have neither cellars nor granaries, but God
feeds them. Consider the lilies of the field how they grow, they toil
not neither do they spin; but I say unto you that Solomon in all
his glory was not arrayed as one of these.

70. Moreover we ate and drank well, for we knew that God had
placed a table before us.

71. And behold, Mary, the mother of our Jesus, came, and He
showed no respect towards His mother, but made as if He did not
see her.

72. For by this indifference He desired to show, that concerning
His unexplained birth, He saw in her only the medium of the flesh
for His heavenly father's higher purpose, a kind of fortuitous
cauldron in which His mighty seed was fomented.

73. And He desired in His far-seeing wisdom, to set an example
for all times to those who were chosen to do great deeds, that they
might say without shame or conscience to each one who is newly
reborn, just as He said to us: forsake your mother and your father,
and follow me, just as I forsook my mother and my father and
followed the Lord!

74. And feigning to know nothing of this, as if she did not
notice His rancour, His mother came up to Him to reproach Him
for bringing shame upon the House of David by His drinking.

75. For it was written that the Son of God should be born to the
House of David.

76. And Jesus said: what have I to do with you, woman? my
time has not yet come but give me and my friends some wine, for
we come in the name of the Lord.

77. And I said: I hope that He who holds sway over the world
thereby also holds sway over the grape.

78. Then His mother, not without the maliciousness of the sober,
told Him that there was no more wine, although it was only the
second day that we honoured Halilieh's home with our presence,
and only the fourth day of the marriage in Cana.

79. And the Messiah became angry, for He did not like to break off anything that He had begun in the name of God, and He placed a curse upon them : it goes hard with thee, Galilee, breed of vipers! It goes hard with thee, godless Cana, that thou hast made arid the throat of the Son of God! From thy grapes, harlot amongst the lands of Hanan, henceforth will flow only water!

80. And then He left off His cursing and pointed to six stone vessels which served for the Israelite custom of cleansing themselves, and He ordered the servants to fill them up with water to the brim. And in each vessel there was about three pails of rain water for the cattle.

81. When the servants had done what He had ordered, the Messiah sent the first vessel to the best man for him to taste it, and he, to the consternation of all of us who knew the origin of the liquid, called over the bridegroom and praised him that contrary to custom he had kept the best wine to the end of the feast.

82. And when the wine had been shared out amongst the guests, they became as intoxicated as if it were the finest Samarian wine which had gone to their heads. And they gave great thanks to the Lord, bowing down before His Son and believing in Him.

83. And that was before they fell down on the floor.

84. And John, the son of Zebedee wondered greatly, and asked : Rabbi, did you make the water into wine, that everyone has thus become drunk?

85. And Jesus said to him : taste it and say!

86. Then the sons of Zebedee, who were used to doing everything together, tasted some of the miraculous wine, and they at once became drunk, and they are still drunk, just as are all people from Cana.

87. And as for Nathanael, or Bartholomew, he remarked caustically that it seemed to him that the wine had been watered down a little, since some mud from the rainwater, which the miracle had not got down to, was left as a deposit on the bottom of the jar.

88. And Jesus became angry and said to him : if heavenly wine is too weak for you, what will other wine be like? Is there any kind of wine that will upend you?

89. Nathanael said : no Lord, there is none!

90. Then Jesus placed a curse on him, saying: let it be so. Thou shalt be blessed with a haven of paradise, but shalt live in filth: thou shalt be brought sweetmeats, but it will seem that thou eatest carrion; thou shalt be dressed in velvet, but thou shalt believe that thou wearest rags; thou shalt have love showered upon thee, yet thou shalt suffer blows!

91. And verily I say unto you, whosoever was not made drunk by that water will never see paradise.

92. And I say unto you, dear brethren in Christ, that for such a man the time will never come to see God face to face.

93. For he will never bathe in the mists of unconditional faith, as in the wine of Cana, nor will he take pleasure in God's shadow when it passes across pitiful, everyday faces, and darkening them, illumines the horizon with incredible visions of an eternally beautiful future without sin.

94. And I tell you of this so that you may see who Nathanael was, and so that you may see to it that there are no such men amongst you that you may banish them from the garden of the true faith.

95. For they will seduce you and lead you into temptation and show you false signs, leading you into the service of the Devil.

96. Just as they themselves serve him from the beginning of time.

97. For drunk with the wine of the Devil, they do not recognize God's wine, but hold it to be water.

98. When, therefore, the marriage guests had drunk deeply in celebration, and fallen beneath the table, glorifying the new kingdom, which if nothing else, gave promise of the certainty of first-class drink, the Teacher decided that it was time that the two of us took a sip of something.

99. So I brought Him a mug of the miraculous water, and He without thinking tasted it and at once spat it out cursing: what is this, Simon, withered fig tree, rock of rocks?

100. Wine, Rabbi, I said humbly.

101. And Jesus asked: what sort of devilish wine?

102. And I answered Him that it was the wine that a little

earlier He had made from water, and from which all the people had become drunk.

103. And He placed me in front of Him and spake thus: eh, my Simon, eh my barren vine, this is just pure water, but what is wine to sinners, to the elect and the righteous can be nothing more than water, and what to the elect and the righteous is wine, let it be as unattainable to sinners as the Book of Life on the day of the last reading.

104. And I asked Him what I should do.

105. And He said: go to the nearest inn and buy some real wine but watch that they do not give it to you from the bottom of the barrel. And make haste, Simon, that I may refresh myself, for tomorrow there awaits me the continuation of the miracle which I began by turning the water into wine.

106. And when I returned with the wine, He tasted it and said: that is wine but the other was water.

107. And we drank thus up to the third day after our arrival, and up to the seventh day of the marriage in Cana of Galilee.

108. And of this, Simon, son of Jona of Bethsaida of Gennesaret, whom the Saviour called Peter, or Cephas, and turned into a rock on which to found his most beauteous Church, bears witness and leaves behind as the first bequest of faith in legacy to Christian elders.

109. To the Glory of the Father, and of the Son and of the Holy Ghost. Amen.

Translated by Bernard Johnson

Bora Ćosić

THE KING OF THE POETS

When Brag the great national poet came to our town – at that time he was quite unknown – he went into the writers' café to look for the king of the poets or someone acting on his behalf.

'What do you want with the king?' they asked him. 'Perhaps we have a king and perhaps we haven't.'

Brag looked grim and gloomy. He had no wish to discuss the matter with just any ordinary poet.

'I want the king' – he said at last – 'it's just that I want to bust his teeth in.'

The poets smiled slyly to themselves. Brag grabbed hold of the one nearest to hand and gave him a resounding thump on the nose – to the credit account of a king who did not even exist. The man he clobbered slumped beneath the table; the newly arrived poet asked his friends for something to eat. They gave him sausages, wine and their poems.

'I am the greatest poet in Serbia,' Brag proclaimed, 'and for this reason I permit you to offer me food.'

The poets began to talk about this, the greatest of them all. Brag caught hold of women in the street by their breasts, got himself beaten up, and for a short while, arrested. He embarked upon an amorous pursuit of Rosy, a one-legged tart from the railway station, of Anny, the decrepit cashier from Kate's café, of fat village wenches who brought cabbages to the vegetable market. He was hopelessly in love with Greta, the cook in the Commercial Hotel; he drooled beneath the window of the lavatory attendant on Republic Square; he flung himself under the legs of a toothless conductress on bus 34. He loved women utterly, devotedly, ceaselessly. He wrote poems about being and about nothingness, about puerility and about death.

His poems were as incomprehensible to the shop-assistants he slept with as to the poets who fed him. They appeared in every magazine. He was the greatest national poet of the first years following the war. Then his great performance began.

He used to burst through café doors, fraternize with tramps, jump head first from the lower storeys. He was beaten up by drunks in the port, by policemen, by the husbands of receptionists, and even, at length, by the poets themselves, who were becoming scared at his fantastic fame. His poems were turbid and well-fashioned. They gave an incredible picture of love, revolution and life in general. Brag became more and more popular and began to appear in school textbooks; the children read him with fear and sweat on their brows. He used to sleep with the gipsies under the bridge over the Sava.

At large poetry meetings Brag, as the first great national poet after so many years of silence, bawled out in his drunken voice the most beautiful things about the Republic ever written. The Republic honoured its son and applauded. The poet went about without socks because of the heat. His poems were powerfully passionate, melodic and frightening. His toothless mistress, the old women he chased, the little, flat-chested waitresses, all listened to his brilliant, drunken recitals with closed eyes, without understanding. The great national poet, Brag, crossed Republic Square in the middle of the day on his knees in homage to the lavatory attendant there. Below, in the stench of disinfectant in the 'Ladies' – ignoring all rules of decorum – he composed four sonnets on the future – the most beautiful of their kind – while kneeling among the lavatory brushes. The girls of the entire city, young undergraduettes, lesbians, activists, daughters of respectable families, were crazy about his poems and not a little about him.

At the evening literary gatherings in the parks, or in faculty halls, or by the pedestals of huge statues, they would ask him in tremulous tone how he succeeded in writing so warmly, so rapturously, so fabulously, above all, so well. He smiled in his innocent way beneath his heavy spectacle frames, showed his small teeth grown awry and explained that he did it to infuriate the others. The virgins were amazed at the simplicity of the poet's reply and he, instead of doing anything else, read another six scintillating sonnets about Eve, his newly acquired mistress.

The poets, eaten away by despair and jealousy, gave up feeding him. Their published verses did not bring in enough even to pay for his drinks. And the national poet, forgetting his pride, knocked on the doors of various national bodies looking for something to eat. They led the king of the poets, ravenous as he was, into their reception rooms, entertained him handsomely and introduced him to various foreign literary figures who were friends of the Republic. Brag devoured fine cuts of meat and swore at the mother of the host concerned in French. Then he stood up and recited his translations of Valéry, which were excellent. At night, he used to return to the windows of the hospitable house and, drunk and cold, pour out great curses on humanity, on the French and on any and everything else.

Learning of their brother's fame through the newspapers, his relations began to arrive from the village: brothers with cudgels; brothers-in-law and finally his father himself.

They took over their forgotten son now that he was a great and highly esteemed poet. His brothers went to the editors haggling for each verse, the father threatened the publishers with an ominous stick he himself had carved. The books came out on time, beautifully bound. The brothers with their bloodshot eyes went into fine shops to buy their brother the most expensive socks. The brothers-in-law chased away the poet's mistresses, the hunchbacked streetwalkers, full of sensitivity, the one-eyed tram drivers and others. Life to the great poet became desolate and because of this Brag set out on foot along the road to the south. He went along wide roads, nibbling coarse grass, puffing at dandelion seeds and gazing at the clouds high over the flat country. After three days he reached the frontier near Subotica.

'Where are you going to?' the border people asked gaily.

'To Budapest,' Brag replied. 'I am a poet and a better one than anyone else, I want to see what the Danube at Budapest is like and to write a poem about it.'

Expressing their regret they informed him that without a passport he could not go to Budapest nor indeed to any place abroad. He looked at them, politely, and asked when it would be possible to go to Budapest and to all those other wonderful places in the world without a passport, to which they replied that they did not know but that at present it was not possible. So the poet Brag returned from the frontier of the Republic, whistling, nibbling grass, happy but a little tired.

On the way he held poetry meetings in the villages, factories, and in football stadiums. The people flocked and, standing, listened solemnly to his endless recitations.

His brothers in their house on the outskirts sorted out the poet's papers, stuck his photographs which had appeared in fashion magazines on the walls and weeded the grass around the house. They even bought a radio. The poet fled from his fine relations, wrote dark and brilliant sonnets on great metaphysical problems, on human blood, on diaphragms and other organs, on chimeras, wars and such things and on life. Only once did he take a fancy to a fair girl; a graceful secondary-school girl, the granddaughter of P. Bosustov, a social confessor. She tried to take him with her fragile, manicured fingers. For six days he wore shirts whiter than white; for six days he sported expensive ties and drank only mineral water. He discussed poetry only in the sublime manner; he listened to classical music, subtle and unceasing; he lived in another great and polished world. That woman lulled him thither with her breasts, her eyes and her arms but on the seventh day, according to Biblical finality, he got disgustingly drunk, ate onions, took off his socks which he found too warm. Bosustov's granddaughter asked him if this meant that something had happened to them and he replied with an alcoholic blandness that what had happened was that he could no longer stick such a fine but hellish life.

Finding himself once more in the street, the great national poet felt an inexplicable coldness in his heart: a loneliness, hard as stone, gripped the poet's soul. He went into a telephone box, that station of human understanding, but was unable to find a friendly number so he called up the world, mankind. 'Oh, world' – he cried out – 'where are you?' But the world, that great community without loneliness and warmth, did not reply.

In the cafés sat circus dogs' trainers, acrobats, gamblers, menders of broken plates as well as very young poets.

In the pungent smelling cafés, propped up against the counter, stood many citizens of the new age, talented short-story writers, impeded by alcohol, do-gooders and lunatics, some of whom recited *sotto voce* with poignancy and enchantment. Their poems turned on the wheels of history, on aspects of the female form, on everything. The poets were young, unschooled in the matters of life and did not know where to turn with their painful and blasphemous poetry.

These noble minds, distracted by history, once more adopted the king of the poets, Brag, as their comrade. He was no longer alone and great festivals of poetry-reading began to take place, the audiences were moved to the brink of tears.

Brag once more took heart and explained at last the great significance of his art – the witness of a new age. Brag became possessed and fired with a new zeal. He addressed the philosophers, cataleptics, idiosyncratists of the whole world. He explained that by means of special electrodes, he controlled the growth of plants. He convinced them, over and over again, that the threads of many important events, even those relating to traffic and contraception, passed through his pulsating brain. Clutching his breast in pain, he confessed what an effort it was for him to renew by his own forces the daylight of every morning at precisely the appointed time. He had no fear of competition from the fearful lady versifiers nor from the vulgar poetasters who gathered around. The poet explained the formula of his inconceivable verse. A great force was in the king of the poets when he spoke.

And then, in the middle of an enormous celebration of great words, the lavatory attendant, accompanied by her three-year-old son, hobbled in on a large crutch. The poets looked at the newcomer in a drunken way, the dog trainers, insulted, began to leave the table. They asked her what she was doing at such a function : the greatest poetry festival since the war. She said that she had more claim on the great poet than any one of them because she had given him a son, the three-year-old urchin she had brought with her. The poets began to swear and curse, calling her a lying whore; the king looked at the child without any sign of recollection. The sweet young things (the sort to be found in a café) wanted to approach the child who, although dirty, looked very sweet, but the frightful lavatory attendant, mother of the poet's offspring, said outrageous things and, dangerously brandishing her crutch, spat at them continuously.

And Brag, the king, denying his paternity, began to stroll from café to café followed by the versifiers, the possessors of great words, the masters of sincere verse, all very drunk. He showed them all what he could do with his enormous brain-force; many of them asked if he could do this, that or the other, and the poet's answer was always that he could.

Then John of the Underground, the critic of life, the classicist of forbidden thought, the great respecter of self-imposed cruelty, stood up and from his tattered pocket drew a revolver captured from the occupation forces and asked a question about the death wish. Looking at the bloodshot eyes of the great poet, he of the underground humbly and quietly asked if the king could answer this final challenge of history. Brag, without a flicker of expression, took the revolver from John, put the muzzle into his mouth and pulled the trigger.

To the cemetery flocked the poets, the revolutionary leaders, the citizens of our matchless city and its outskirts. At a discreet distance, behind the other tombstones defaced by the rain, stood the great loves of the national figure, those little old lame and syphilitic women.

You will find in P. Bosustov's study an imposing collection preserved in formalin. The collection includes an index finger, allegedly belonging to Brag and reputed to have been lost in a café brawl. For many years poets, blinded by grief and drink, have been paying the unemployed social confessor a small income to kneel before the legendary formalin unicate which, in defiance of chemistry, is dissolving in the green Chartreuse-like liquid. It is not really known, however, whether the great poet was buried without or – which is more probable – with all ten fingers. In favour of the latter conjecture we animadvert to the curt notice, inserted by the proletarian writer, D. Vidović, in all newspapers on the day of the death of this young leader: 'STRANGE EVENT – HE HAD EVERY-THING.'

Translated by Harold Norminton

Tomaž Šalamun

ECLIPSE: II

I will take nails,
long nails
and hammer them into my body.
Very very gently,
very very slowly,
so it will last longer.
I will draw up a precise plan.
I will upholster myself every day
say two square inches for instance.

Then I will set fire to everything.
It will burn for a long time,
it will burn for seven days.
Only the nails will remain,
all welded together and rusty.
So I will remain.
So I will survive everything.

THINGS: IV

He fell as the sun falls on the sky
only he wasn't fulfilling that sort of function
he was disturbed by the clinging Moloch's clammy skin
so with a small gold machine
he detached the peel
peel with hair on the inside
using a code of the
higher mathematics he sorted

his passion into four groups
and put each group into a cardboard box
then he spent a long time
arranging this library of his
just leaving some specimens as a reminder
hung up like clocks
sometimes when the sun was going down outside
with that quiet way of dying it has
he would creep up
and with white thread listen to the explosions
in the cardboard boxes
and to the differences in sound
between group A and group B
and group C with its gentle pulse

THINGS: V

Have you seen god yet
running to arrive in time at half past two
responsibility responsibility
you can't get it near the beginning or end
immobile tethered
instead of dangling its legs any old how
responsibility responsibility
a world without nature
a world without talk
trees are irresponsible while they grow
and what does the word have to do with it
the sun has no need of it when setting
nor the sky which is just blue and nothing else
who did god ask
when he created the butterfly the way it is
when they could have had legs made for it six inches in diameter
responsibility responsibility
baroque the nations victuals

THINGS: VII

I shall draw a cross

                +

s-bends on my rocking chair
how sadly the shirt hangs
when vacated by the body
but it's still a shirt
and there's the nub of our defeat
and the suitcase and the t-square
have you ever seen a chair
scampering from the bathroom to the kitchen
or in the opposite direction it's all the same
and asking hysterically
what about my life after death
have you ever seen a balcony railing
saying i've had enough
        i've had enough
        i've had enough
i am fond of my little life too
i want to get something out of it too
and have you ever been down abraham street
and seen between number four
and the well an old boot that's lain there
ever since the year of
those last night regattas when Mario won
did the boot say to you
good morning excuse me
for troubling you here on the street
but don't you think
don't you think
don't you think
Incomprehensible are things in their artfulness

inaccessible to the rage of the living
invulnerable in their incessant leakage
you can't catch them
you can't grab them
as they stare immobile

POKER: IV

It's here again that damned dry wind
with the spittle of all the summers
when we lay on the scorching stone
and Piero sailed by in his old boat

Lorelei lily lorelei
said the wizard
and then forgot
that's why I too play poker

That's why I too play poker
but still I hear the noise
of those old pulleys
when we dried the wash in the street

That fig tree will have to come down
said mother one morning
and leaning out of the window
sang our old song

Translated by Veno Taufer and Michael Scammell

Ljubomir Simović

THE FIRST BOOK OF MOSES, CHAPTER THREE

Eve, cast out of earth and heaven's eden,
amidst the world of future people wandered lost,
alone and naked in an unknown region
one hand between her thighs
the other held across her naked breasts.

And in the future at the sight of Christ
and of the nail that pierced his open palm
and at the vision of tomorrow's sins
her startled eyes were overcome with terror;
but by her stubborn sinning
from one exile to another
the world gradually drew nearer
to that part of heaven
which had got drunk upon the apple.

DANUBE

Whose head do you carry along
through my vineyards
whose lifeless head
crowned with its flecks of hoarfrost
do you bear away from its body, Danube?

Where do you bear it so well loved
into the sky over autumn
towards a better body
a stronger blood, a more fertile kiss
to some winter less cold, Danube?

Look well once more at the land
towards which you bear it
see once more to ointment and balm
that after its heavy blood may not stain you
from the blood that splashed on the axeman, Danube.

Better to turn again to your source
and return into darkness
to the battlefield where the steed rears up
at the writhing serpent
a black raven in the saddle, Danube.

Better once more to cast it forth dead
in front of its wounds
that the sun may not see it again
alive like this
over your cold waters, Danube.

'TOTING OUR ARMS...'

Toting our arms and our sawn off legs, soldiers!
and with these as our weapons
let us gallop across the fields filled with smoke
to batter to death our leaders!

Then let us light up their heads like torches at night
and lit by their flames
carry them off to regale the dogs and the fish
with the wine of their skull and the seed of their hip and their
    thigh.

And when the beasts have their fill, let us rest on our spears
and with their aid
leaving the land to winter and sleeplessness
let us all go back through the dark to our graves.

SHEPHERD TO PRINCES

Yours are those flags
all those towers on every hill
all those dungeons, all those henchmen
all those thrones in the clouds
all that armour, all those bridles
and all those roads with the sword as signpost
but mine is the wheaten cake,
a basket of apples, a glass of milk
and a wife who eats supper with me
on the other side of the table
and the cold pasture beneath Sopotnica
when bare through the night mist
from the edge of the last sky
a new sun appears to us.

Translated by Bernard Johnson

Matija Bečković

'IF I KNEW...'

If I knew that I would hold myself proudly
In prison and before the courts :
I would roast and burn but still bear all
Resisting everything with my bare limbs !

If I knew that I would push away
The table with my feet, myself put on the noose
My soul would earn itself eternity
And my hangman weep after me.

But I fear that I would entreat
And weeping, kneel, betraying all.
So as to keep at least my naked life
And spit on everything, agree to anything.

'I UNDERSTAND NOW...'

I understand now why the guilty die
punished deservedly and dying voluntarily,
but why does a man die
when he has done no ill,
when he obeyed his parents, studied –
as if that's all in life he ever needed.
I thought that just the guilty died
that death was there to separate the guilty from the good,
for if it made all equal what would be the sense?
Whoever died had sinned in something,

Socrates, Heraclitus and Christ.
Knowing I'd die tomorrow I'd die now,
but I'm not sure that I shall die at all,
and so I live !
Perhaps I'm an exception : I'll not die, perhaps I can't,
perhaps I'm just incapable of death,
perhaps one day I shall be known only
as someone who can never die at all !
Surely because of that I shan't be called abnormal
or caged in as a monster or a freak,
I shan't be killed off simply for the reason
that everybody hopes some day I'll die !
But I'll just keep on living without rules,
for only thus can I avoid wrong doing.
There is no reason for a guiltless man to die,
the innocent must keep on living always,
that is their right
but not in heaven : rather here on earth
where they may have such all-eternal heritage.
And that this never yet has come about
is just perhaps the proof
that up to now there's been no guiltless man
Or that some man somewhere throughout the ages
in some secluded place is living secretly
and cannot speak about his happening.

TWO WORLDS

And very soon the day must be near
we shall send a request to the prison governor

To preserve us from fear, freedom and cold
and accept us for penal servitude !

And when we are thrown into chains and servility
may the world at last lose its shameful stability !

And of those two worlds which this world embraces
may the world of prisoners become the greatest.

And then may our guards out of shame or fright
ask to come over one night to our side.

Translated by Bernard Johnson

Ivan Slamnig

COLUMBUS

It's my nerves that drive me to pace out the deck.
And I feel all the men's eyes upon me.
At least they are lucky, they can find sleep.
If only I'd find at least some small island.

I am fretful now beyond all endurance.
The horizon is flat.
How foolish it was to risk all this
as if I hadn't foreseen it:
emptiness, endlessness, my own apprehension.

What good fortune it would be to come upon
some small island, any sort of land.
For me to say: I wasn't mistaken, at least not entirely.
I pace about anxious and piss overboard from the closets.

Darkness all round, no horizon is near
therein I can feel just a little at home.
It's good that the dark should hide us a while.

Why is it I haven't got strength?
Did I really believe it just wouldn't matter?
Everything slips through my fingers.

At the end of it all I want to find something
not just for the finding
but I need to show proof
for my voyage to these men here.

India, India, only to find you
is too much expectancy.

THE GOSPEL WRITERS

Three working men : a plagiarist, a drudge
and a physician, angular and old,
with not much hair and almost toothless
and at their side a none too clever boy
who read all books and saw right through them.

The print of effort on their wrinkled brows,
short-sighted and with furrows in their palms
Matthew and Mark and Luke set down their Gospels;
But then it was the boy who managed
to start off writing thus : In the beginning was the word.

And they began to wonder not a little
at him, and he at them,
so that they all began to wonder greatly.

And while they wandered, following after Christ
the boy would lean his head upon Christ's breast,
and while for Christ the others were a rock,
their names were rocklike and their shoulders too,
the boy was gentle, wayward like a child
and like a woman sensed the ways of Jesus.

UNKIND DIVINITY

When he strikes you, it's a real blow
with his panzer fist of wolfram steel.
Your side is weak, his prow is high
he runs upon you boldly and with skill.

Brute-like he purposely courts an encounter!
Jabs with his elbow, springs on you down from the roof
until with your new automatic rifle
you scatter buckshot like a farmer blasting

a regiment of crows. When you raise your sword
at his strong form, there is no one there. So
you slice smoke! You smash in the fuse box,

batter the plaster, sunder the gas-meter,
and he is there but you just can't get at him
to cut him down, you only hear his laughter.

RETURN FROM THE MOON

There was something quite natural about
going on that journey. Of course
there was something about it quite special too.
The long, long absence. The uncertainty
and the impossibility of foreseeing everything.
On the other hand people so regularly
and seemingly quite without fuss go off on such journeys,
(we often saw a flying saucer's captain on the screen,
always a man the girls could fall for).

But when I come back from that distant journey,
but when I come back, what will you see of me?
(You will be glad at my return.)

But I shall grow cold and changed
And turn green at the touch of the air,
An unseen Selenite, remote and meaningless.

SAINT

A plum-tree, three wild cherries,
a hazel-bush and half a sunflower,
here it was the saint grew up
his hands crossed
upon his breast.
Grew up out of the ground
without ever passing through woman.
Eating figs for sustenance
he was like a white boat newly painted,
and took the sky for eyes.

Saint Ioann Stylites
never coveted what was his neighbour's
nor knew of passion
for he grew up out of the ground :
no possible fleshly contact
could temper the fever in his spine.

He didn't know what
he could sacrifice to God,
so, clambering on to his column,
he sacrificed curiosity
for that was all he had,
Ioann.

                    Translated by Ivan V. Lalić and Bernard Johnson

Aleksandar Tišma

PERSONALITY

There is nothing more unnatural than the murder of a sleeping man. The victim is thereby deprived of the most fundamental human feature: that of perceiving the approach of his own death, a characteristic which has been bought dearly by the species in its progression from the animal state by the sacrifice of the animal's blissful limitation to immediate impressions.

Of course someone who dies naturally in his sleep is similarly deprived of this visionary capacity. But only in the conscious part of his being. It is certain that at such moments of extreme peril the human organism sends corresponding signals to the brain, and even if these are not transformed into comprehension or answered, because the body is asleep, they are nevertheless registered in some kind of change, perhaps only within the context of the sleeper's dreams. Yet what signals can be emitted by a healthy organism, when the weapon which in the next instant will split open its skull is already poised in the air? Doubtless only a jumbled impression of the last unendangered moments.

In the case of Radovan Predić who was sleeping in just such a situation with the axe already raised above his head at a certain moment in the afternoon of New Year's Day, this impression must have been still warm with the satisfaction of possession. It had been stimulated by his wife who even then was holding the axe in the air. The next moment the axe came down and it was all over.

This unusual act put an end to seven years of discord, which, judging by all external signs, was nothing particularly out of the ordinary in that dismal suburb with its squat, uninteresting little houses and their tiny gardens. Predić, a worker in a factory producing screws, and a prominent citizen of that squalid district, from time to time beat his wife Gina, was unfaithful to her, swore at her, and made love to her just as ecstatically so that their life was as sordidly stuck together as a lump of tar thrown away in the dust of the unpaved courtyard. His wife secretly lamented her sufferings as though they were some kind of punishment. She often threatened to leave Radovan, but (apart from the fact that they had a growing child), in that world of identical, one-storeyed houses, built with the labour of a lifetime to last a lifetime, her words made little sense, since leaving would merely mean circulating in the same streets and among the same people, face to face with everything she was trying to escape from. Where could she go if she left him? When Radovan had married her, marrying for the second time, he had left a room in his mother's house for a room and a kitchen in an identical house belonging to Gina's father: just as his sister-in-law had taken over another room and kitchen in the same house when she married Gina's brother; just as Gina's father had once moved there when he got married; just as Radovan's mother had moved into her house when she married; just, in fact, as Radovan's first wife was still living in a room in the house of her former mother-in-law. It was like moving about in a morass: in pulling one foot out, you pushed the other further in.

Perhaps it was the impossibility of moving, or only of moving in the same circle, in the same mire, that created in Radovan that sullen malice which poisoned his second marriage, to Gina. The harder it is to leave, the bleaker a place becomes, particularly for a man who feels that he has it in him to move around. Radovan felt that he was capable of moving, even if Gina did not. He was a big man, handsome, a skilled metal-turner which in that half-village atmosphere with its bourgeois aspirations represented the most coveted of male qualities. Predić made good use of them: he was known as 'the Actor'. He grew a black moustache and combed his black hair back from his high forehead; he bought a motor-cycle on credit and kept it until it broke down; he continued to go to dances alone even after he was married, and afterwards slept with the girls he saw home – this was how on one occasion he got off with Gina.

But then he had married her, divorcing his first wife after an entanglement which had just suited his violent, grasping nature. It was summer then, with long, bright days and he was spending more time with Gina, who believed him single, than his wife, usually more words than action, was prepared to tolerate. She lay in wait for them one evening in front of the 'Adria' cinema, in a summer coat, bristling with anger, and carrying an umbrella with which object – brought along perhaps with this very purpose in mind, since the sky was cloudless – she proceeded to lay about Gina's blonde waves. Gina could only shelter her head from the blows and Predić had to grab hold of his irate wife by the arms and drag her off into a side street, where he explained certain things to her and packed her off home. When he returned to the cinema entrance, Gina had gone.

He ran after her (he did not yet have his motor-bike), and caught up with her in the market square between the stalls; spread out in the evening light beneath their pointed awnings and arranged in two parallel rows, they looked like a frigate under full sail. She was walking alone amongst their shadows, dazed with humiliation, and it was some time before Predić could get her to stop. He leaned her against the nearest stall and confessed what had in any case already become apparent : that he was married, but that he loved only her and would get a divorce as soon as possible so that he could marry her. She listened, her head turned aside towards a piece of water-melon rind which had been thrown away and lay underfoot in the roadway, giving off a strong smell of decomposition. He sat her on the stall and made love to her, amongst the rubbish left over from the day's market and right next to the stallholders, sleeping on the neighbouring stalls, within sight of the passers-by whose heels clattered on the asphalt of the street along the side of the square. Then he took her home with his arm round her waist and constantly kissing her – because she was far shorter than he – on the crown of her head, which a short time before had equally meekly submitted to his wife's blows.

At the time it probably seemed to him that his affair was a means of escape into some more exciting form of love; but when he had brought it to a conclusion in the way he had promised, he must have realized that it was a trap. Far more of a trap than his first marriage, which had never taken on the form of an escape because it had begun in complete youthful freedom; whereas over this one there hovered the image of that shadowy summer night among the stalls, sprinkled with the smells of over-ripe fruit and framed by the footsteps of the last passers-by. But the reality was removal from one one-storeyed house with a garden to another, from one occupied bed to another, from where, in the morning, when it was time to get up and go to work, could be seen the same hopeless vista: the low roof of the hen-house framed by the window. Gina's father was an old, sickly grumbler, who tapped on the partition wall all day long; her brother was half-witted and always drunk and his wife a slovenly, prying busybody. It could only begin all over again : he would arrive home bad-tempered after work and the local bar, and in the evening set out, changed and shaved, the real 'Actor', for dances and crowded places, to pick up other men's girls and wives.

But all this no longer satisfied him because Gina had once been an exciting affair and he knew instinctively that he could not expect to find something better or more exciting than her. It was from her that he wanted to achieve and preserve that illusion of male strength and freedom which she had conjured up for him that night amongst the stalls in the market. He wanted her to be just as submissive, desirable and new as then, and as she could no longer be so of her own accord, he tried to make her so by force, to abuse her so that she would take on that grey, night-time colour, her head turned away from him, to crush her dignity so as to strip her of the other unnecessary human qualities connected with that house and garden, her drunken brother and whining father, and have left only a woman, a naked woman.

'Those legs of yours !' he would say, staring with hatred in his black bull-like eyes at the floor across which she was walking. In fact Gina's legs were the best part of her body. Beneath her small, oval head, which was half hidden by wavy, blonde hair, beneath her underdeveloped breasts which narrowed down into her waist like a young girl's, beneath her firm, muscular hips, they spread out in luxurious femininity. They were full and mobile and it was impossible not to notice them, they swelled her skirt although it was wide and pleated, making a deep line between her thighs which stood out like full distaffs at every step, or even when she was just standing or sitting. Only her feet were small and turned slightly outwards, like those of people who walk a great deal. That was perhaps why her legs both attracted and repelled him at one and the same time; he wanted them as they were, but without the distraction of those tiny, pointed asides which seemed to take them away, to remove them into the miserly triviality of workaday preoccupations.

'Those legs of yours!' he would say, sitting at the table, angry and tired after work, while they moved to and fro bringing him dinner. He was not satisfied with her cooking: he said that the food she prepared was too greasy, but if she made something light he complained that he was still hungry. Then he would ask her for an account of what she had spent, and when, trembling with fear ('humph, those legs of yours!') she brought her notebook, he would shout that she was robbing him, ruining the household. On the other hand, he would not allow her to look for work although in her child-like naïveness she longed to earn something independently. 'Of course, you'd like to knock around with those salesmen!' He would glance down at her legs, at that slit between them and his face would grow pale. He shouted at her because she was slovenly and stockingless in her sloppy housecoat, but if she put on a decent skirt in the house he would screw up his eyes at her in disgust: 'Who are you trying to impress?' And he would shut himself in the bedroom to sulk, though not forgetting to order her to get him some hot water and a clean shirt: in other words, he would be going out that evening. Sometimes, just as he was setting out, he would demand that she go with him, and then the whole evening in the street or bar he would make malicious fun of an unruly strand of hair, her lipstick, her skirt or her expression. He drank more than usual when she was with him and slapped her face if he thought any man was looking at her. Or else he would angrily send her back: from the café or even from the very doorway of the house. And then he would set off to amuse himself on his own, to chase after women and see them home, impress them with his imposing male strength and make love to them, in bed or under a hedge. Enthusiastically but without brutality, which he had no need of here. But these were only breathing spaces which seemed to be necessary to the other half of his double life and which in no way affected the more sombre side. With or without them, titillated by jealousy or desire, he would always return home at night looking for revenge.

Then, with Gina, he would start those unseen activities which lead to violence. In the locked room, behind closed blinds, using their little boy's precious sleep in the kitchen next door as a threat ('sshh, we mustn't wake him up'), he would work away at Gina's legs, now naked, and drive out of them by exacting exercises that utilitarian lameness. He, who always took women with spontaneous appetite, would force her, who was made only for passive, submissive surrender, to perform all the erotic acrobatics he could devise. He got hold of pornographic pictures and put them on the table under the lamp, like a map for some military operation; then he made Gina look at them, holding her by the neck and pointing at them as solemnly as a judge or a prophet : 'There, you see, that's what I want.' She begged him to stop, but this of course only increased his determination. She wept and weeping knelt, stretched and contorted herself; then she would lie rigid, soaked with the cold sweat of nauseated resistance, coughing and retching until at last he tired himself and pushed her away, angry and disappointed that she could not be that blank, impersonal face turned aside which he thought he had found amongst the market stalls that night.

She was like that on one other occasion, but only to get rid of the doubt, her own or his was not quite certain. Nor is it clear when she decided upon it, at which point of the long New Year's Night, which dragged on over half the following day's holiday, although if there was a crisis or a turning point it was probably during one of the brighter moments. She had become hardened to the darker moments and she accepted them that night as meekly as usual. Radovan had first announced that they would see in the New Year at one of his haunts, the 'Partizan' or the 'Park Hotel'; but whether because Gina gave some sign of interest in this idea, or simply because his intention altered independently, a few days before the holiday he let it be known that there would be no night out after all. So Gina neither got her dress ready nor prepared herself mentally; she listened calmly to the neighbours and her brother and his wife discussing their programme for the evening and announced then that it had been decided that they were not going out anywhere in just the same impersonal way in which she was accustomed to disguise her domestic troubles.

But on New Year's Eve itself Radovan returned home from work and having run through his usual list of reproaches (including 'those legs of yours!'), he suddenly reminded Gina irritably that she had better get ready quickly because the Jelesins were expecting them at eight. 'The Jelesins!' she let out in surprise, knowing that Radovan's friend and frequent companion on his evening sorties had been separated from his wife for at least a year. 'That's what I said!' he snapped without any kind of explanation, and went into the bedroom, slammed the door and threw himself on to the bed. She had no alternative but to use the few gloomy hours left of the afternoon to make hasty preparations: a shirt and suit for him, a dress and underwear for herself, to wash, and to heat water for him to wash and shave. And indeed at six he emerged and began to make himself ready with what she had prepared; they could already hear excited footsteps and voices outside in the yard and the street, and their little boy came in from playing, asking for something to eat. 'What shall we do with him?' Gina betrayed her anxiety; in a free moment while the iron was heating, she had run over to her brother and two or three neighbours to ask whether anyone had cancelled their plans, but without success. 'We'll take him to my mother's,' replied Radovan, shrugging his shoulders and revealing despite himself that the sudden change of plan nevertheless contained a certain amount of forethought.

And so it was. Jelesin, a turner at the same factory as Radovan, had become reconciled with his wife two weeks earlier, and amongst many other things, he had promised her that he would not get as drunk as usual on New Year's Eve, but that he would spend the evening respectably at home. But so as to guarantee himself some gaiety he had all the same invited Radovan, for whom he had an almost feminine weakness and whose company he sought constantly, round to supper. At that stage, as he was still intending to spend the evening at some bar, Radovan had laughingly refused;

but when Jelesin had pleadingly repeated the invitation that very day as they left work, Radovan's original plan had been abandoned, he had prepared his mother for the role of minding her grandchild, which in any case was what she enjoyed more than anything else, and now it was only a question of taking advantage of this arrangement.

Gina had no knowledge of these details, but this was a perfectly normal condition of her marriage : details, small but crucial in coming to decisions, remained hidden behind Radovan's scowl, reaching her only eventually as abusive claps of thunder, generally so invariable that she herself realized that they were only symbolic. So she simply accepted the decision and since, exceptionally, it was not unattractive to her, she even allowed herself to feel a certain amount of hurried pleasure. She had not spent an evening in company for years; whenever she set out anywhere, Radovan would vindictively send her home; she thought that this time the innocence of their purpose would be her protection.

Holding her son by the hand she followed behind Radovan, who was striding ahead along the provincially wide, uneven streets that this time as always were to be the signposts of their short but strained journey. They walked the full length of the street where they lived, turned into another, shorter one, Ćorović Street (all the streets were named after writers), took the second on the right and entered a house similar to their own. Radovan's mother was waiting for them with her usual frightened, suspicious expression; for a second Radovan's first wife poked her untidy head out of one of the rooms off the courtyard. They handed over the child who pressed himself happily against his grandmother, expecting some special treat, and left. When they reached the corner they turned back into Ćorović Street, this time taking the opposite direction to the way they had come, carried straight on and eventually, with some difficulty because the street lamps were weak and Radovan could not remember clearly, they found the Jelesins' gate in a row of identical houses.

Here a certain festive bustle was already to be seen, or perhaps rather the unnaturalness of renewed domestic activity : there were lights in the sitting room and the kitchen and the door of the flat had been left casually open. Jelesin's wife was running back and forward across the yard because the food was kept behind the larder on the other side. Jelesin, freckled and shaky, was standing in the middle of the kitchen doing nothing and looking guilty. But soon everything was ready. The table in the room was laid with a white tablecloth and silver-edged plates and Jelesin's wife brought in a dish steaming with sausages and black pudding, a gift from her father who had killed a pig, while the host dragged a keg of wine across from the corner. They switched on the newly purchased radio which began to pour out a noisy New Year programme of comic turns followed by music for dancing.

With these promises the strained atmosphere of the artificially united group gradually thawed out; Jelesin's wife and Gina, who had not met until then and who had both found out about the invitation that afternoon, and Jelesin and Radovan who were used to each other's company but in a completely different atmosphere. So they drank dedicatedly, saying very little, while the women, circumspectly and with ingenuous lightness, exchanged complaints about them with the men sitting in front of them like dangerous defendants. But as the evening wore on the balance of merit turned more and more in the Predić's favour and Gina felt this. As against the Jelesins, they had behind them like an invisible cash-box an established household and an already grown child; as well as this she felt herself to be better looking and more imposing than her new acquaintance, and it was not hard to see how subservient Jelesin was to Radovan. At one point their earnings were mentioned: Radovan, who was an excellent worker, made about five thousand dinars a month more than Jelesin. Thawed by the wine and the buzz of conversation, she saw that, in the midst of all the fear and revulsion with which her marriage was filled, she had never given a thought to this very real superiority of her husband's and now she looked at him through new eyes. He was dark and well built; the skin of his face had become red from the wine, he was handsome, gay and she even managed to dispel her constant image of him, of his unprovoked vindictiveness that made him the torment of her days and nights.

Radovan too felt the difference, he felt Gina's newly aroused awareness, which was of great importance to him. Had he not, after all, tried to force that awareness into her, moulding her to be obedient to his unrestrained desires? Perhaps he could have abandoned those demands if only she would give him proof of her submission to them. His feelings of superiority gave him the impression that it was so, and at one point when they had begun to sing and when Jelesin took hold of his wife to move round the table in time to the music, he too stood up, a little scornfully, to dance with Gina. And when the radio announced midnight and Jelesin, now drunk, urged them to welcome the New Year in the appropriate way, Radovan patted Gina's shoulder, – without following it with a kiss, it is true, but with a conspiratorial wink from his shining black eyes.

But from then on it was too much for him. He caught the answer in her expression, which was not at all impersonal as he would have liked but, so it seemed to him, rebelliously self-aware. He stood up to go with the excuse that they had stayed long enough and would not listen to his hosts' pleas, which in any case were not altogether unanimous, since Jelesin saw in Radovan's caprice an opportunity to get away from the house again. He explained to his wife, who would not make a scene in front of strangers, however angry she felt, that he was just going to see their guests home, seized his coat, pulled on his cap and followed Radovan out almost at a run.

The latter, perhaps because of the unexpected company, which prevented him from settling accounts with Gina at once, right there in the street, from crushing her rebellion and moulding her to what he wanted, proposed that they continue celebrating at the 'Partizan' which was not far away. The other two followed without objection.

Now they were again walking down the shallow troughs of the streets with their low houses and it was quite natural that Gina walked beside Jelesin, behind Predić, who was striding ahead. They did not talk but just occasionally one of them would utter a word or two to point out to the others the groups of travellers who appeared round the corners, on their way home or, like themselves, changing the location of their celebrations. The nearer they got to the centre, the more frequent these apparently aimless groups of people became, and at the edge of the suburban area, not far from the railway line and the first bus-stop, they seemed to stop moving: the groups stood around the signal box in the trampled snow and mud, talking at length, shouting across to each other, taking their leave and exchanging New Year greetings. Then one or another group would move off, making its way slowly towards the bus-stop or back the way the three of them had come. At the corner, by the open level-crossing, two lights were shining under the enamelled tin shields high up on the prominent yellow façade of the 'Partizan' Sports Centre.

Here the noise and excitement of New Year's Eve was still at its height. The doors of the gymnasium were wide open but still the new arrivals were met by a blast of hot, dense air, like a bad breath, from the crowd crammed inside. While Gina and Jelesin were looking round dazed, Radovan had already penetrated to the cloakroom improvised from parallel bars and vaulting horses, taken off his coat and was waving to them to do the same. Then he pushed his way into the hall ahead of them to where the lights were festooned with bunches of bright paper garlands, wine-stained tables were groaning under the weight of the elbows leaning upon them and in front of the rostrum at the end of the room a crowd of couples was buzzing like a wasps' nest. Just at that moment the music from the stage blared out and a shout of 'Radovan' went up: unseen hands dragged the three of them to a table in the centre. Somebody, purple in the face, was trying to outshout the band and women were laughing shrilly, thumping their hands on the table; chairs and empty glasses were conjured up from somewhere and they all drank to the New Year.

Gina did not know these people either; she felt that she had seen some of them in the district where she lived, but dressed quite differently, and of course, very differently disposed. This somehow made them even stranger, grotesque, but as she was with Radovan whose glass everyone was trying to fill, patting him on his broad back, she was included without hesitation in their circle. Gina laughed at jokes she did not understand, explained to a still sober woman opposite her where they had started off the evening, and when a waltz began and her red-faced, thick-set, balding neighbour whom she had scarcely noticed until then made a comically gallant bow towards her, she stood up to comply with convention, having first assured herself from Radovan's indifferent expression that he had no objection. They forced their way into the crowd, he took hold of her round the waist and began to spin her round swiftly and expertly in a way she would not have expected from his heavy body. She felt herself being carried away and that it was both pleasing and worrying at the same time; and for the first time that evening this feeling aroused a kind of remorse in her, a sensual apprehension at the thought of what that New Year's night would probably have in store for her on their return home. She tried to see where Radovan was but they were separated by the moving curtain of dancers, and then this barrier became even denser, swaying and surging with the pressure of the new heads, shoulders and arms of a whole group of new arrivals with paper hats pulled down over their faces which shone with sweat and laughter. The dancers bobbed up and down as they turned and Gina realized to her surprise that she was seeing first one, then another and then yet another – a whole group of acquaintances from her long-past girlhood days, whom she had rarely seen since and whom as a married woman, the wife of a stern, jealous man, she had only been able to greet with restraint. But now they were all coming back to her, their faces flushed and refreshed across that gap of seven years, with their old familiarity. And she herself must have looked more like she used to for a host of people suddenly surrounded her and in the general chaos swamped her with greetings. She found herself being kissed by soft, firm and prickly pairs of lips, brushed by thick, greasy and silky hair while necks reddened by the effort of shouting loomed over her. Now she felt the danger stronger than ever, knew that there must be some punishment for this moment of pleasure, that something terrible had to happen to redress the balance of this spasm of happiness which was shaking her and forcing her lips into a smile; panic-stricken she held herself back from the hugs, the lips and the hands which were dragging her into disaster as into an abyss. But it was too late. Radovan was standing in front of her, pale, his black eyebrows rising to an angry peak, his lips green and trembling with fury. 'You slut!' he hissed in the silence which his sudden apparition amidst the dancers had carved out. 'You dirty little slut!' And his heavy hand fell like a mallet across the lower part of her face and neck. Then she felt his hands pick her up and push her roughly through the crowd. 'Home! Get moving!' She did not quite understand and holding her hand to her left cheek she stopped involuntarily in the middle of the empty circle which had formed around her. Radovan reached her in one stride and pushed her forward with both hands like a volley ball. 'M-o-o-o-ve!' so that she slumped, staggering, out of the hall.

A murmur of amazement came from the circle of dancers but only for a moment. Then the music started up deafeningly and the couples, glancing at the furious Predić, nervously took up the dance again. He reeled back to his table with clenched fists. Nobody there asked him to explain himself, not even the bald accomplice who had followed behind at a respectful distance; it was his own family matter and some even tried to console him. But this he rejected impatiently; he emptied his glass and at once refilled it, he wanted to get drunk.

But he found no solace in drink. He kept seeing her, smiling as she danced, her face flushed under the rain of kisses, the open rebellion of her wanton female stubbornness and he regretted that he had only hit her once and sent her away without thinking, that he had not beaten her, crushed her there and then. He was no longer able to join in the conversation at the table, he misheard questions, looked at the faces around him as though he did not recognize them. Finally, at about two-thirty, he suddenly got up and left, hardly saying good-bye, determined to complete the punishment with which his palms were itching.

He hurried home through the monotonous streets without seeing anyone, unlocked the door and only then, bathed in sweat, did he remember that Gina had no key. She would not have been able to wake her half-deaf father and there was no light from her brother-in-law's room. Nevertheless he unlocked the door and went in – everything was ghostly still, empty. Then it occurred to him that as she could not get in she might have gone off somewhere by herself and be wandering about with that flushed face, her shapely legs turned slightly outwards, free, uncowed, perhaps even ready for some capricious revenge during that night of folly. But he knew her too well to take this last possibility seriously; when her fear had passed a little she would begin to look for him.

So back to the 'Partizan'. But he did not have the patience to retrace his every step once again through those same streets, so he took his bicycle which was leaning against the wall (he had sold the motor-cycle), and vaulting on to the saddle, he set off into the snow and slush. As he got near the 'Partizan' he slowed down and looked carefully at all the people hanging around in the darkness, young couples who were still loath to part, but he did not see her. He went in, took off his coat, glanced round the hall which was somewhat emptier now; of the people he knew he could see only Jelesin standing between the tables with a glass in his hand in drunken indecision. He took hold of his sleeve and pulled him to one side, but he too knew nothing of Gina's whereabouts.

The two of them sat down at an empty table, spattered with wine, to continue drinking. Angrily but in silence. Jelesin was not used to starting conversation with Radovan, he was happy just to be in his company. Radovan for his part had nothing to say to his blissful friend who, having escaped from his wife, had long since forgotten that she existed. Radovan could not forget his : he kept seeing her flushed face and the curve of her full, taut legs, slightly apart as she stretched her body forward to be kissed. How dare she not come back to continue her chastisement? How dare she leave the house at all without him, without her child? Only then did he remember where their child was and that Gina must be with him. He gave a sigh of relief. He stretched himself up straight beside the table, feeling the blood flood through him in alleviation. Then he paid and got on to his bicycle.

Gina was indeed with her son; Predić saw this at once from the resentful, anguished look on his mother's face when he awoke her with his old signal, a knock on the window. As she opened the door she put her finger to her lips so that he should not wake them. This evidence of her knowledge of his temper only exacerbated him more. Pushing her aside he went into the kitchen and shouted frenziedly: 'Where's that slut? She'd better come out here and quick – I'll show her. ...' As all he heard from the room by way of answer was the rustling of a straw mattress and someone whispering, he concluded that Gina was reassuring the child, that now she was thinking of him and not of her husband, so he opened the door and threatened hoarsely: 'Come out here at once, do you hear?' because he sensed that in bed with the child she was protected from him.

And she came out, her face already swollen from weeping, in her slip which hung loosely down to her waist and clung tightly to her hips and thighs, barefoot with her soft, narrow insteps turned slightly outwards and stepping carefully, wary of the impending pain. He grabbed hold of her as soon as she came through the door so that she stumbled, but when she tried to use her fall to crawl to the door, she found him standing right over her. He thrust his fingers into her thick hair and tugged at it so hard that she writhed and straightened up, crying out with the pain. Clutching her hair in one hand, he dragged her round the table as if on a leash, hitting her with identical, measured blows with his free fist across her neck, shoulders, breasts as though he was thrusting a knife into her. 'That'll teach you!' he shouted and he did not stop hitting her until she collapsed unconscious under the heavy blows. Then he saw his mother's face between Gina and himself and heard the child whimpering in the next room: 'Mama, Mama.' He sensed that she was not shamming and that she was a dead weight on his hands and he only hit her once more, in the softest part between her thighs for good measure to see if she would give herself away by crying out. Then he let her fall face down on to the floor. He quietly allowed his mother to push him aside and drag Gina's inert, sack-like body through the open door into the bedroom.

Without taking his coat off he sat down on a chair by the wall and lit a cigarette. Bent double he listened for a long while to the murmurs, groans and crooning which reached him from the other room, his attention suddenly blunted by a satiated drowsiness. He saw his mother hurrying from room to room carrying bowls, rags, water, and glancing at him, terrified, out of the corner of her eye.

But he no longer wanted to hit anyone. The longer he rested, the more clearly he saw the storm of a few minutes earlier, how and where each blow had fallen and with what effect, and it seemed to him at one moment while he was twisting Gina's head back with his hand caught up in her hair, that for an instant he had seen an expression of strange, maddened, frantic humility. Had he been mistaken? Was what he had seen the first sign of physical unconsciousness, or had he really broken her this time at last? The thought excited him. More and more strongly he could visualize her body suddenly falling, her lips parting, her eyes rolling upwards to show the whites. No, perhaps he had not been mistaken. He breathed heavily, his heart beat so strongly that he could feel it thumping against the back of his chair. His mother was coming out of the bedroom; she was not carrying anything this time and her walk and her whole appearance seemed calmer. Did she know too? An absurd thought took hold of him. He could not wait any longer to find out. He was in the middle of his third cigarette but he threw it away into the waste basket where it went out hissing slowly. It was gradually getting light outside. He stood up and twice walked towards the door. 'Gina, let's go home,' he said, his voice hollow as if in prayer.

He waited there standing up without moving while she dressed; when she appeared he did not even look at her, afraid that her present, her true expression might disappoint him. He went out without a word to his mother, took his bicycle and pushed it into the street. He stood holding it by the saddle and Gina understood: with a moment of hardly noticeable hesitation, she sat on the bar. He climbed on to the saddle and set off.

Now he had her in front of him again, under him, clasped in his arms, legs and breath as once before, a long time ago; but never in such meek proximity. He rode attentively, the street was already half-light so that he was able to avoid all the puddles and not splash them. A new day was beginning in the houses: they could hear voices, small windows were being opened and dusters were appearing out of dark rooms in housewives' hands, like flags waving in greeting. But untouched by all these innocuous activities, hedged off from them as if by a railing, he bore his prey back

to the cave which he had constantly and vividly before his eyes –
to their room.

The main door was open, his brother-in-law's door ajar, but he
did not let his eyes, nor those of the woman he was pushing in
front of him wander from their course. He leaned the bicycle
against the wall, unlocked the door of the flat and stood by it to let
her in. Then he went in himself and locked it from the inside,
pushed the bolt home and drew the curtains. He looked round the
room. Inside it was dark as evening, the door of the bedroom was
open and he could just make out the bed at the other end. The air
was cool and that gratified him : it suggested some kind of dead,
unchanging state which seemed to hold time at the point attained,
time that he now wanted to stand still.

She was standing in the middle of the kitchen, looking to one
side as if not understanding, her lips crooked as if in great sadness.
Yes, she was just as he had always wanted her to be, he had not
been mistaken. He went up to her and took off her coat; in the next
movement he tore off her dress, slip and underwear and pushed her
forward, his hand on her neck, undoing his own buttons with his
other hand. His coat, suit, shoes fell to the floor. Now they were
both naked and he threw her on to the bed.

He was hungry, desperately hungry for the embrace he had
wanted for so long, and his physical strength, excited by the
alcohol which had seeped down into his every cell, gave his desire
endurance. He bent her backwards, pounding, twisting, pinching,
biting her, submerging the tunnels of his protracted suffering in
her, no longer feeling the necessity of erotic pictures to inflame his
imagination which was obedient to the urgency of his spontaneous
need. In fact there was no call for variety now, his goal was
attained from the beginning; he had only to assure himself again
and again that its fulfilment was complete. He looked at her face,
those eyes, lips, the spasms which contracted her forehead. It
changed but no longer in substance. Her mouth let out cries, tears
streamed from her eyes, but no longer out of indignation, disgust
or rebellion but from sheer pain; no longer from her will but from
impersonal, physical hurt such as he applied and regulated. He
could never weary of it. Each time he had finished reassuring him-

self and she had collapsed, exhausted, beneath him on her back, her eyes rolling upwards, her lips shapeless, her legs without their sharpness and individuality which had been so beautiful in their inviolate form, he would take new vitality from the sight of her, new ideas for new reassurance; and pull her up to renew his investigation. Only when her face grew a deathly ashen, her body cold and dry, did he, calm and indifferent, push her away on to the floor so that she fell on her knees, elbows and belly beside the bed. He got up, went to the door, picked up his jacket and looked for cigarettes and matches. He went back to the bed, lengthening his last step so as not to tread on her, stretched himself out and lit a cigarette. Everything had been accomplished, he had nothing left to do.

It was the same for her, as though they had agreed upon an impersonal, harmonious outcome. The stimuli were extinguished, now it depended only on what she could do and the speed with which she could gather her strength to do it. First of all, with a great effort she pulled up her right leg, crying out involuntarily at the pain, and moaned weakly several times. Then she drew up the other leg, raised herself on her hands and knees and remained for a long time in that position like some sick animal; she leant her hand on her knee, stood up shaking all over and slowly, her legs wide apart like a sailor, made her way towards the door, dragging the scattered clothing along with her feet into the kitchen. There she slowly collected each garment, dressed, wrapped her coat around her. She pushed back the bolt of the door, turned the key and went into the yard.

It was almost midday. The sharp winter sun blinded her eyes. Her sister-in-law was standing opposite in the open doorway of the flat holding a ladle. As soon as she saw Gina she called out inquiringly: 'Well, how was it?' Gina made a non-committal gesture and hurried to the closet at the bottom of the yard. From there she went straight back into her flat, into the kitchen and sat down on a stool beside the cold kitchen range from where, without turning her head, she could see what Radovan was doing: she saw him stub out his cigarette on the matchbox, stretch out and lay his head on the pillow to sleep.

She could not restrain herself enough to wait until she could hear his breathing grow regular; she went out into the yard again. Her sister-in-law immediately appeared in the doorway and called her over; behind her, Gina caught a glimpse of her brother in a sweater and slippers. She crossed the yard and went into their kitchen : the fire in their stove was burning brightly, they offered her wine. She drank it while they asked about the evening. She said they had had a good time. But then she broke off the conversation impatiently and returned to her own flat.

As she expected, in the meantime Radovan had fallen asleep. She had only to glance into the room to make certain and make out his pale face and tousled black hair. She went back to the kitchen range, bent down and pulled out a small axe from under the oven; she straightened up and, carrying the weapon alongside her leg, went into the bedroom, right up to the bed. Yes, he was asleep, his face was completely relaxed, distant, his lids firmly closed over the shadowy hollows of his eyes. But the axe, which she swung easily to test its weight, seemed too small; she went out and put it back in its place.

Back in the yard, she crossed over to her brother's of her own accord and standing in the doorway, talked until they offered her a drink. She felt the need to build up her strength, like a woodcutter. She drank a glass of wine, said good-bye and set off to the shed for her father's big axe. With it she returned to the flat, the room, the bed. She swung it; it was heavy. She raised it and turned it in the air, as she had often done when she wanted to split a log in which the blade had got stuck. It came down straight on his temple. She saw Radovan give a slight shudder as though he were simply easing his body into a more natural position; she raised the axe a second time. But as the axe came down she saw it was unnecessary, the wound was already there, deep and gaping. The axe-blade slipped into it easily like a well-used tool into its slot.

She left it there on the body; she looked at her hands to see that they were not stained. She turned round, collected his scattered clothing and folded it over a chair. She went into the kitchen and picked up his shoes and coat. She tied a scarf round her hair, took one more look into the room to see whether it was reasonably tidy, and went out, locking the door. Her sister-in-law was watching her and asked her where she was going; Gina waved without replying. Until the detective arrived, nobody in the house knew that Radovan was lying dead in the bedroom. It had all passed unnoticed, unremarked, externally, as with Radovan himself, who probably, at the last hundredth of a second before death, had embarked upon a dream full of the realization that he had at last conquered Gina, reduced her to nothing more than a woman. Objectively that was quite inaccurate but it might also have been quite true for her from some very personal standpoint, which had induced her to kill Radovan on that particular day after she had voluntarily submitted herself to his tormented passion.

Translated by Celia Williams

Živojin Pavlović

FIRST LOVE

1

We were on the farm which used to belong to Mr Pusić; he had just
been shot. We were sitting in a circle of cut buckwheat; it was
rotting where it lay, scattered across the furrows. We were watching Mile and we too were trying to squeeze that white liquid out of
ourselves, but no matter how hard we tried it wouldn't come. 'I
just can't imagine anything,' I said unthinkingly, tired out by the
monotonous rubbing : my hand had begun to ache. And while I'd
been straining away, hunched up over my own navel, Mile had
twice already wiped the sperm off his palm, laughing triumphantly.
'You've no imagination,' he said, while he laughed at us, and
wiping away the sweat he lay down on his back, buttoned up his
trousers and gazed up at the white clouds. 'Think of a naked girl,'
he said to me a little later when his elation had subsided. 'If you
can just visualize her like that, it's easy,' he went on and smiled
dreamily.

I knew that, but – I asked myself – how can I imagine anything
with all the others there? I looked at them, I saw them panting, I
saw the laboured expressions on their faces and their eyes screwed
up in strained expectation. I just couldn't manage to cut myself off
from them, and I'd have had to have been alone for the images to
have intoxicated me. I knew that Mile was right, but I needed
solitude, for only by myself in the darkness, in complete silence,
when I could hear and see nothing, could I imagine the body of my
landlady, and then I was seized by a trembling as if I had touched
an electric wire with my bare hands. I'd caught sight of her one
evening when she was taking a bath and the memory of her sturdy
thighs and the dark triangle between her legs aroused in me an
unpleasant, but uncontrollably bitter-sweet sensation which I had

never experienced before. But in any case it was difficult for me to imagine the outline of her body again now, because I was overcome by shame; the others were shouting: 'Oh, but he has his Slavka!' reminding me of the little urchin girl with the close-cropped hair whose frightened eyes followed me everywhere.

2

Lazica left the churns on the other side of the road and came through the orchard. Each one of us was wondering whether he had noticed anything whilst he was coming towards us through the buckwheat. The boys were still sitting on the ground just as they had been a few minutes earlier, but now they were lolling about on their sides playing with dry twigs, or lying on their backs gazing in front of them, or chewing silently at a straw as if they expected something from him.

'Come on and show me *that* then,' he said to me and I got up. I'd always preferred to be with boys older than myself. 'Come on, it's on our way,' he said and turned away.

'Where are you going?' but I didn't tell them: I wanted to get away from them after their unbearable jibes. I went off after Lazica with my hands in my pockets; I felt them looking at the back of my head with envy certainly, and perhaps even with hatred, for they knew where we were going. But I didn't look round once: it would have been enough for me to look at them for them to have got up and come with us, to go crawling along by the fence and to join us again when we already had the bombs in our hands, as they always did. So I walked in front of Lazica without looking round, helping him to carry the milk churns which he was bringing back from the town, where every morning he sold the milk to the officers' mess, and then I crawled through the wire to Pusić's farm.

It was abandoned, for the workmen had gone to the front at Srem: magpies were cawing in the ruined barns. We went past the padlocked stables, past the concrete bunkers filled with rubbish, skirted round the motor-pump and I clambered up the ladder to the loft of the outhouse which once had served as a pigeon cote. 'Catch!' I shouted to Lazica and I threw down a grenade which he caught with the awkward movement of a man taking hold of a glass of finest crystal; then for myself I picked up a German anti-personnel bomb and climbed back down.

'Where shall we go?' he asked me, and without speaking I went past the rubbish dump, leaving the outhouse behind us. I walked along confidently, listening to the rustling of the lizards in the dry leaves of the hazel-nut trees. Lazica strode behind me, allowing me to go first, for he had to learn something that I had known how to do for a long while : he wanted to learn how to throw bombs.

Behind the stone shed in which were the cauldrons for melting down the pig fat and the big distillers for making alcohol with the dark green film on their copper domes, there were three concrete reservoirs filled with wine pressings. On those days when the sun warmed up the ground, its bitter smell wafted across the meadow and the maize field as far as the cemetery where we usually played football.

We left the milk churns behind the shed, and went up to the reservoirs, pushing through the thick weeds with difficulty. 'In there?' asked Lazica and I nodded my head affirmatively. He laughed out loud but it had a nervous tone in it. I knew why he was like that and taking the bomb from his hand I explained how it was done. 'Hold it like this so that the spring is in your palm, then just pull the ring and don't be afraid. As long as you hold the lever down tightly along the iron casing, the bomb can't go off,' I told him. 'But don't throw it until I throw mine, I want them both to go off in the pressings at the same time.'

I knew that hesitation would only make him more afraid, so I quickly unscrewed the safety-catch on the handle of the German anti-personnel bomb. 'Now!' I shouted. He tugged at the ring and looked at me uncertainly. In a flash I'd pulled the ribbon and as soon as I'd counted to three, I hurled it as hard as I could into the nearest reservoir. He did the same. A second later two muffled explosions went off one after the other and an enormous gusher of stinking pressings spouted into the sky, splashing the trees, the roof of the shed and the concrete paths. We picked up the milk churns, they too were spattered with the red liquid and with plum-skins, and we ran back up through the hazel-nut trees to-

wards the meadow, fleeing from the bitter stench. Lazica was laughing loudly, happy at last to have accomplished something which
he had hankered after for a long time, but which up to now he
hadn't dared to do. I looked at him proudly, because he wouldn't
have been able to do any of this had it not been for me.

3

'Have you got a girl?' he asked me while we ran panting up through
the trees. We were on the top of the hill. We were sweating, for
the milk churns were heavy. For a while both of us were silent.
'No, I haven't,' I answered, 'and you?'

'Yes, I've got one,' he said. 'You ought to find one too. It's better
to do it with a girl than without one.' I couldn't bring myself to
look at him. I turned away and looked down from the brow of the
hill at Pusić's fodder store, at the hedge, strengthened with barbed
wire, at the narrow, dusty road behind the orchard through which
could be seen the field of uncut buckwheat which stretched almost
to the first houses on the outskirts of the town. It was clear that he
had seen us. Now there was no one in the buckwheat.

'Go on, why don't you try with her,' I heard his voice suddenly
behind my head: he had come out into the clearing which divided
the hazel-nut grove from the meadow.

I climbed up after him and to my horror saw the crop-head girl
standing there on the open ground, the edge of which was crisscrossed with trenches, the same girl whose soulful eyes followed
me everywhere. She was quite alone, dark against the sky: she
was looking down at her feet, and her hand was holding a cord
which was tied round the neck of a pair of sheep. 'You could do it
with her,' said Lazica. 'She's fond of you.'

I raised my eyes to look at his face, but I saw that he wasn't
making fun of me. 'Go on,' he said, 'I'll get lost so that she won't
be embarrassed.' But I hesitated. 'Try it just once,' he said again,
pushing me forward. It had to happen like that: his hands turned
me away from the clearing which divided the grove from the
meadow, and I moved towards her, all the time feeling myself resisting more and more.

I got nearer to her, but her shape began to swim before my eyes. First I stopped seeing her thin legs and the bumps on her knees, then her hands got lost somewhere in the mist, and her short, dirty dress went off somewhere into the greyness. I could only see her close-cropped head clearly and her big, translucent ears which seemed to me to stick out from her head.

When I got right up to her, I told her to come with me, and she did so without a word. She opened her fingers and the cord dropped on to the rough ground; the sheep went on grazing, while we, not looking at each other, set off towards the crumbling trenches. I jumped down into one, not turning round to look at her and I don't know how she got down over the banked earth on the top. When I looked round, she was already standing behind me, her back pressed against the damp earth. I told her to lift her skirt. I said the words quietly and jerkily, but I knew that she had heard them, for her shoulders began to tremble. Her lips became dry; at that moment she looked more like a boy. I repeated my demand, not knowing what to say, although I sensed that she had already done what I asked of her. Now I had to look at her, and with a great effort I brought my eyes down over her body with a feeling of unbearable revulsion: the skin between her thin legs was white and hairless. Instantly and without knowing why, I hit her across the face with all my strength. Perhaps I wanted to destroy some mysterious world. But it was not her but I who burst into tears.

Translated by Bernard Johnson

Dragoslav Mihajlović

WHEN THE PUMPKINS BLOSSOMED

It was there that me and the Apache rubbed up against each other.

Just at that time I was trying to drop a dolly of mine. She'd begun
to chat up the old lady, get round the old man, take my kid sister
to the pictures. And I was a bit careless with her, used to take her
home. Andra, my old man, had started to nag me about her:
'What do you think you're up to with that girl who's always hanging around the house?'

Ah, so that's how it is, I think to myself. You wait, you bitch.

I had this mate, Lale, a real fast worker, a type-engraver with
Borba. And just as nasty as he was handsome, a really vicious type.
'Lale,' I say to him, 'do me a favour. I've got a date with a bird
tonight, but I told Desa I'd take her to the pictures. You take her.
Here's the tickets. Tell her I got held up at the club. And be nice
to her, she's a real fine dolly. And still whole.' That's what I said,
whole! She was too, once!

'Don't worry about a thing, boyo,' he says, 'It'll all be O.K.'

I didn't like giving any girl of mine the push like that and I
wasn't at all happy when some lousy character took over from me,
but I was really choked with that one: I wasn't going to get married, was I? So he took her off to the pictures that night, and
another time I said I couldn't get away again and the third time
they fixed it up themselves. Then he went for her like a maniac.
She ran off crying.

The next day she comes whining to me: 'See what kind of
friends you send me!' I act quite dumb. 'What sort of friends?
Why come to me? You take up with all sorts of rowdies and then
you have the cheek to come and moan to me! Not any more you
don't.' And then I wrap it up for her with Pa and the old lady.

'Just you find me another doll like that Desa,' I tell them, giving out as if I'm really angry. 'She wants to marry me but at the same time she's knocking around with two or three others.'

'We found her for you?' Andra asks me, 'Who are you having on? Who's she going around with?'

'I'm not having anyone on,' I say, 'and she's going round with the smoothest operator in all Belgrade, Lale the engraver from *Borba*, that's with who. I saw them myself last night.' Desanka comes round two or three more times. The old man gets lost at once, the old lady acts as if she's busy. She starts moaning to her about me, but all she gets is : 'Well, my lass, a girl ought to watch what she gets up to.' So good-bye, she doesn't come round any more.

That evening I went round to the 'Zvezdino' with an old oppo and sparring partner of mine from the club, we'd picked up a lot of birds together, a great guy and a fine boxer, Draganče Stojil-ković. He was a welter-weight international later on for years and he really was a great artist, but it was only just before he left the ring that he became Serbian and Jugoslav champion for the first and only time, not until after those sharks Šovljanski and Toma Hladni retired. Because you couldn't get past them any other way than by taking an airplane. And on the way there some insignifi-cant character from my factory by the name of Mića latched on to us.

When we got there I spied a real lovely bird, like a dream she was, tall with long blonde hair, a pretty face, pointed tits and real shapely legs.

'Jesus, Draganče,' I yell, 'take a look at that over there.'

'I already did,' says Draganče, 'terrific !'

'Let's try and get off with her.'

'You mean,' he says, 'you try and get off with her?'

'Yeah, of course,' I laugh, 'me. She's too tall for you.' And it's true, he's not over tall.

'But why don't you get off with that piece that's with her? Look her over, she's not bad either.' So we're just fixing things up like that : 'You lousy bastard,' he says, 'how long do I have to go on being the sparring partner? I always get the next best bird to yours' – when the dance starts and who pads up to her from nowhere at all but – Stole the Apache! He gets to her first and takes her off. Up pops Mita the Monkey with him and lifts the other one. I take a quick look round and sitting down a bit further off I see two others of the Dušanovac mob – Pretty Boy Ivica and Steva the Knacker.

That's spoilt it! Where did they spring from?

'Ljuba, did you see that?' asked Draganče.

'I saw it,' I say. I'm busy thinking about what to do. 'You know what,' time to change tactics now, 'let's go for those other three who got left out.'

So we take off with three other hoary old birds – she's with a crowd of others, seven or eight perhaps – everything else has gone already, it's like at the racetrack. We dance that dance.

Then we go back to our places.

'Now, we'll do it like this,' I say. 'We'll get a bit nearer so that we don't get shut out again. You take mine and I'll take your one.'

'That's right, you just share 'em out!'

'Come off it, next time I'll do the sparring for you. You too, Mića, make your mind up which one, take one from over there too.' I wanted to bring him into it. If it came to a punch-up, at least we'd be three, although he didn't know a thing about roughing it up. He'd at least have a go.

We move in a bit and the minute the saxophonist starts up, we're alongside. 'Like to. ...' I dance with the smaller one, Draganče's – she's really not bad at all. I look across at him. He's mouthing something, all turned on, but it looks as though it's no good – she's almost bigger than he is and turning her nose up a bit. I take a quick squint at the Apache and company: all four of them are sitting there and sizing us up threateningly. We'll be up to our knees in blood here tonight.

'You know what, Draganče,' I say afterwards. 'Now we'll get one jump ahead of them. We'll go there again but we won't touch those two.'

'O.K.,' says Draganče. 'It looks as though I wouldn't get anywhere with that one of yours, anyway.'

This time we take three others. The Apache and the Monkey

grab the other two at once. And I see it looks as though things are all right again. Ivica and the Knacker were holding on to see how it would work out, but they too have got hold of something or other now.

When that dance is over, I say: 'Now you've got to watch it. They mustn't get in before us this time. And if you see the Apache and the Monkey and the other two sidling up or hanging round us, then the fun's over, chop the first one you can get hold of, don't wait for them to start it. And don't get split up. Keep close to me.'

And that's how it was. We made it in front of the Apache and the Monkey by a whisker. They went off with two others so as not to look silly.

Ivica and the Knacker fidgeted a bit on their bench, but when they saw Stole and the Monkey dancing, they got up too.

I realized we were going to get through that dance without a bundle. Now I had to work fast.

I started to chat her up – I haven't seen you here before, I usually notice all the pretty birds, do you come here often – and so on. She looks me over a bit – she's got big, sharp, green eyes – but there's something she doesn't take to. From Kragujevac, she says, came to Belgrade this year, fresher student. I try something else, and still not much reaction. Has the Apache already knocked her off, I wonder? He really is the great lover-boy: if he's tried it on she's sure to have fallen for it, or the world's got turned upside down. And if he hasn't yet then I've got to work fast to get her. Otherwise I never shall.

Draganče and me, we had one play that never missed, we'd tried it on a hundred times and it worked every one; women are all just barmy, really. It's probably that way I got my nickname.

While we're dancing, I move over towards Draganče. 'Draganče, mate,' I say, 'How are you making out? I'm not getting anywhere at all.'

'Hey, Champ,' he says, 'I don't know about you, but it'd be easier for me to go the whole distance with Šovljanski. She likes me like she likes a dead horse.' They give a bit of a smile. Then we go on at each other some more like that, and they – that's done it –

they thaw out. His one looks at me, mine looks at him: they've still got to act refined, but now they're interested.

I hold back a bit and – now the climate's quite different. After the build-up I fool around a bit in my own way. She keeps on looking at me more and more; she's got eyelashes like curtains. Then she asks: 'What was it your friend called you, are you really a champion?' So there we are! And I'm so modest it hurts. Of course not, nothing like it. I'm not the champion, only the Serbian one that is, not for all of Jugoslavia, but Draganče now, he's a great boxer, not a champion yet but he will be for sure, he's a brilliant boxer and a great guy – and I give out a tremendous line about Draganče. We're old hands at the game: he's doing the same for me with the other one. And as soon as the dance is over, they'll swap notes.

The dance ends. I start off to take her back to her place and modest and polite like I am, I say: 'Excuse me, you're a beautiful dancer, I've hardly ever met a girl I got on so well with and I'd like to ask you to dance again. But I noticed you dancing a lot with that dark boy over there,' – that's for the Apache, – 'if he's your boy friend, or you're already booked, please tell me, I shan't be angry.'

'No, no,' she says, 'there's nothing like that. I only danced with him two or three times. And besides, he gets on me a bit. And he stinks of tobacco.'

The next time we get in first again at the last minute – the Apache isn't used to this holding back, usually the girls can't wait to get at him, and the third time, as soon as the music starts up, they start off towards us by themselves.

And then – the three of us agree to bring them over to sit with us: even Mića's getting on all right with the third one – across comes the Monkey.

'Hi there, Sparrow,' he says.

'Hi Monkey, what gives?'

'You shouldn't lift birds the way you do.'

'I don't know what you're on about, Monkey,' I say, 'when did I lift any birds of yours?'

'Not mine, Sparrow, don't act dumb, the Apache's. He sent me. That's his bird.'

'Tell me, Monkey,' I say, 'is she really his bird or does he just think she is? Has he had it off with her yet?' I'm still that bit doubtful.

'Well maybe he has,' says the Monkey, 'and maybe he hasn't. But he will. He says she's his. And he sends you word to keep off. We've been operating round here for three weeks. He's been hanging around here for three whole weeks. My own doll's got to stay at home because of it. And you ought to know, Sparrow, that it's not healthy to muscle in on the Apache's girls.'

'I know it, Monkey,' I say, 'but now I'll tell you something: we're old partners but it could turn out very unhealthy for you, bringing me messages like that. And since you mention your doll, you're not worried about the other one who's with another old partner of mine, Draganče here?'

'No,' he says, 'I'm not pushing it.'

'I'm glad about that. And tell Stole that I don't want a feud with him and I've never moved into his patch. It's not just that this bird isn't his: she's mine. And tell him too that she's hooked on me. And tell him that I've been after her not for three weeks like him but for three months; it's because of her that I've given the other dolly I had before the push. And last of all, tell him this: it doesn't do for the Apache to ask someone to keep off a girl so that he can step in. The Apache either takes or leaves alone. Tell him not to lower himself. And I've somehow got the impression that this bird isn't worth us carving each other up over. So give my old partner the Apache my greetings.'

'All right, Sparrow, if that's what you say,' says the Monkey, 'but it's still not healthy to lift our birds.'

The Monkey goes off and the music starts. All three of them come towards us, even Mića's. We start to dance and at once move over into the opposite corner: if there's going to be a bundle, we might as well be able to see them coming in time.

Over there – the Monkey's making his report. Stole's gnawing at a matchstick. Then he thinks for a while, thinks, and gets up. He comes towards me. He smiles and I can see he's pale.

He holds up his hand.

'Ljuba,' he shouts across, 'It's all O.K., Ljuba boy.'

I wave back.

'It's all O.K., Stole boy.'

And they go out.

O.K. nothing, Stole boy, I think to myself. You'll remember me – and he did too – you'll wait for me in the moonlight, Stole boy, you'll wait for me in some dark spot when I'm least expecting it. But don't you worry, Stole m'old partner, I'm not so dumb either.

Afterwards the three of us and the girls all left together, on the lookout every step we take, and all three of us take each of the dollies home in turn. And then Mića and Dragančе come right to my home and then they go back into town and only there split up to go their separate ways.

It was at about that time that Stole the Apache was the king of Dušanovac. Just like Stole himself, all the tough guys of his gang when they stripped off were tattooed like woodpeckers all over their bodies, they all carried knuckledusters, they all had special razors in their pockets; they made them themselves. And they all hung on Stole's every word, as if he were God.

And it used to be that one knew who was liable to get beaten up: now everybody got it in turn. Nothing was certain any more. Once in Dušanovac they only went for wide boys and strangers; now no one knew what to be certain about; whether you'd reach home after getting off the trolley-bus in one piece or with broken ribs was more and more a matter of good or bad luck, a lottery, a chance. When they caught some cop on his own, he'd know about it; then they wouldn't sleep at home for a few nights and then everything was back to normal. They used only to go for dolls outside; now they even molested them in Dušanovac itself. And it used to be known that there were some they wouldn't touch; those they'd been at school with, or the younger ones who were at school with their brothers and sisters. Even that could no longer be counted on.

And the law at that time – well, they probably had more important things to see to. They were nowhere to be seen. And when it did happen occasionally that they came into Dušanovac, they came along in threes. And then they'd hang around the market for a bit as if the wide boys were their biggest problem, glance in at the doors of the cafés and the cinemas, and then off out of it. Everything was quiet and everybody was happy; they were probably the happiest of all.

But two or three months before I went into the army, there appeared in Dušanovac a certain cop named Sulja. Somehow I don't remember any of those who came there ever being small, but he was a real mountain of a man. At first he too only came to Dušanovac in a group, and like the others, behaved quietly : if you can't do anything the least you can do is shut up. And then, bit by bit, and as time passed, more and more, things began to be heard : last night Sulja caught someone or other in the moonlight and did him over properly; Sulja met so-and-so this morning; Sulja arranged so-and-so's ribs for him ...

What he was like before I don't know, only that the time came when for Dušanovac Sulja had become a real punitive expedition: no less than the Apache and his gang. You didn't know who to defend yourself against first. Outside Dušanovac Sulja was quiet and orderly. Here, as soon as he came out of the station, he stripped down like an unfrocked priest, rolled up his sleeves and took out his truncheon. And he stopped going around in company : he was always alone. And by the time he got to the bath-house – he'd already worked over two or three on the way.

And like the Apache, he wasn't choosy. When he caught someone from the Apache's mob by himself, he'd chop him before he even had time to open his mouth. That's how he beat up Pretty-Boy Ivica, that's how he did for Mita the Monkey, and the Knacker went that way too. And then he'd come on a whole group with the Apache – and not one of them would lift a finger! He'd walk through them, they'd look at each other, but no one would so much as mention the feud. Except that he'd drawl out to one of those he'd already caught on their own something like: 'Well what happened to you, Mita, fall off a trolley-bus?'

But that was how Sulja smashed up a lot of the boys, and a lot of other quite harmless people too, even Pera Manojlović, a cripple with no legs up to the thigh who never had anything at all to do with the Apache. Pera shouted at him: 'Watch out, I'm a cripple, can't you see!' But Sulja just said: 'You got that with the Četniks, didn't you?' 'Of course not, with the Četniks? I was at the front!' 'Oh yes you did, with the Četniks, if I say so!' And he bashed him even harder. And when there was no one in the street who took his fancy, he'd simply go into a café and as soon as he saw two people sitting together, without saying anything or asking questions he'd start on them. 'What yer up to, on about the People's Government are yer?' he'd say. And the other people didn't want to know about it, they just went on drinking their beer.

At first one or two of them tried to complain about him to the police. I don't know whether they did anything to him there or not, but afterwards Sulja would come looking for the poor sod and fix him even worse. So everybody buttoned up. The cafés in Dušanovac got emptier and emptier.

Stole – well, he was near to blowing his top, he was so mad. 'You must have all had nancies for mothers,' he'd shout at his lieutenants, 'to let that great crap heap get at you! You useless lot of yobs!' And he'd threaten: 'I'll fix the bastard.'

And from then on Sulja was on the lookout for him. If he'd met him somewhere at night alone, he'd have settled his hash for him. But in the daytime the whole gang was always there . . .

So they sent messages back and forth and looked out for each other, or when they met in the street, they had a good look at each other – and then just went straight on by.

And then one evening that summer, my first in the army, Sulja appeared for the first time ever in Dušanovac without his uniform.

The whole gang were standing outside the cinema, they'd just got back from the Sava: Stole, the Monkey, Ivica, the Knacker, Nature-boy Milanče, the whole lot, ten of them or more.

Sulja walked right through the middle of them. He looked each one of them straight in the mug and grinned. All around him – silence.

When he'd got a little way past them, Stole took a last pull of smoke and stamped out his dog-end.

'Hey, Sulja?'

'Yeah?' says he.

'So they've slung you out of the police, have they Sulja? They're choked off with you too, then?'

'That's right,' says Sulja, turning his head round and grinning.

'So I've been waiting for you for a long time, Sulja. If that's how it is, maybe we could sort things out a bit.'

'Fine, Apache, I've been waiting for you too. Can't seem to meet up with you anyhow. But this'll do jes' fine.'

'O.K. Sulja,' says Stole. 'If you're sure you haven't got some nice little rod tucked away somewhere? Nice and clean, eh?'

'Well, waddya know, Apache, you wanna keep it clean? But if you say so. Where'd it be?' and he throws his coat wide open.

'Well, if it's clean, it's clean,' says Stole, 'I'll leave my hatchet alone too.' And he hitched up his pants and unbuckled his belt.

And that's how it started. I doubt if anyone's ever seen a better fight around here before or since.

They say that up to then no one in Dušanovac ever took such a bashing as Sulja that day. But – he was as strong as a horse. Stole would draw him on and then hit him with a series of three or four blows which a horse wouldn't have stood up under. But Sulja would just wobble a bit like a ripe pear, look cross-eyed – and stay on his feet. Then in the scuffle he would stretch out his arm and the Apache bounced off three or four yards into the dust. Sulja rushed up in a hurry to finish him off. But he really was too ponderous and clumsy for Stole: he'd be waiting for him on his feet. And they'd start to mix it again: the Apache hit him nearly every time. Sulja went on swinging and missing. But at last he'd get one home on Stole again and Stole'd nosedive into the dust once more. And then it'd start over again . . .

Like that they progressed slowly from the cinema to the market place.

But still, strength is strength. When they got to the market place you'd hardly have recognized Stole: his back was all torn from the cobblestones. And though they were both groggy, the cop, who'd stayed on his feet longer, was getting more and more the better of it. At last, in the market place itself, he managed to lay another one on Stole. Stole went up in the air and came down somehow so awkwardly that he fell right under a stall. And while in the half-dead state that he was, he was trying to drag himself out some way or other, Sulja's suddenly standing there right over him !

Sulja hit him once as if he wanted to knock his head off : Stole flapped his arms like a yo-yo and took off again. Sulja got to him as he was getting up and again used the same surgical procedure on his head : again Stole made a hole in the dust for free. Then he went up to him, like a navvy going to finish some hefty job, more slowly now, but more certain, to really finish him off. He didn't wait for him to get up this time. He bent down to drag him up: Stole was already crouching. He caught hold of him by the hair, pulled him forward, and half-dazed as he was, lined him up for the kill. And that was the second mistake he made that day.

How the Apache, half-dead like that, when the grey matter just isn't in a state to work at all any more, at that very moment managed to remember what was really a cheap trick, I don't know, but like a flash he grabbed the fist at his head with both hands, just dropped his knees to a squatting position – and the ligaments cracked like glass. Sulja just managed to let out one yell.

Now Stole's job was an easy one. He got his breath back, kicked him in the balls with his foot, hit him with his fist in the belly beneath the belt, and then again in the eyes, the throat and the back of the neck. He just kept on till Sulja toppled over. And then, for good measure – he kicked him a few more times in the kidneys.

Then somehow or other he staggered off somewhere, and left Sulja lying in the middle of the Dušanovac market place like a heap of rotting tomatoes. Eventually they had to get the blood-wagon to cart him off.

Translated by Bernard Johnson

Veno Taufer

HOSTAGES

day after day the warders search
Christopher Columbuses
walking past us distrustfully
but we have hidden Eldoradoes
in our grins
day after day the warders search

day after day we walk
night after night we walk
along a thousand and a thousand thousand
walls
in each a different country
in each a different river
by each a different sea
under the bunk a stream and a meadow
and windy herds of deer
on a thousand ceilings the birth
and funerals of clouds the silken love-making
of the planets

an amorous woman
comes to the bars at midnight
a left breast of sand through the right bar
a right breast of wind through the left bar
and through the lower bar a belly of white fire
we invent a multiplicity of grins
sink long caravans of words
our hips are squeezed
by summer's sweaty thighs

the morning counts our bites
on the iron bars
then we march off
to the stakes on which
with quiet fingers
the sun paints numbers

but we have hidden
a thousand and a thousand thousand
Eldoradoes
in our grins
pierced eyes look inwards
and fill
with earth

A PERIOD OF RAIN

sailing sailing through the pouring rain
high blue bows are heaving before us

sinking sinking in the frothing ooze
gunwhales black getting heavier heavier

we stand on deck and listen to the rain
with wax in our ears sinking calmly to a rainbow shipwreck

sailors the captain is dead in his glass cabin
playing grinning fish for a handful of pearly droplets

the captain is dead sailors our sails have no wind
with hollow ears we listen on deck to the rain
the captain is dead playing cards and he sings sings

VOYAGES

everyone circles his own circle
grows flowers in it wards off wolfish mists
in the dead centre feeds a snail with his own spit
fears the snail's horns and obeys

into his quiet head he hauls stones quietly
he will need them for quiet loving or a quiet kill
only the circular thought of circles in circles disturbs the rest
as from his hair he brushes the stardust nightly

at night the circle is a soft ball
with itself playing ball
till the circle dwindles

the ball is his head when he wakes
he trails again after flowers stones snail
and in ever widening circles circles his circles

ARTIST AND MODEL

he paints her
lips which darkly
parted call
and paints his tongue

he paints her
breasts which rise
to battlemented towers
and paints his fingers

he paints her
belly which scorches
him with its horizon
and paints his forehead

the painter paints
her closed eyes which
torture him so
wide and moist

that before he sleeps
he dreams of snakes
her copper hips
not finding

on the canvas
his kisses grow
into rubber balls
where he sought

seashells between the ebb
and the flow of her
skin still white far
beyond the horizon

from where tiptoeing
over the waves
on tall legs o god
those tall legs

rustling the leaves a
lady in still veils
steps from the canvas and
cringes clinging to his feet

away death you
bitch crawling
after me from the
wall where i first

mixed myself the fine red
pigment of your pelt
don't lick the painted blood
the model sleeps do you hear

but maybe you hear
the rustle of other
steps let's go
further along the shore

OPEN-AIR CONCERT

she with tin legs
hourglass in mouth aquarium in her head
he with all the towns staircases on his back
under his arm a heart that can be wound up or stopped

they open a book and look for a road
to water sky and blossoming grove
where there's no sweating paper no fumbling eyes
where like in a B picture pretty birds twitter

she opens her legs unlocks the aquarium
starts hunting for fish
he climbs the stairs and winds his heart up

nude bodies drown in sand from the hourglass
fish flick through their veins
with dark designs concealed in their bloody gills

AT THE END OF THE JOURNEY

you step into apeland
you step up to a green apish eye
you remove necklaces of thought strip off the rags of travel plans

come closer to the green apish eye
come and join the ape princes
all apes are princes you too will be a prince

bow down to the green apish eye
come on to the branches of sawdust bananas
you too will be a banana all apes are bananas

smile to the green apish eye
you will have a tail of long curly love
all princes have the tail you will swing by love

come come or stay or else make a bow
give a wave a wink a laugh or else cry
you are always a prince swinging among princes

or you can die as well and not be a dead banana
nor a skeleton of love nor a dead tail
the green apish eye won't gaze on you you won't be a prince among
    princes

you are a grain of sand or a drop of water you are watched
by your own eye alone or heard by a grain or a drop
only when you touch it on your common way to the great sea
to the pupil of darkness to the eye of the stars

Translated by Veno Taufer and Michael Scammell

Jovan Hristić

MNESARCHOS

The gods have decreed that Mnesarchos the sculptor shall have
   talent richly bestowed upon him:

They visit him in his dreams and show
The sculptures which he will mould. Sculptures
Of which even the boldest sculptor would not dare to dream.

But Mnesarchos was a favourite of the gods
And they desired to help him.

And in the daytime Mnesarchos took his chisel and set to work:
The stone cracked, the chisels broke, but he was
A favourite of the gods and what could thus resist him?
People stopped and stared in wonder: each sculpture more beauti-
   ful than the next.

For Mnesarchos was a favourite of the gods
And they had richly bestowed talent upon him.

The faces of his sculptures blazed with the wanton glory of power,
In their triumphant orgy they were equal to the gods, but
Those who stopped and stared did not look round or return:
For no one had breathed into that victory the soul of defeat.

But Mnesarchos for certain was a favourite of the gods.

CANDLES

He wrote : 'the days of our future stand before us
Like a row of tiny lighted candles.' Is this only to be
Our lot to be accepted, or were they kindled
By gods whose favours we had won unthinking?

Reading his lines I can make out that pathway of beauty
With its glimmering ending – is it a flame that awaits us there
Or perhaps the light of a distant, burnt-out star
which still travels towards our desiring eyes?

For while I admire that shining carpet of welcome
I ask myself : is this a gift given to us by the gods,
Or a treacherous song enticing us into darkness?

In the dark all lights are shining, and as is known
The gods may not give anything for nothing,
and who knows, who knows?

ISLANDS

Again the season comes for me to turn the pages of his book :
And sudden rains sweep away feelings of winter
Like sand which winds have carried to the rooftops,
When walking through grass trousers become heavy with water.

Can this be some old fever left by February
forgotten in my bones? Or is it the flapping of sails
from some long-over dream? Come then. Drops from the leaves
And lovers laughing in abandoned bowers.

Footsteps pass. The sea breaks against cliffs.

In the small hours and wiser after rain
Sea gropes towards stone. Waves roll up
On to the seashore. Women turn in bed.
The wind is off the islands. Rain falls out at sea.

Darkness. In the harbour hausers chafe the deck.
Do these islands still come to you in your dreams?
The window is open, summer enters the room
Traversing the flimsy curtain of memories, memories.

ALEXANDRIA

DION CHRYSOSTOMOS

He came to build a homeland for the world and for his name :
Since all the cities were already glorifying their kings
For him only the sea was left, and the lands across the sea –
Yet he must be a king and greater than all others.

The gods gave him many lands and many victories,
But he was too young to know the balance must remain;
And so they led him to a fickle shore, to where the winds
Tossed his name back and forth from sea to desert.

They gave a city where all brought different gods,
A homeland for foreigners, an insecure eternity for exiles,
Where only now and then the evening wind whispers in Greek
Amongst the houses already peopled now by other odours.

TO PHAEDRUS

And this too you should know, dear Phaedrus. We have lived
In desperate times, making of tragedy
Comedy, of comedy tragedy.

But that reality, seriousness, measure
Uplifting wisdom, eludes us always. We have been
In some uncertain land, neither ourselves
Nor someone else; always a step or two away
From what we are, what we should be.

Oh dear Phaedrus, when you walk
With heroes upon the Island of the blessed
Mention our names at times amongst your talk.

Let their sound spread along the vibrant air
Upwards, towards the sky they never reach
To find at least within your speech their rest.

Translated by Jovan Hristić and Bernard Johnson

Vasko Popa

THE WANDERER

Earth has been rising in him
To his waist to his throat
Ever since he saw the light

He drags himself along on his stomach
Grabs the sunbeams

He hangs himself on each sunbeam
And each breaks
He drags himself on

What is he trying to weave
Out of the sunbeam

A golden ladder
Or a sacred noose
Or just a swing

What is he hurrying to weave
Before night overtakes him

THE PROMISED LAND

Through the wolf's ribs my son
I see our promised land
It has the form of the Easter lamb

The wolf's heart shines upon it
Amid the crimson sea

Perhaps it was swallowed long ago
And is now neither dead nor alive
Or it is just ready
For a second birth

It depends on the wolf's hunger
And on our guiding star
On nothing else my son

THE LITTLE BOX

The little box grows its first teeth
And its little length grows
Its little width its little emptiness
And everything it has

The little box grows and grows
And now inside it is the cupboard
That it was in before

And it grows and grows and grows
And now inside it is the room
And the house and town and land
And the world it was in before

The little box remembers its childhood
And by most great yearning
Becomes a little box again

Now inside the little box
Is the whole world tiny small
You can easily put it in your pocket
Easily steal it easily lose it

Take care of the little box

TOWER OF SKULLS

For the gold eyed sunflower you gave us
Blind stone your unface
And what now monster

You made us one with yourself
With emptiness in your empty poison tooth
With your dock tailed eternity
Is that all your secret

Why now flee into our eye sockets
Why hiss with darkness and sting with horror
Is that really all you can do

That's not our teeth chattering it's the wind
Idle at the sun's fair
We grin at you grin up to heaven
What can you do to us

Our skulls are flowering with laughter
Look at us look your fill at yourself
We mock you monster

IN A SIGH

Along the highways from the depths of the soul
Along the blue black highways
The weed journeys
The roads disappear
Beneath its steps

Swarms of spikes violate
The pregnant seeds
The furrows have vanished
From the field

Invisible lips
Have wiped the field out

Space rejoices
Contemplating
Its smooth hands
Smooth and grey

ON THE COATSTAND

The cravats have gnawed through
The necks of suspended emptiness

The gloves
No longer have kittens
In silken pockets

Underground streams
No longer ripple
In the warm absence

Fingers of darkness peep out
From the widowed sleeves

Little fish
No longer leap out
From the deep buttons

Green fear arises
In the tame pleats

ON THE HAND

On the quick sand
Dumb crossroads
In hesitation

At each crossroad
An inquisitive glance
Turned into a pillar of stone

Rosy desert

But all that comes to it
Bursts into bud with sense
Bursts into flower with hope

A unique spring
Or a blessed mirage

Translated by Anne Pennington

Vlado Gotovac

DEAD JOURNEY

First the alcohol evaporated out of us
And we returned to the world we had just left
Our feast ended the bottles were empty
And we began once more to go about our work
There was too little alcohol for all around to be stunned
And rebukes were shouted at us from all sides
It was even said that we might be wastrels
For who could apply the word feast to such an orgy
For whose sake we forgot even our nearest and dearest

After that we began to lose all moisture
And the fever gnawed at our normal strength
We stayed away from our work and took to resting
But everyone sympathized looking at our skin
The cracks they saw in it were not bleeding
And we resembled the earth after a long drought
We withered from the head down like flowers
And you could already hear rustling as when they are stirred by
    the wind
The furniture in our rooms began to crackle
And all who visited us coughed from the dryness of the air

In the end we had dried everything up around us
And the wind was whirling more and more things along with us
The noise was getting louder we were carried along in disorder
And our dust was spreading out in all directions
Many places looked already deserted
Suddenly individual objects began falling corroded
And then even entire tree trunks from an entire house
And as the dust rolled ever outwards

No one knew whether we were already dead
And whether that would help in ending the drought

But we had already been long dead
   For there was no other world

OUR NEW SUN

The sun that we persisted in making
Now consumes us
We were clever enough to destroy tried and tested worlds
But no one insured us against the infinity of the account
Maintained by the universe
The stars will never get drunk on this human liquor
The universe about us is sober
We though have created a barren sun
A puny sun with a desert stretched underneath
We created a sun and the earth empties
But the universe is untouched
There is nowhere for joy to spring from
O how pathetic is the drunken human heart
So left to die

ORPHEUS ALONE

For Juri

More and more do I seem to hear the clouds
More and more are my ears my servant
Voices of many things come to me
No more can I retire into silence

I can already express the mosquito's sobbing
Or the pain of the stuck fly shuddering
Man fades more and more from my ear
And his words change to the noise
That is proceeding steadily from all things
A huge violin without strings perhaps
Reverberates softly across the azure sky
And the stars shudder with passion
And grow still and fade and die
Until fresh strains are heard from the cold depths
Like some drum summoning to creation
The clouds answer everything easily
And only the children sing with them
More and more it seems to me that words are fading
Less and less of that poetry is in them
More and more are my ears my servant
                    I could descend among the dead

FOREVER LOST

The same star above me and in me
And the night growing with thoughts of the dead
And their sky is visible and peaceful
Clouds float freely through sleep
Across our boundaries like heartbeats
Poems tales and other lessons of many years
For each a special star has been selected
And shines now
Or falls
And its ancient lesson
Is a tangled paradox
On earth as in heaven
Forever lost.

AFTER ALL MY ILLUSIONS

So I sit here helpless now
Among the snapped threads of my secret worlds
Each one breaking more at each touch
The paths of the once-upon-a-time kingdom are overgrown
Each one led to a new world
I sit here almost invisible
In the earth's quiet embrace
I am on the path it traverses
With its own and the sky's things
I can still see only what never changes
But that is all I need
The combined radiance of earth and sky
        After all my illusions.

                        Translated by Michael Scammell

Miodrag Bulatović

A FABLE

He was a specimen of the coleoptera ! The size of one's finger nail !

Those who watched him didn't pay any special attention to him, even though he was no ordinary beetle.

This didn't anger him, for he knew their attitude meant nothing, being of little significance.

People usually passed him by.

He looked up at them through eyes that saw insignificance, ephemerality, illusion in everything and he was unafraid of being crushed underfoot. For he knew this must happen one day and whether that day be now or tomorrow was a matter of complete indifference.

From his very first moment of self-consciousness he had been aware of this truth, this end, this way out of everything. He lived pretty well as all other coleoptera with fiery mauve hairs on their legs and under their wings, preparing himself against that final moment of pain and agony. It was the pain he feared and not the end. For he was of a weak and cowardly temperament that every contact with people hurt.

He hated no one. Indeed he considered hatred an evil. Yet he couldn't get on with others, be they of his own kind or of the human race on whom he relied, in fact, for crumbs. All contact, no matter with whom, disgusted him, made him want to vomit, evoking a feeling of strangling revulsion. Then, usually, he would curl up in a ball of resistance, rolling on to his back and remaining so until whoever was touching him had departed.

He sometimes felt, living in that dark pit where people mingled with lizards and lizards with spiders, that he would die without ever having glimpsed the light of day.

He thrust his neck out of his armour and cocked his head up towards the small, barred window.

He made little distinction between lizards and men, often concluding that the former were far less harmful than the latter, thereby demanding greater regard and value. For the former had always treated him with the greater consideration.

Yet, in spite of this, he continued to afford the greater respect to humans for, no matter how they behaved, he couldn't do without them. Without their crumbs and refuse which he hungrily awaited in the gloom of his corner, he couldn't even exist.

It was a question of attitude and esteem. People never noticed him and passed him by without paying a thought to the fact that they might crush him. Perhaps this was why he didn't respect them. He had no reason to be grateful to them and, as for death, he was prepared for that at any moment. On the other hand, lizards, why who can tell, always favoured him with a long and thoughtful glance. Even had he known they were merely debating whether to eat him or not, he wouldn't have been angry. For then he'd have known that he represented a tasty morsel for someone, that he was important, that something, no matter what or for what reason, needed to pay him attention.

Of the moment of death he thought but rarely. He knew it must be a simple matter, like the death of any other living creature; his soul – whatever the soul was – would quit the body, depart, dissolve or else be changed into dust and light that would then sting and burn others from below and above, while his body would turn into water or some other element and torment other living and half-living beings with its stench, with bones and memories of a loathsome disharmony with self and with others.

There were even times when it seemed a moment of release, of escape into eternal peace; a particle of the truth he'd always loved and served faithfully; a particle of the light, fatal in its intensity, brilliance and insubstantiality, the light he'd so often dreamed of in the darkness, imagining it as a great cloak dripping fire, as a suit of red-hot armour shaped like the sun, like the stars, its light effervescing like foam, pouring from its metallic outlines into people's eyes so they saw more clearly and penetratingly than did other creatures the life around them, for human eyes were larger and able to absorb more light. Smaller eyes absorbed less and so radiated less around them.

Such thoughts usually came to him on days of hunger and conflict with other beings that had vegetated in this dark lair as long as he had himself. He had no fear of death and so, often, on days of hunger and weariness, he saw it as a revenge and as a prolongation of his own existence and duration.

This coleopterus! This many-limbed devil with his multiplicity of feelers!

Those who saw him paid him no special attention, even though he was no ordinary beetle.

Yet he wasn't angry because he knew that this was only their normal egoism. He knew, knew well, that he'd always be unhappy till the moment when he ceased to regard himself and grasped that life was a naked vanity, when he admitted to himself and others that the desire for distinction and immortality brought with it only a hateful torment, a grey suffering, with a soft, algally, slimy death at the end.

He longed to remove his presence and all his desires from both himself and all the things and beings he knew.

I must live purely, without desires or thoughts. I must lose myself in what is greater than I and all things I've ever seen.

He knew too the need not to think of himself, but rather to forget his own existence and that of all things around him. And so he paid no attention to the people who watched him nor regarded them as being of the slightest importance. All he was certain of was that they were capable of trampling, of crushing and grinding him into pieces and so delivering him to a higher wisdom, a wisdom entirely his own. And this was all they *could* do. He looked on them as one does dead and useless objects. He felt no regret at the lack of speech which prevented him telling them how harmless and superfluous they were.

He rejoiced in being so small, so disregarded, so unimportant that he hindered no one's living or breathing.

All he wanted was a serene life and an easy death.

To realize such a desire demanded much of him, among other things, that he paid as little attention to himself as he did to others. So he remained silent for some time, meditating both on himself and others.

The people were still bickering over the lizard, a quite ordinary, many-tailed lizard. They went up to it, quarrelling as they did so.

Their tormented and naked bodies drew nearer, grew more visible and uglier. He caught their smell, the strange stink of their hairy, bristling bodies. His stomach turned over.

Between him and them, beside a heap of broken bricks, a small man gazed sadly between half-closed eyes, his ribs and knees protruding from his long hair and beard. He looked at the approaching people tearfully. And it seemed that this man too desired to avoid contact with them and for this very reason wept.

The man's teeth were chattering. His face was tiny, handsome and wrinkled, his arms thin, dirty and too long for his body.

The beetle believed that this good, frightened man, from whom, a few minutes ago, they'd taken the lizard that belonged to him, saw everything, watched it, yet paid it scant attention.

But he recalled that to seek love of one's fellow is as mad and senseless as to nurture love for strange, alien, non-existent things. I have resolved to spend my short existence entirely alone and without envy and not to allow such thoughts to possess me, he thought, and caught himself in yet another transgression; he loved these people who were fighting and squabbling over the lizard, pulling at each other's ears, hair and skin.

Is this love I feel a senseless, insane and ill-considered thing? he asked himself. And there arose in front of his eyes the image of the other beetle he'd left behind the bricks, feeling that any commingling with other creatures was unhealthy, morbid, unnecessary and dangerous.

He watched the people attacking and beating the unhappy little man.

This sad, wrinkled little fellow uttered obscure sounds and noises, embracing their bare knees and kissing their thin hands.

He saw the tears that flowed abundantly down his cheeks. And he pitied him until he was struck by the thought: No! I shall never lose myself in what is greater than I or they, if I go on thinking of others and if I allow love, hatred and pity to work inside me. It will mean good-bye to an easy death and a serene spirit. To mix with others is to enter hell, a universal hell.

He felt sad.

He watched the people tormenting the small man, whose knees and elbows stuck out from the hair of his body.

He even felt disgust.

He longed for a little light. The window through which there came a faint gleam of light was so far away that, small as he was, he couldn't imagine himself able to stand in it.

Nor could such a light find space inside him, he thought.

Still, this thought didn't perturb him greatly. He wanted to climb up there, no matter how impractical, how impossible it might be. He was unconcerned at the vast space which he knew lay beyond the bars. For that space was so great, so vast and limitless, that he didn't dare envisage himself as one tiny particle of it all. He was afraid the light would poison him, that he would be spellbound, lost in it.

He decided to curl himself away still tighter in his shell.

The little man lay on his back by a heap of bricks, the blood flowing between his teeth.

I'll think of nothing, not even of these people, the beetle thought, for I shall only disturb my everlasting peace that I've won with such effort.

He set off, his legs moving beneath his armoured shell. He crawled over people who lay weary and exhausted beside the hairy one. He hated doing this, but his way towards the window lay in that direction.

He crawled on like an old man, his armoured body wobbling from side to side.

The wall was only a step or so away.

He looked round for the lizard they'd been squabbling over, but it was nowhere to be seen.

Then he noticed the small, hairy man was gazing at him and he hurried on.

But he was already half-way up the wall, too high to be reached, or knocked down.

The man crawled towards him.

From below, his wrinkled face looked up. There was much hurt and longing in those large, dark eyes and this startled the beetle even more.

He knew what the hairy little man was up to. He wanted him, to tame him, to make a pet of him. Coleopterus was horrified at the very idea.

None knew how deep his contempt was for personal happiness or how he cherished the idea of purity and serenity of spirit.

All he wanted was to climb upwards to the light, no matter how hungry he was.

Two arms stretched up towards him from the mass of hair. When he was half-way up the wall, he stopped and looked down. People were scrambling over the floor and whispering to one another.

Never had they seemed so small to him, so useless and miserable. He was glad not to be amongst them any more. Never – he thought – will I go back there to them, even if it means the abyss of death. Down there is disease-ridden and the sun's rays scarcely ever reach it and I want to drown in a sea of light.

He watched the student, the baker and the stranger rushing after the lizard.

The lizard dodged round a pile of bricks and filth and round the hairy little man, hiding from them.

Then they caught it and mounted it, the great lizard, and it tried to move but fell down.

Clinging, pressed to the wall, the beetle wondered how long all this would go on and whether there was any term to human misery.

The answer came immediately, as he moved slowly towards the window. These people were unhappy because they were cursed with the desire for pleasure. And they would go on being unhappy as long as they wanted to ride on the lizard. But I have no such desire and I'll die a happy hermit. All I want is Nirvana, eternal peace and serenity.

At last he gained the window.

Seen from above, the people looked quite different. They were scarcely visible. They were trying to make the exhausted lizard move, but to no avail.

The hairy man, the lizard's erstwhile owner, watched them sadly and amazedly from his corner.

Coleopterus felt no pity for him nor did he make any attempt to understand him.

He stopped thinking about them and turned his back.

The dense light blinded him. He didn't know which way to look; upwards, to the sky, empty and limitless, or around him. He saw the flames sliding along the roof-tops and vanishing into the smoke and haze. He saw the charred, top-heavy spire of the church from whose belfry poured the sound of bells and the blackened minaret of the mosque with the muezzin doubled up over the parapet. The muezzin sang in a tone of desperation and coleopterus could not tell whether he was only fooling or whether he was calling for help, summoning the faithful to prayer for the last time.

He saw people rushing headlong, panic-stricken for the edge of the town and the forest. And they appeared strange and almost unreal, for never had he seen man other than in the dark prison. Seen from above, like this, his first sight of the mass of people shocked and terrified him. He had imagined it all so differently, living down there, as he did, in the pitch darkness, among the insects.

He was afraid rather than disappointed.

But he quickly drew back, remembering that it was wrong to demand anything of others or to meddle in what did not concern him and that one should always be satisfied.

He was at a loss as to which light he should concentrate on most; that which poured down from above or that which seethed below in the form of infernal flame. He settled the matter at once by looking at both.

He was surprised to find how little what he saw excited him. It all seemed quite commonplace.

He was seized with a sense of vacuity, of vanity and ephemerality.

Why did I bother to climb up here when it's all so ordinary? – he wondered, scenting the bitter tang of smoke, soot and scorched earth in his nostrils.

I'm glad, very glad, I've climbed up here, he thought, glad I didn't stay for ever down there with those people. Yet, he concluded, I really will become unhappy if I go on grumbling and complaining. Those people down there were unhappy just because they would chase that poor lizard and try to ride on its back. I must stop wanting and hoping for things or I'll disturb my peace of mind and body.

The light was so abundant that coleopterus could not contain it all.

And coleopterus was so hard and black and shut up in himself that he was unable to change himself in any way.

And so they stood, confronting each other, like two stars; coleopterus, a small, black smudge with violet-blue legs under an armoured shell and it, the light, like a massive, fiery, yet useless shield.

The light permitted no one to enter into its depths.

It was endless. It lit up the whole window.

It rocked, borne like smoke on the wind. It smelt of the young, silky fronds of maize, the downy seed of the dandelion and the moss that grows on the bark of plum trees.

The beetle rested on the window-sill and wondered what he should do, once his desire to see the light was satisfied. But he had no idea which road he should take.

He thought he was standing firmly, but such was not the case. The wind and light rocked him to his very soul and he maintained his footing on the window-sill only with difficulty and effort. He listened to the babble, the human babble, doubtless, that was going on down there on the ground and he wanted to see these terrified people who shouted and fled from the fire. He didn't dare lean over, not for anything. He knew that if he fell he would never be able to regain his present position. He knew that nobody could be in the same place twice. Also he felt a great affection for this place. He wouldn't have exchanged it, even for a better. It was his one and only true and rightful place.

In front of him welled the terrible light and the fire, while, behind him, the darkness pressed about the walls. He didn't want just the one. He desired a spot that had both darkness and light, every kind of light there was, be it that which dripped from above or that which welled up from below or even that borne upon the wind, every sort of darkness, known and unknown. In a word, he wanted to see everything that existed and to live in the new-found light that was all around him.

He didn't even want to lift his eyes, for he felt that what he was seeing now he would never see again.

He was afraid that, were he to look any higher, he would absorb too much light.

He sat motionless, squinting.

He grew afraid in case the babble of voices from below might engage him too much and he drew back.

Still, he stretched his neck through the window bars.

He saw people fighting, killing and tearing at one another. Some had red stars in their caps, others did not. Others wore yet another kind of badge, a rounded insignia. Most were capless, barefoot and in rags.

He wondered why they didn't run away from the fire that was licking at their heels, roaring above their heads and scorching the soles of their feet.

As he gazed down, the people fought, drawing knives, brandishing pitchforks and prongs and grabbing stakes.

But as he felt himself losing equilibrium, coleopterus ceased looking directly at them and, in a second, the entire pandemonium, edged, as it were, with blood and fire, vanished from its place in his eye-sockets.

Tottering to the depths of his being, the beetle looked round, but slowly and with little attention. The two lights flowed one into the other, forming a single glow, a single sea of whiteness into which he could fall.

Unable to get a firm footing, he watched how the light nearest him mingled strangely with the darkness behind and how the window bars, the people and everything he could see from where he stood, were transformed, not as he had imagined it when he was down below, nor as it had been when he had first reached the window, nor as he had thought he might one day see it, but somehow strangely inverted, chaotic, ugly and dangerous. The entire chaos terrified him and he strove to regain his footing.

He couldn't.

He could neither encompass the light with its angry gaze, nor the darkness. He felt nothing, remembered nothing.

His one desire, his one aim was to retain his hold in the same, familiar place. This and nothing else filled his mind for the time being.

But he was already falling.

He fell slowly at first and at an angle and then headlong, his legs spread out in all directions.

To the dual light, the dense light against the walls, the striated darkness, the mingling of the two uncomprehending miracles – the light within and the light without – he paid not a thought. He had no time for thinking.

In reality, he fell in the normal way, through a milky, white mass that he knew neither how to name nor determine. His legs hung down, stiff and tensed.

Perhaps, with some slight physical effort, he might have saved himself. But he felt no wish to do so. Maybe, by some movement of his legs, he might have found a footing, but once more he lacked the will.

In other words, this fall was what he needed, what he had so long desired, reckoning that only then, only by a long fall, would he learn of eternal peace and serenity.

He heard nothing, a fact that caused him joy, as being the first sign of rest.

The hunger he had felt up there on the window-sill had vanished; a further sign.

And again he had no desire to return where he had been; yet a third sign of oblivion.

He fell as if for the first and last time.

Soon he became aware that he was not falling as he should, as he wished to fall.

He was falling sideways, his head twisted over to the left. He saw the wall of the building where he'd spent his entire life lying on its side, the sky and the fire lop-sided.

Everything was topsy-turvy, stood on its head; the roofs that smouldered and burned, the minaret of the mosque from which came the faint sound of the muezzin's song and the church spire that was dissolving in the peal of its bells.

The more his fall angled to the left, the more lop-sided everything grew, until he felt as though it would remain so for ever. Even prayer would be upside-down.

He didn't want this. He didn't want everything to remain one-sided. He wanted to be honest, if only for the last time, to plunge straight, headfirst, on to the earth.

He moved his body, trying to regain his correct position.

He couldn't.

He tried again, but to no avail.

The third attempt brought tears to his eyes with the effort.

He twisted himself slowly, just as he fell.

He was no longer falling head downward, but in exactly the reverse position.

Now everything was lying on the right; the chanting muezzin was on his right and the bells too. The light which, a moment ago, he had so venerated from the window-sill, appeared now to be almost without substance. All that reminded him of its existence was its warmth.

This light was treating him unjustly. It was this, he thought, that was preventing him from falling headfirst.

Quietly he cursed it, hating himself for doing so. If I must fall, then I want to fall straight on to my head. If I have to die, then I want to die from the head down. Will I get into the right position.

He was certain one ought to fall on one's head and no other way. In fact I'm not falling at all. I'm just drifting sideways and I'll never get as far as the earth.

Before him he saw the emaciated faces of the people with whom he'd lived so long in friendship and enmity. And their faces too were leaning over to the right. And they were weeping because they couldn't get the exhausted lizard to move. And then it seemed as if they too, these people above, were vanishing into the terrible, white liquid of the light.

But their faces remained as ever, solid, rock-hewn and unforgettable. They were looking at him with contempt.

Had coleopterus dared think of himself and his immortality, he would have been angry with them.

But instead he smiled at them as he fell. And, still falling, he loved them and drew close to them.

At last he wished he couldn't see them. Their faces intruded. He thought, over towards the right; perhaps they're not persecuting me. Have I ever done them any harm? Indeed, am I very evil, when all is considered?

If I am evil – he replied to his own question – then, what of it! I'll go on in the same way. One must sin, for in sin lies meaning and redemption.

The faces were no more. He supposed they had turned into light – so is it with all living and non-living things and beings.

At last he attained his correct position. His head was pointing downwards and the light was upright and flowed straight and true along his wings and legs.

He fell rapidly and he saw ever less of the church spire and the pointed summit of the mosque around which licked the tongues of flame.

The directness of his fall gave him physical pleasure, nor did he realize how fast he was falling.

Already he could discern even the smallest objects on the ground; bits of bone, broken weapons and insignia on empty caps, tattered banners and dead bodies.

He saw, too, many laughing and hiding themselves behind the fire. Their appearance surprised him. He saw that he was falling very rapidly and that he would be smashed against the earth. What of my life? he wondered. Nothing so very terrible – he thought, I'll be saved by the very fact of being crushed. The one and only way I can save my life, such as it is, is to lose it. Ah, how good it is to fall on one's head!

Everything was upside-down. The multitude of magnified objects filled his vision.

He could think of nothing save his close and happy end. He'd imagined his last moments differently.

He plunged with increasing velocity, his fall ever more fatal. The milky light paled and turned to ashes, to the many insignia on the caps of the blood-stained people, to the mouths of the rifle barrels and the burning eye-sockets of the skulls.

It seemed as though he'd left the light far above him.

Everything was ashes. Ashes everywhere. And the fire that consumed the earth. Ashes poured even from small objects.

He could scarcely credit the speed with which the ash choked the eye-sockets of the dead man by the fire. It was like leaves in a forest, like light over roofs.

Soon he was dazzled by its greyness.

The sharp outlines of the flames, the space of the earth beneath the fire, the silhouette of the people long at rest beside their weapons, all of it had lost its original distinct contours.

He thought he was going blind.

Such a happy, merry ending he wished the poor, tormented lizard, unable to move with the man on its back.

He felt himself being broken.

He saw nothing, not even the abandoned human weapons on the ash-strewn battle-field. It was the fourth and final proof of peace.

And the fire raged...

Translated by E. D. Goy

Lojze Kovačič

MESSAGES FROM DREAMS: GOD

Together with others I step through the velvet curtain of the cinema into a big room with an immensely high ceiling and crammed tight with furniture of all shapes and sizes. Here and there, in among the pieces of furniture (stands, couches, glassware, china, tables), are standing the buyers – dark married couples and salesmen in black coats, talking soundlessly with hands gesticulating: a nodding of heads, a turning up of corners of mattresses, a glittering of crystal and an opening of drawers in sideboards. Remember that this hall is the exact replica of the antique furniture shop that used to be in Lower Šiška before the war, which now holds the Sava cinema, but whose balcony, which extends up to the dark blue moulded ceiling, is now occupied by an agglomeration of narrow and wide wardrobes of varying heights, old and brown, with black doors, and tables and chairs (stools, armchairs, Venetian chairs, rocking chairs), with their backs or legs sticking up in the air, and where a tiny old white-haired woman, wearing a brightly coloured robe and a headscarf tied turban fashion, and with a gaudy duster in her hand, standing amidst a clutter of piled up furniture – washstands and dining tables, painted vases, tattered chaises longues, rolled-up tapestries, flower stands, carpets, old pictures with no frames, jewellery boxes, pilasters, rectangular and oval mirrors – pointed out to my mother, who was wearing a black coat and hat, one of those huge wardrobes with three sides showing, exactly like the sliced-off triangle of the D.O.Z. Insurance building on Miklošič Street, and then went off along the far wall and up soft, yielding stairs to the balcony in order to point out the wardrobe in question from there, and then, completely insignificant at that distance, shouted down to us to follow her up because there was a much better view of the whole premises from up there.

And so, suddenly alone, I am walking along a corridor formed by wardrobes to right and left over thick rugs (which they sell here too), and go on past rows of open shelves into an emptier, airier part of the hall which is extremely high and where a sweating, dishevelled lady is sitting on a yellow couch, her coat unbuttoned, resting her shopping; she has a coral necklace round her red neck and is surrounded by parcels and bags; just past her the premises become still higher and deeper, two reinforced concrete walls stick out from left and right something like the doorposts of a huge loading bay and there, at the far end of the hall, at the edge of some sort of hole, I bump into a group of discriminating buyers, who are standing surrounded by filigree cupids, dishes and faience ware, examining the last little pieces of furniture on display. When I get closer to them I see that it is the edge of a yawning, quadrangular pit, above which is the empty shaft of an enormous staff lift, faced with roughly mortared walls, full of cracks, patches and the thick soft rags of spiderwebs, and a drill disappearing into the cold and utter darkness of the upper regions, which at the first stage can be seen to be crisscrossed with girders. I turn round to this group in their respectable city hats and suits, into whom my shoulders and back keep on bumping, although they are standing some way away from me by the far doorpost, and ask: 'Who is up there?' One of them, wearing a coat of sporting cut, gestures with his slender, white, intellectual's hand towards a certain spot in the shaft: 'God is up there,' he says. Slowly they all raise their heads and gaze upwards in silence. In the corners of the shaft, on vertical rails, are two milkish-white cylindrical tube-lights with rounded ends; they are off, each one is secured to the wall by an iron hoop that divides them into two. Suddenly a pale yellow flash lights up the upper part, winks like a kindled spark and goes out. 'What's he doing?' I ask. 'He's angry,' answers a gentleman from the group. I wait for the tube-light to go on again and indeed it fills with a pale glow, but instantly dies once more and all that remains is the greyish, milky glass. I look up at the dirty concrete, into the blackness, whence a cold, freezing draught is blowing; nothing can be seen in the gloom, which is growing more and more dangerous and black. like coal-smoke in a tunnel. I go past the lady, who is still resting from shopping in the midst of her purchases and taking no interest in the universal dismay around the shaft, and on through the wall, through a miserable little hole in the shape of a rectangle at floor level; I crawl into the darkness, which extinguishes me on the painted pavement among the puddles of Hajdrih Street in Moste by the railway, lit only by a flickering street-lamp above the bend of a rise in the distance. My hands are gleaming in the darkness. I can feel the presence of a blackened wooden paling against my hip, it is preventing me from leaving the building; beyond the fence is a dense thicket – a magnified shadow, around which I walk for a long time, unable to go away; close to the pavement are the glazed slits of woodsheds and cellars. I look the house over – it is dark and gloomy and ugly, just a normal suburban house, everything is asleep – I look at the shuttered windows, full of stony mysteries and the pitch darkness of absences; it is between half past twelve and three o'clock in the morning, when the sky presses its forbidden life down on the earth, leaves and grass; a faint glimmer of light shows above the gutter, a moonwhite ray. Previous dreams come back to me: I throw my hands in the air, stretch them over my head and fly up to about five or six inches above the parapets and the black windows with their motionless, woven curtains. Sticking out on either side of the pitched roof is a mansard with a flat roof and a double cross carrying power cables; one window is dark and the other light. I step off the gutter on to the steep, sticky tiles and press my face to the cold wet pane of the black window. Inside I can make out only the reflection of a massive writing desk with the aluminium cradle of a blotter in the corner. I go up to the lit window along the centre wall, but without daring to press my face to the pane. Sitting inside on a high made-up bed and around a broad round table are a number of slim, long-legged girls in flowery miniskirts and with their hair dyed and coiffed in various fashionable styles – for the most part black, smooth and with an oily sheen. They are sewing and knitting something white in tambourines and singing in unison. A single light, in the ceiling, illuminates the room's yellow walls. When I look at them, I see that they are as white as ivory, with narrow faces, long slender necks and slim hands, but their dresses are made of nylon, silk or crepe paper; they are singing separately, each one to herself, but more

harmoniously and strangely than I have ever heard before. Then
the white-painted doors from the attics open and a light shows in
the darkness between them – round like the light from a pocket
torch – then slips down across the threshold and approaches
through space – a crystal-clear fruit in the form of a pear – ever
nearer to the light in the room. That's God, explains someone in my
shoulders, in my leg, in my back. The girls jump up startled from
the bed, from behind the round table and from a big chest covered
with the green and red striped cloth from the picture of the Last
Supper in Jerusalem in Bible Stories, huddle in a tight knot, and
with their arms raised above their heads begin to say something in
a language never before heard. The spherical light comes nearer into
the middle of the room, floats about a foot above the floor-boards,
slowly, all on its own, travels between the foot of the bed and
the chest, past the orange skirts of the petrified girls, by the round
table with the abandoned sewing and knitting on it and comes
straight towards the misted-up window with my face behind it. I
step back and down towards the gutter; the light, shining without
a source, like in dreams, comes nearer, slides across the narrow sill
inside and then suddenly changes, and something dark sticks to the
windowpane – it is a big black sheet of emery paper. It is starshaped,
so that it is like a missile, it has cut-out eyes, a slightly bulbous nose
where the grainy paper folds, a grinning half-moon of a cut-out
mouth which does not move. It stares at me. I feel a stab of sharp
pain. It is unbearable and incessant. It has in it the majesty of the
operatic. It lights up the railway tunnel behind the roof, the garden
and the sky, as though judgement day has come. With a mighty cry
that wakes me, I turn away from the wall and jump into whiteness.

Translated by Veno Taufer and Michael Scammell

Mirko Kovač

UNCLE DONATO'S DEATH

there is a gap here for I lost the eight
best pages during the revolution – the
Croat appears simultaneously with Uncle
Donato – Daria had the nickname of Juliet –
this is the only chapter in which Jakov isn't
mentioned – it ends with tears and a priest
chanting and then a cold wind begins to blow

Uncle Donato was the only and possibly also the very last Dalmatian in the whole of this part of Hercegovina. And it is doubtful
whether any event in Varoš ever evoked as much excitement as the
extraordinary death of Uncle Donato, which for us Hercegovinians, or rather for us Hungarians in Hercegovina, was and remained the most mysterious of events, occurring as it did extremely unexpectedly – one fortnight after his birthday feast,
while he was still reasonably hale, and just when, under his wife's
supervision, he was taking his bath and changing his underwear.

Donato was born at Kaštel Stari beside a spring, in a year when
the cherry trees blossomed and birth and death were the two
highest virtues. Beside that spring his grandmother Ana, who came
from Biriš, had used American money to repair the little chapel of
St Rochus that stood on their land beside the road to Trogir, which
she did one night and the following morning she and signora
Andrica kept uttering holy words and saying:

'Behold the Virgin Mary, my soul has seen, my soul has seen,'
and the villagers came to pray and leave gifts and alms, 'upon my
word, it is,' they said, 'it's the holy Mother of God,' and Donato
took the money and placed it in his grandmother's cashbox, which
she left in trust for Donato not to be opened until his marriage,
but Donato opened it when he was twenty, that is when he first

slept with a woman, some tart from Trieste, and promised her the cashbox if only she would do him one favour and satisfy his curiosity by opening the cashbox and counting the money, for he believed there was lots inside because it was holy money that accumulates and multiplies.

Then a theatre came to Kaštel Stari and the first woman in his life went off with some peculiar fancy man and from the trap she was leaving in she tossed the empty cashbox at Donato's feet and he, out of a feeling of shame and some sort of extraordinary paralysis, neither waved nor even picked up the cashbox to look inside, as Dalmatians usually do, to see whether anything had been left there.

Donato told the little knot of Dalmatians gathered on the jetty that on the highroad above Kaštel Lukšić he had seen golden carriages carrying the Serbian heir apparent, the son of his Highness, King Alexander. He was cradled in the arms of some lady, so Donato said, and so feeble was his body and so diminutive his head that he couldn't even sit up without being held by one of the ladies in his entourage. And when they came to the chapel of St Rochus, so Donato said, they bore out the heir apparent on their arms supporting his head on little pillows and he looked with loathing at the Catholic chapel and then was carried to the spring where the heir apparent, in all other respects a fully grown man, began to weep when he felt the cold spring water on his face and refused to drink, so that he was borne back to his carriage on the ladies' arms and there started to kiss one of them and in front of the other ladies to put his thin lips to the warm nipples of her plump white breasts and then drove off in the direction of Trogir, and with some sort of terrible shriek the carriages disappeared in the distance, 'and I went over to the spring,' said Donato, 'and found this gold coin there which must have been dropped by the king or one of his ladies and also this picture of a naked English duchess dedicated to King Alexander.' Later it was said that the young prince was a nudist and that he used to appear on the nudist beach clad only in a white robe, surrounded by his retinue and his band of lady attendants who supported him and encouraged and massaged him before he entered the water. He used to pronounce himself

'King of the Serbs' and told them to keep a close watch so that Serbdom did not drown, but they say that in spite of his skinniness and undeveloped body his male member was enormous and that all those court nobles used to blush to the roots of their hair and insisted on trying to conceal this paradoxical fact, but that the king himself deliberately paraded this superiority of his and was supported in this policy by absolutely all of the ladies, including even some quite elderly dowagers from the court.

But soon the stories about the young heir apparent died away in Kaštel Stari for there appeared a certain skinny scholar of world renown, believed to have been born in Gospić, who started to photograph the Dalmatians so that Donato has a number of photos of the two of them together in front of Miljenko's house in Kaštel Lukšić, and that strange scholar of renown didn't want to tell them his name and merely asked the Dalmatians to call him Nicholas and none of them knew what was the source of his renown. Then he began to appear alone and they thought that he wished to settle down here, but some people from Zadar brought a rumour that he was a stone carver and had come to organize people and get them mixed up in some sort of party and then they began avoiding him and destroyed the photographs in which they appeared together with him. Donato was informed that the authorities knew he was responsible for bringing him here. That same night they were both taken away and for eleven whole years nothing was known about signor Donato, and then towards the end of summer he reappeared in big black shoes and a wide-brimmed hat and for a long time nobody recognized him and he himself said not a word but lived for a time like a stranger and at nights used to go alone to the jetty, where they stared at him in vain to see who it was and who knows how long this would have gone on if the whole thing hadn't seemed suspicious and only after he had been questioned did it come out that Donato had returned and that he had been away somewhere in some famous prison where the communists had been jailed, so that he had changed and become silent and withdrawn, with chain marks on his wrists and his face all seamed and wrinkled. He was informed that none of his family lived here any more and that his house had been sealed. The villagers said that his family had been driven out as a punishment for the son's sins, some dark soldiers had raped his sister and left her for dead in the house, then they had stuck danger signs over the doors and windows together with the skull and crossbones so that no one had dared to open them and go inside.

'Only for many years,' said the villagers, 'we could smell an unpleasant odour that came from that house and which, to our great surprise, instead of disappearing grew greater from year to year, and if we went close to the house we could feel a strong draught blowing through the dead doors and cellars.' As the years went by the house was filled with reptiles who could be heard slithering among the moss and nettles, and some sort of huge great birds used to fly through the roof and would attack one another, and sometimes indistinct voices could be heard.

'That's the way it is when a house is empty,' they said, 'and when misfortune strikes,' and they asked signor Donato what had happened to that skinny man who had caused him to be driven out.

Donato said that he was dead and that he didn't know any more.

He stayed in Kaštel Stari for a few days longer and married one of three lonely sisters who were living almost destitute, and it was said about the eldest, signorina Fila, who had been ill and exhausted-looking her whole life, that she had once had an affair with Telso though it was hard to believe because for the time of his stay in Yugoslavia he didn't show the slightest interest in women and they say that in America he led a retired and modest life in some sort of attic, where he spent his free time photographing live or dead birds with which he had filled the space under the roof.

Donato married signorina Tone, the youngest one, and then disappeared without trace.

He knocked around Croatia for a bit and then looked up Gustav Gaj, who was a relative of his, and he sent him to Hercegovina, to Varoš, and Donato got a job there as a servant to my sister Elida and in addition carried out the duties of market inspector, and here in Varoš he found his true home and refuge after the long years of wandering and longing for his native land.

The first incident in Varoš connected with his name was the long-awaited birth of a baby to the idiot-girl Zazija, who, said the locals, had been carrying the child for over a year, in fact since the day when Donato had arrived in Varoš. On the day when Zazija's delivery was expected Donato came too, wearing his clean best suit and with a rose in his buttonhole. He knew that the whole of Varoš thought it was his child, although we happen to know that Donato had never had anything to do with the luckless Zazija. On Elida's insistence he even accepted congratulations. The Varošites waited a whole morning in the heat of the sun for Zazija to give birth in a basement and amused themselves by betting on whether it would be male or female, dead or alive, and no one could have possibly imagined that it would be neither one thing nor the other, and truly not even today will those of us who know say what it was that was born that year, which in any case was under the sign of amazing and incredible happenings. And that child was taken more as an omen of disaster than as a living human being, which we throttled the instant we clapped eyes on it and in the evening dumped in the cave where we used to throw dead carcasses. But for us the spectacle at the mouth of the cave was a horrible one, for no sooner had we tossed that thing (and we still can't say what it was) into the cave than Zazija appeared just as she was in her post-natal sickness and with a fierce impulse of mother love and began to weep and climb down into the cave and we tried in vain to explain to her what it was she had given birth to, but it all came out well in the end for we promised Zazija another child that would start at once to walk and talk. Zazija was happy, put her hands to her belly and said: 'It will be in here again,' for if we knew one thing it was how much Zazija had changed during the time that she was carrying her child, her marks of madness and spiritual paralysis seemed to have completely disappeared in the presence of that sense of happiness that filled her entire being through those months. Filled with a warm, aching, human desire for happiness to show itself in her, Zazija had expressed herself by striking her belly. It was never discovered who the true father was.

Elida used to reproach Donato for his love for Daria, which was also known to his wife signora Tone.

But really he was past eighty now and for over four years already had been smelling most unpleasantly from some kidney disease and the only one who could put up with it was his wife who said that he had accustomed her to everything and had been humiliating her for fifty whole years now if you excepted the war when they were separated for over three years.

'That was the only rest I ever got,' so signora Tone, his wife, said, who on the day of Donato's death exclaimed, 'Oh, my God! Oh, my God!' and also at the grave, but nobody paid any attention, not even Father Jeftimije, not even the little girl who carried the single wreath that had been sent seven years earlier and all this time had been hanging on the wall of his room. It must have been repaired a few times for otherwise it would have disintegrated at the first touch. As long ago as that, his daughter, who had run away with an American subject, had thought that he would die and since her job was making wreaths, on which she had supported both him and her mother for a time, she had written:

> To my dear Daddy, may this Rose stand over Him always,
> Your daughter, Marija

which really needed several yards of red crepe-paper, but she wrote it in two lines in tiny silver lettering, which had already faded and which Father Jeftimije with the best will in the world couldn't read, which showed in the way he didn't move his head; then he had such a fit of coughing that we had to interrupt the funeral for over forty minutes.

It was supposed that the funeral would also be attended by the Russian woman, Daria, who was the same age as Uncle Donato and who had turned pale and bowed her head when she heard what Zazija had given birth to, because she too believed it was Donato's child and Varoš had been talking at that time about Donato's queer disease that he had brought back with him from exile and later infected women with, though not out of desire to infect them but simply that the illness appeared to make him feel a constant desire for women, so that it gave him no peace until just before he died. For over fifty years, ever since she had come to Varoš, Daria had been giving music lessons on the piano belonging to the mentally retarded daughter of some old Austrian officer and for an equal length of time had been going for a walk each evening with her dog, which to all our respectable citizens seemed positively indecent. The only time she hadn't taken the dog had been that evening in 1921, just as if she had known that she would be approached by some Croat who was a synonym for masculinity and who was talked about even by people of consequence : officers and the railway staff. He caught sight of Daria as she was strolling past the railway station in her grey mantle buttoned only at the neck. She had yellow sleeves and a pure white baton that she used to wave whenever she tried to sing something and which in truth she used more in conversation, for she would frequently poke it into her companion's stomach and once when talking to a certain Šaranović she had lifted his cap with it and when she saw his forehead had laughed and said :

'Good God, I knew it.'

By some miracle or other she never praised Russia to the skies and often said that she herself was from Poland which none of the Varošites believed because during the war she had sung with the Russian soldiers.

She was wearing an excessively short frock which wasn't at all the fashion at that time, what's more it was much shorter at the back which is what the Croat also noticed. For a wonder she wasn't waving her baton in the air or trying to sing something, but was simply strolling along the little path for she had just taken some medicine and would soon have to go to bed.

The Croat went up to her and said :

'Oi'm goin' to fuck ye.'

Daria walked past him with dignity, not deigning of course to look at him, and then whirled round and with her white baton, as if pointing at some smelly object, prodded him in the trousers and said :

'You are not a gentleman. Aren't you ashamed of yourself ? You stink !'

'Ah but mebbe ye doan't know what oi got yere in moi trowsers,' said the Croat.

'My god it's absolutely incredible,' she said, 'all these years after the war and you still stink,' and then she pushed him away with her baton and turned her back on him.

If the Croat had wanted to he could have seen her thin legs and the too-high heels that only just held up under those legs. Very likely he would have noticed other details too, such as the creased white stockings that she wore solely because they went with her baton. But how could he look when he was practically touching her from behind and she knew why his breath was coming in such short jerks but she didn't want to pay any attention. And when he said:

'Danged if you ain't a witch, why doan't ye turn round,' she swiftly turned and truly there was something to see, some say that she even let out a shriek which is not very likely with regard to Daria's dignity, and even if she did she was only putting it on for she knew in advance, most likely she only exclaimed 'Ooh!' even though she also used that exclamation whenever she ran into some acquaintance or when, on the road from the station to Varoš, some cat or a chicken would suddenly jump out from somewhere.

But so as not to get too carried away by a description of Daria, we must at once confess that three days later, in a hurricane of ecstasy, love was born between Daria and that Croat, and on Sunday the ladies came to see her as soon as he had left for the small town seventeen miles from Varoš where there was a Catholic church, and inquired whether he really had what people said he had. The god-fearing ladies were amazed and even looked upon the matter with disgust and one by one they all said how happy they were with their husbands. Some say that because she grew extremely poor at that time Daria must have been paying people to exaggerate the masculinity of her lover, but that was the sort of tall story that could happen in America or indeed anywhere else you like to name, but at all events a long way from Hercegovina.

The ladies maintained that it was abnormal and crossed themselves. Some of them even registered to wash him and lay him out on the day of his death, which was really absurd, but soon it was learned that one of the officer's wives had merely said it as a joke. The ladies were also scandalized when Daria said that in spite of everything he still hadn't managed to satisfy her, which was

immediately put down to something else : he didn't want to. Now,
however, it has been established that the Croat never did sleep
with her, not even that night in 1921.

To continue our narration of these events would take us altogether too far from Uncle Donato's burial and lead us to forget
even that he died, but the Croat's fate attracts us also because,
although we don't know how much of it is true, Uncle Donato was
also mixed up in it.

The terrible love that tortured Donato brought distress to his
whole family. Because of his anguish and jealousy they didn't
burden him with any more hard jobs to do, his wife signora Tone
watched over him, the doctors kept coming to see him and Elida
tried to calm him and persuade him of the absurdity of this love.
But Donato in spite of his anguish and loneliness was plotting revenge on the man who had caused him such unexpected pain. At
that time he received a letter from his daughter, but they say he
didn't even open it although he had always shown great love to
her. Preoccupied and withdrawn, Donato upset the whole family
even though it was clear to no one what Daria had to offer him at
that age, and even less did they understand Donato's need of love,
especially at a time when the Varošites expected him to die. The
whole of Varoš knew about his love for Daria so that many of our
most prominent people came to persuade him against it and told
him that Daria was an unhealthy creature with black, puffy,
flabby rings under her eyes, that she was nothing but a bag of
bones with dark shrivelled-up skin, that she was no longer living.
To touch her body meant touching death. And actually to apply
one's lips to it meant truly to die. Maybe Donato's love was merely
an urge to die, although it is absolutely certain that he didn't
realize it. All he knew was that he loved her. Moreover some people
maintained that no Croat existed and that Daria had been living
for years in the Austrian officer's attic completely alone. And they
told him that it was unimaginably filthy, that all sorts of lice had
bred in there and that insects turned the nights to pure horror.
Donato was ready to believe in anything but the non-existence of
the Croat. The children explained that they had seen her with the
Croat and that he looked very like Donato and even had the same

gaunt face and the slow gait of a man who was nearing life's end. This similarity that they described to him enraged Donato even more for he became convinced that Daria had loved him only because of his similarity to the Croat and had accepted him because he was dirty and had prominent signs of masculinity. This unhappy love more and more got the better of Donato until it reduced him to such helplessness regarding the Croat that he no longer even planned to kill him – he was so crushed that he was ready to commit suicide first. Apart from that he was unable to imagine the appearance of the Croat, whom he had never seen, as being similar to his and thought of him in the shape of some monster possessing supernatural powers, and every attempt of Donato's to drive him away ended in helplessness. Then Donato even began to doubt at times that Daria loved him, for if she did she would have got rid of this Croat. However, he found an excuse for her and came to think that she was doing it in order to whip up his love for her even more. Perhaps all every woman needs to know is that she is loved, even if she lives with some creature for whom she feels nothing herself. A woman that is loved, thought Donato, needs to be at a distance. Jealousy of the Croat had so exhausted him that he conceived a desire to fall at his feet and worship the power of that phenomenon that had succeeded in winning Daria's love. Suddenly Donato's feelings took an unexpected new turn. The growth of his love for Daria was matched by the growth of his admiration for the Croat. It seemed to Donato that only now when he felt excessive love for him was he able to kill him. Daria was forbidden to appear in the streets of Varoš for fear of worsening Donato's illness. For the first time in her long life Daria was satisfied with her filth and insects. Her life, which was drawing to its close, was filled with unexpected happiness; the lethargy of old age was lit up with the rays of some inner radiance. Her entire being was filled with a sense of aliveness, so that their lives flowed in parallel, only Daria was filled with joy while with Donato it was anguish. But even this anguish was but the consequence of love and the whole of Varoš was saying that both of them had expressed a desire to be buried together. This weird love of an old man for an old woman gave rise to all sorts of stories and one day,

before he died, a disembodied voice came to Donato and informed
him that the Croat would be killed at exactly eleven o'clock, upon
which Donato desired that he too would die as soon as possible,
and then an incredible and amazing thing took place: *at exactly
eleven o'clock they both died.* It seems that Donato's death was a
little trick which could be seen from that brief smile that lingered
on his face even after his eyes had closed for the last time. The
children truly said that the Croat had disappeared – either he had
died or somebody had killed him – but the trouble was that the
children were confused: they could never tell the difference between the Croat and Uncle Donato. Before his death Donato just
had time to draw up his will in which, apart from everything else,
he left all his land in Dalmatia to Daria.

Daria didn't come to the funeral and thus never learned of the
will, although it included, among other things, the following:

'The greatest aim of my life was fulfilled on the day I met Daria,
my darling Dashka as I nicknamed her then and as I call her now
after I am dead. The tenderness she showed me transformed my
life. Be merciful to her, oh Lord, and reward such a creature with
eternal life. Tears well up from the depths of my soul, for now I
understand how great is life when one possesses even a secret
faith in it. Oh, if I hadn't met her I would have long since been
dead already, or rather, I was dead until I met her. I welcomed the
day of my death for I had long wished to display a bravery in
dying that would equal the tenderness with which she knew how
to live. Here my tears leave me and my only hope is this cold dark
world, this new life in absolute freedom. Daria, darling Daria, I
am no longer able to speak of you so affectionately for wonderful
death is spilling over my lips, death which will come to every man
only when he understands the nature of this life. Oh Lord, who
ever fails to meet in his life one such wonderful creature, for whose
sake he can happily die, will find death painful, humiliating and a
terrible loss. But I, darling Daria, bequeath you my land with its
wonderful vineyards so that you may soon wish to retire to the life
that you have long craved. Draw the blinds over your windows
and when you see the dark, understand that that was my life
before you. And when you raise the blinds and the sun pours into

the room, that, Daria, is my death. Do not blame me for those weak comparisons for I am no poet, even though I am composing this will "with a heart that would burst with pain were it not already thine" – forgive me for quoting Elida's poetry for I know you could never stand her. Before my day of judgement I bequeathed you my property bit by bit so that I could be sure it would all come to you...'

This will was destroyed as soon as they had sorted through Donato's possessions two hours after his death, and the Varošites never found out that it had ever been written, otherwise on the day of the funeral, as has been done these last few years, it would have been read over the grave, but as it was Uncle Donato was buried without any speeches, peacefully and in almost total silence, except that every half minute the bells were tolled somewhat too hollowly and sadly by hand.

Jožef was noticed at the funeral, holding a scarf in his left hand and crossing himself with his right until Father Jeftimije chanted:

'The Lord have mercy on us.'

The thing that attracted most attention, however, wasn't Jožef but the corpse, which was sitting beneath an icon in the centre of the church in the big leather chair otherwise reserved for the archbishop on his pastoral visits. His eyes were closed and his arms rested on the chair in an attitude of peace. He was shaven and clean, with that peaceful, submissive expression characteristic of corpses. Perhaps he had chosen such a position so that his death would not be believed in, or in general the death of a man who has experienced love at the very end of his life. Candles stuck into the funeral cake flickered over his head and one old man said:

'He looks as if he's asleep.'

Somebody noticed that he seemed to be smiling and from the way he sat and the position of his body one got the impression that he could hear everything, probably because of the gentle smile on his face. Those who in his lifetime had mocked the late love of his old age now felt ashamed before the dead visage of Uncle Donato. Maybe that was also part of Donato's deliberate plan to shame and alarm, if only for a moment, those who had disbelieved his anguish and the powerful emotion of love that had visited him at his life's end.

We walked around him and tossed flowers at his feet, while his wife stood on his left all in black, together with her sister Clara, who was holding Donato's walking stick, and then the rest of the family.

The priest swung his censer.

The small group of his friends walked past the corpse, crossing themselves.

Some of them lingered longer to look at him and it occurred to a certain Ramadhan, a Moslem vagabond, to raise his upper lip, but just as he was approaching him he suddenly began to tremble, bent low and kissed him extremely awkwardly on the knee. Many people thought that this was a Moslem custom.

Some people didn't even dare to go close, probably because of the dead man's extraordinary position, and to some the whole thing seemed like a dream or some fantastic story out of Gogol.

Everybody expected him to be carried like that in the chair because perhaps that was what the dead man had wanted. But to the astonishment of certain more primitive Hercegovinians and of the relatives too, his sister-in-law placed a flower in his buttonhole. Donato's hand, like that of any corpse, was stiff, and at the beginning they experienced some difficulty in prising it away from the chair arm and thrusting the stick into it. This giving of a stick to the corpse provoked still greater astonishment and when this hand convulsively tightened on the cane it introduced a real sense of anxiety, fear and helpless dread. A cold sweat broke out on the faces of those present and also on the dead man's forehead. It was clear to everyone that this was in fact from the strain of trying to stand. At the first attempt, assisted by the cane, he didn't succeed and only when supported at the sides by signora Mande and his wife's sister Clara did he straighten up and stand unsteadily for a moment on his feet. It was a pitiful picture of a dead man rising to show how invisible are the borders between life and death. Anyway, at that moment he evoked far more pity than a corpse could have done. Nobody saw whether he gave some sort of sign to start off or not, but the procession, with the priest and Uncle Donato at

the head and escorted by several old men, one tall woman, Jožef
and the rest of the relatives, moved off extremely slowly, with
Donato, assisted by his stick, stepping out towards his ready-dug
grave, and, as his wife explained later, they had only ten minutes
to walk to the grave, taking into account, though, that they were
forced willy-nilly to listen the whole way to the tapping of his
stick on the cobblestones, which made Clara regret that they hadn't
put rubber on the tip and so spared Japhet, who was carrying the
cross ahead of the cavalcade, and they were afraid the whole time
in case he dropped it for it was well known that he couldn't endure
the tapping of a stick because the greater part of his youth had
been spent in jail and for more than four years he had had to listen
to the dripping of water in some notorious Austrian dungeon.

However there are certain incredible stories in existence that
were put about by signora Mande and that we won't pay much
attention to, especially since signora Mande is known that week,
in fact that afternoon, to have laughed and sworn aloud at Uncle
Donato's death, although on the other hand that does not mean
that things couldn't have been as she said they were. According to
her she saw, or thought she saw, how he turned his head several
times in the graveyard in order to read the names on the graves,
how he licked his left hand and wiped the sweat from his forehead,
and how once he even paused to get his breath back for that is what
he used to do during his last days on his way to the market: on the
steps alone he would stop twice to get his breath back.

Signora Mande asserts that at one moment he wanted to urinate
and that with his left hand he attempted to unbutton his trousers,
but then his wife said in reply that never in his life had he been
able to unbutton his trousers with his left hand and pass water
and that whenever his right hand happened to be full she herself
had had to do it and that it had always, so she said, been extremely
unpleasant for her.

But if he didn't want to urinate, said signora Mande, then he
must have stretched out his left hand to touch Clara's breasts because she herself was holding him on the left and had her hand
under his armpit, which didn't tickle him in the least, but we were
all convinced that there was a grin on his face and we sensed under

his closed lids an expression of tiredness or concealed satisfaction with himself, with his handsome and attractive appearance as a corpse.

Signora Mande's stories really are incredible, but what we saw at the very graveside baffled us at first, although later we became convinced that this was the way it had to be: the dead man wanted to try the wine that was to be poured over his tomb. We all refused to comply with this wish, though nobody could explain why. They say only that this gesture of the hand towards the wine looked as though it reached out of hell itself and that at that very instant a wind stirred the leaves and a cold drizzle began. At the moment when he left us all in silence and descended the little steps into the grave, the priest began to sing 'Requiem aeternam', and one old man chanted the responses from time to time, intoning: 'Amen, Amen.'

When he had descended no one could see him any more. The grave was deep and it would have been a bit awkward to watch him settling himself comfortably and scraping at the damp soil with his fingers.

His wife burst into tears and was the first to toss a lump of earth into the grave. She should have done it more carefully so as not to damage his eyes or some other part of his face, but she was so distraught that it was hard for her to make out which end he had chosen for his head and which for his feet.

The moment they started to throw in the earth, Clara cried out that Donato had forgotten his stick, which she slowly lowered into the grave, and when he was already covered with earth signora Mande threw in the bottle of wine and then she too started to cry for the first time and everyone realized that signora Mande's heart wasn't as hard as she said it was.

Thus Uncle Donato left us too, so said one old man and begged signora Tone, Donato's wife, to give him some old overcoat and shoes of Donato's, for even in 1921 we still shared everything.

We dispersed as soon as the drizzle had stopped. Birds were crouching on the ends of the graveyard crosses. We trampled the rotten leaves that kept sticking to our feet. A cold wind was blowing.

A few days later Varoš was talking about the fact that Daria had disappeared. They say she met her death in the same way as Uncle Donato and they say that certain god-fearing ladies saw her go off just before nightfall in the direction of Donato's grave wearing the same clothes she had worn when they first met, and she was never seen again; then on the marble slab which was placed over Donato's grave they carved in old Slavonic letters: *peace to the lovers.*

Translated by Michael Scammell

Kajetan Kovič

MAD DOG

He rebelled against the slowly and carefully bred
mind of the average dog.
He saw through the bones
that, before they were thrown to him,
had been covered with flesh.
He rebelled against their naked insolence.
He now hated the chained water
and sensed
that his thirst was different and greater.

He had sniffed the great bitch freedom.

They heard when he broke his chain.
Then they saw him run
with lowered head
through the great squares and back suburbs,
saw him standing on the hill
and drinking from the well,
until through some dark unknown corridor
he came running into their dreams.

Now they awoke with the faces of slaughterers.

But he who before had submitted
to their pity
no longer feared their rage.
He knew only for the road beneath him,
and the wearying but sweet motion of his legs,
and he felt
what dogs never feel.
Then he saw them closing the street.

That's the chain, he thought.
But he did not turn back, nor tuck his tail between his legs.
This side life, that side death.
He chose freedom.

They beat him to death like a dog.

THE VOICE

Listen, a voice is coming from the lava,
from mute volcanoes,
from ore, from deaf fish it comes,
a voice that slept,
o give it lips,
a voice without form,
o give it a body.

Listen, those are elephants.
And those are bees.
A flood of ecstasy,
a flood of terror.
You are a compass,
brace yourself in the door
to withstand
the earthquake of the voice.

Listen, the wall is trembling,
the sky trembles,
yes, in your mouth
the sky trembles,
that's the voice coming,
o miserable quarters,
where will it find
a big enough ear?

O mighty ear
for peace and stillness,
for that great space
beyond the voice,
ear for silence
that falls on the lips,
huge as a whale,
an iceberg.

BLACK PRAYER

Come, black word,
last desperate passionate voice
on the tip of my conscience,
bashful and daring voice
of love and anger,
word pure as fire,
razor word,
listen,
they are sounding the charge.

I am alone
in a trench on the edge of night.
No more do I have my golden spear
or golden shield.
Armies are bearing down on me in hordes,
greedy and sullen.
That's why I call on you, word of despair,
and draw you from the scabbard,
my last blade,
that's why I kiss you,
black
naked
sword.

Black word,
we are taking arms against black gods.
I shall look calmly into their faces.
I shall leave you on their brow,
leave you there mute.
For I shall not speak again
of those who are worth no word,
either white
or black.

ROBOTS

Robots are on the march.

The first robot is rectangular.
The stone in his hand
is a cube.
And a cube is a cube from time immemorial
and all that is, is a cube.

Robots are on the march.

The second robot is round.
The stone in his hand
is a sphere.
And a sphere is a sphere from time immemorial
and all that is, is a sphere.

Robots are on the march.

The stone in the sky, the stone on earth
has no choice.
Today it is stone, tomorrow a cube.
Today it is stone, tomorrow a sphere.
Today it is stone, tomorrow a robot.

Robots are on the march.

The cube smashes the sphere.
The sphere kills the cube.
For the cube is a cube forevermore.
For the sphere is a sphere forevermore.

Robots are on the march.

For as long as the cube is rectangular.
For as long as the sphere is round.

Translated by Veno Taufer and Michael Scammell

Radovan Pavlovski

WITCH BOY

Pools of water amidst green grass
were our mirrors
I who once used to come among them to love
Now am deceived in love
the grass undulates with my unquietness
See over there on that black peak
my star burnt out
I witch boy of verse
call to the sea in vain I murmur
words of tenderness
The years like thistledown
float by over my native soil
On the grass as on my lovesick brow
bitter hoarfrost will fall
Forgive me for the things broken in love
that became nocturnal glowworms
the escort of my pain

I love the wilderness of the roots your face
which was a picture of a bright-eyed summer's day
If I turn back
vestiges of storm pursue me
If I look forward
The vastness has merged into a dark vista
For the poet who in writing errs
even the ant unforgiving is a tyrant
Oh summer
faithful wheel of my wanderings
I murmur my love like a sleep walker
in the starry membranes of the night

All is innocent
You lovely head suffer
you artists
Play out the summer tragedy of the flower
On the stage built of cards

Sleep and I wakeful
with a touch will restore you
a whisper of grasses
Gloomy we wandered the whole day through
like prospectors of gold
A magic seed closes in sleep
Awake for your solitude
it opens a vastness
We loved in the deserted garden
now a wind wafts us towards autumn
Sleep and I wakeful
Draw out of the air
a magic kerchief
and turn the storm to stone

THE YOUTH ASLEEP AT NOONDAY

The sound of death
Is carrying you off to sleep
Oh youth
Awake
Your field is resounding with plants and mattocks
The morning sun is a great table
on which the ploughmen break their bread
Noon hides the black threads of night
You have buried stones and moonlight beneath you
Ten horsemen from an ambush
fly up like waves of fear

A tender plant binds your fingers to the earth and will not release
   you

until you give it
a sombre kiss at noon
Out of the grass arises a chorus of dead lovers
Awake oh youth
My boat built of vine tendrils
is at sea with a hoarse throat
There are moments when all is dead in sleep
There are moments when I study myself to see if I am mad
It is evening
And many people come to wake you up
You are drawing a map of the stars
and breathing deeply
Awake oh youth
and tell us your dreams
and on a good horse we will ride to the Iron River
that the wind from the watermills may refresh us
With a wounded flower I button up my shirt against the wind
and go home oh love

Say what potion you use in sleep
that you do not awake oh youth

FLOOD

I

The blue black drum of the Flood
beats on the mountains
Terror in the house on the shore
The heavens will fill our heads
with heavy water

oh lovely world
Let our race bury itself below earth
Oh bird complete your flight
carry no weight
Our feet are beaten and bruised
I took fright at the quick sprouting of the seed
in the dark granaries
and on the seventh day in the heavens appeared
the dread shadow of the Flood

II

Sharp thunder of the heavy summer
My horse gallops over
From dark to light meadows
Seeing him I fill my song with fear
The heavens come down with axes
which make night full of noon
You there my black headed horse in your gallop
Shoot out sparks
and set fire to me
I spend the night in the lair of wild animals
Plant speaks to plant above my head
Oh deep flowing waters
I have a star
that discloses your thoughts of drowning

III

My horse is in the seventh heaven
All I sowed gives birth to weeping first
A cross on the bread and cold wines
In the heavens appears the dread shadow of the Flood
No bed will receive me to sleep
The water yearns for me as a drowned man

Translated by Anne Pennington

Branko Miljković

TOWER OF SKULLS

Dirge of black birds and lament of sad praises
The empty name after death and the sightless gaze
This is not love it is suffering only and shame
When echoes quicken the lonely places and shores.

The wind beneath ground enslumbers the sleepers
A rock and twin-silence stand guard at the entrance
Not love but suffering here and a wall
Of skulls where stars which once shone now decay.

Losing existence I wake to become voice and time
Flower greater than night empty wave unremembering
Over my head the stars come alight
By which I changed face and name of direction
O boat without helm filled with wind and unmemories
The heavier shades of some other world have fallen.

ORPHEUS DESCENDED

Do not look round. At your back is revealed
the greatest of mysteries. Over your head
birds rot and decay, endless suffering
boils up at your glance and a poisoned rain falls.

You wander wounded by stars in your sleep. Shining
she follows behind in your footsteps, but of all
you alone may not see her. Her light
is upon you let it cover her too as she falls.

For you the way in lies where two hounds lie dozing.
Sleep, for the time is of evil. You are cursed for ever.
Evil at heart. The dead will proclaim
you living if they exist. That's he
at whose back comes the world
intrigue without end and a sad backward glance.

THE DARK PROVINCE

Entranced by an alien song. The weight
Of their treachery hides in their fast-beating hearts:
O nightingale wanderer. The sun is an error
Redeemed by horrors within the blind's sight.
The fire's guile gives night in exchange for eyes,
But men stand infected within the exhausted air
To follow out their vision in different ways,
The plants and stars have moved up now into hearing.
The abyss that doubts in them fills them to overflowing
Only the weak need have no fear of the danger.
Even the sleeper takes part in the evil deed.
There is no one left to help the strong by forgiving
That within the dark province to which they descended
They found the gold that was not theirs for the taking.
Whatever you do is evil for that same mud
From the nether region is ever greater in glory.

POET

He knows all roads and winds,
winds and their orchards,
orchards in which grow words
and the roads from words to hopes.

He is carried away by the road
down the world and the devil in words,
to pay court to his own shadow,
to sing in a false orchard :

The chaff of his spell-binding moonlight,
the dog-rose, the vileness within him,
to blind the bounds from another's eye
to give back the night in the name of tenderness.

CHRONICLE

On the first day the birds died, their nests became homes for ser-
pents and winds
On the second the fish left the water, the water flowed empty
On the third the forest came into the town and the town was no-
where
On the fourth they erected a tower of skulls and grinding of teeth
On the fifth by the river the forest assembled the headless corpses
On the sixth a small fire lovingly looked like the sun
On the seventh day the angels did not begin singing
On Monday the eighth day for the first time the bird made of ashes
sang out and the wall began speaking

Translated by Bernard Johnson

Dane Zajc

THE CHAFERBUG

All night the quiet chaferbug
rubs with its six legs
the white bone.

Buried in ash, the white bone
is planed by the black legs,
gentler than thistledown,
of the quiet planer,
with an unreadable intention
in its speckled eyes.

What does it want.
What does it bring.

Perhaps the mad creator placed him
Everything with the thoughts not theirs
thought by six rhythmical legs.

Perhaps the mad creator placed him
with two fingers on the brow,
on the bright brow of the bone:
Do this job for me.
Do this quiet job.
Do it well but without a sound
because I am going to another star
to create a new world of madness.

All night the six legs
are rubbed on the white bone by the quiet chaferbug.
And when it picks off a scale
the chandeliers of the galaxies sway :
thus the insane creator
revels in his work.

ALL THE BIRDS

We will kill all the birds.
All. All, said the ravens in the dark.

And in the stillness of the night I heard
someone in the garden killing my birds.
And I knew that my mornings would now be
songless
and I felt
grief closing its hand round my soul.

All. All the birds, they said.

And fluttering about me
I felt
black wings and
watching me from among them
a raven's yellow eye.
What are you looking for, raven, I asked.
There are no birds hidden
under the crust of my skull.

All. We will kill them all.
All the birds, he said.

And I was afraid
that one night
through my dark dreams
he would split open my skull
and with his crazy beak
search in the nest of my thoughts
for any songbirds hidden there.

All. All the birds, he will choke.

Everywhere I feel now on my neck
the raven's yellow eye.
My soul has been pierced.
My soul is a slain bird.

All. We will kill them all.
All the birds, croak the ravens
under the dark sky.

THE GARDEN

He came back shrivelled.
Only the furrow behind him in the yellow sand
showed that he was moving.

From their perches the lookouts reported:
something is coming out of the desert.
They gathered on the border.
They pulled him into the world of green.
I am the one you sent, he said.
It was like pincers talking
when he spoke.

Then his head slumped down,
impaled on a willow wand.
He's not one of us, they thought,
and gazed at his doggish tongue
licking the grass.

What news from the Forbidden, they asked.
It's all true, he shivered,
and the pincers of his mouth closed shut.

They dropped water on to his tongue and demanded:
Isn't there a garden on the other side?
Isn't everything we don't have in that garden?
Everything you know is true, he rustled.

This isn't the one we sent, they said,
and slit his vein.
When the slow grey liquid came oozing out of it
they were sure
he was a hostile being.
They left him there. (His ribs thinned to
sticks of brushwood.)
They chose a new messenger.

SNAKE KILLERS

When you meet a foe
your snake bites him.
But this is done only by those
who are fond of themselves
and very self-confident.

People who are not fond of themselves
go off in secret to meet their snake.
To look it in the eye.
To stand up to its gaze.
Soon afterwards they are found dead
with a wound as imperceptible as the bloom of starvation on purple
    lips.

We know little of the mysterious power of snakes' eyes
for they kill only in secret,
and the traveller mostly mistakes them for the gleam of dew on a
    green leaf.
When we hear a cry in the wood we think a hawk is killing a bird.

It's not a crime if we kill someone with our snake
nor if we want to meet it.
Both are just agony for oneself.
Worse is to kill someone else's snake:
that person will then crawl into the first deep shadow
and be sucked up in the evening by the little bit of sun.

We don't know what happens to snake killers.
Probably they are not punished and don't suffer.
They are from a universe we cannot apprehend.
We don't know if it was them leaving on the stroke of the moment
    just past.
We don't know if it is them commanding us from under our finger-
    nails
or if it is them stepping out from the dark wall of the future.

We never know which snake killer
is hunting us through the quarries of the world.
And we never know where our snakes are
although they will always come at our call and do our deeds.

Everyone has his snake and his star.
But only occasionally do the stars' invisible rays
pierce a leaf in the thicket of our moments.

FAITH

Your heart comes to rest
deep under the ruins of your broken body.

And you think you are laughing.
But that is a sob running through your perforated throat.
And you think you are sobbing.
But laughter's sadistic fingers
stretch the skin of your cheeks.
Laughter rolls pebbles
around your mouth.
Then you toss into the air the coloured beads
of your words.
Catch them with your mouth
and swallow them voluptuously.

For you can never fall.
Not to the bottom.

Then comes a stray dog
and laps the rainwater
from your open skull.
Lively mice gnaw
your ears.
Your lips.
Rats weave a nest
in your breast.

Then you laugh gaily
with your naked teeth.

You get up white pure and insensible.
You stand on the threshold of a new day.
The sun puts a bugle to your lips.
A hot brass bugle.

You have never fallen.

THE BIG BLACK BULL

The big black bull roars into the morning.
Big black bull, who are you calling?
The pastures are empty.
The mountains are empty.
The ravines are empty.
Empty as the echo of your call.

The big black bull roars into the morning.
As if the heavy black blood was spurting
to the tops of the dark pine trees.
As if over the wood to the east
was opening to the morning
a bull's bloody eye.
Big black bull, who are you calling?
Does it give you a thrill
to listen to the echo
return your hollow call?

Big black bull, the morning is bloodless.
Your voice falls into the ravines
like a ragged flock
of black crows.
Nobody hears your loneliness.
Nobody drinks
the black blood of your voice.
Shut up, big black bull

The big black bull roars into the morning.
The sun in the east sharpens
the gleaming slaughterer's axe.

Translated by Veno Taufer and Michael Scammell

Meša Selimović

DEATH AND THE DERVISH

The image of man, lonely but braving out the difficulties on the path of life, accorded with the sense of destiny I had at the time. Had I been in a different mood, I might have been upset by the suggestion of hopelessness, of being condemned to a dreary march, but at the time this image struck me as a reasonable reconciliation, even as a form of defiance. I do not know what was in good old Hussein-Effendi's mind, but it seems that he was a little amused by himself and by others.

Hafiz Muhamed came out of the tekke and stood by the fence above the river. His face was pale, agitated. He did not even glance at me. Was he ill?

'How are you feeling today?'

'Me? I don't know. Bad.'

I could sense he did not like me, but I did not resent it. He was also dancing on the rope hung between the two banks, as best he could. Sometimes he was even trying to be good.

I asked him, smiling, still in my good mood, ready to understand everything, ready to be grateful:

'Tell me honestly, you knew what the kadi's wife wanted, and this was why you sent me there, wasn't it?'

'What kadi's wife?'

'There's only one kadi in the town. And one kadi's wife. The sister of Hassan.'

He was angry, almost disgusted. I was not used to seeing him like this.

'Don't mention their names together, please.'

'So you knew about it. And you didn't want to interfere. Was that it?'

'Leave that filth alone, for heaven's sake. I wanted to help you, that was why I didn't go. But don't mention them now.'

'Why not?'

'Haven't you heard?'

'No.'

'Then I'll have to tell you.'

I could tell by his broken voice, by his effort to force himself to look me in the face, by his restless hands incessantly disappearing into his deep pockets and coming out again, by everything I had never noticed in him so far which made him appear a different man, by the fear I was feeling, I could tell that he had weighty news.

I asked him, eager to drown in these black waters:

'About my brother?'

'Yes, about your brother.'

'Is he alive?'

'Killed. Three days ago.'

He could say no more, nor did I ask him.

I looked at him: he was crying, his mouth crooked: he was terribly ugly. I know I noticed it, and I know I wondered why he was crying. I was not crying. I was not even saddened. What he said flashed like a blinding light, and then there was peace.

The water murmured peacefully.

I heard a bird in the branches.

Well, it's over, I thought.

I felt relief; it was over.

'That's it,' I said, 'so, that's it. On the water gleaming gold in the sun.'

'Calm down,' Muhamed said, horrified, thinking I had gone mad, 'calm down. We'll pray for him.'

'Yes. That's all we can do.'

I did not even feel pain. As if something inside me had broken, and was no more, that was all. It was strange that it wasn't there any longer, quite incredible, quite impossible, but it hurt more while it was there.

Mustafa came too – Hafiz Muhamed must have told him about my misfortune – he brought a little food in a copper plate, friendly and gentle as he was, even clumsier than usual.

'You should have something to eat,' he offered me some food, making an effort not to shout. 'You haven't eaten anything since yesterday.'

He put it in front of me, as a medicine, as a token of his tenderness. I ate, I did not know what it was, the two of them kept looking at me, one by my side, the other in front of me, like inadequate sentries staving off grief.

And then, between two mouthfuls, what had broken in me began to hurt.

I stopped eating, taken aback, and slowly, slowly got up.

'Where are you going?' Hafiz Muhamed asked me.

'I don't know. I don't know where I'm going.'

'Don't go anywhere. Not now. Stay with me.'

'I can't stay.'

'Go to your room. Cry if you can.'

'I can't cry.'

Slowly I was becoming aware of what had happened, and drowning in pain, as if quiet waters were welling up; while they were only ankle-deep, I was anxiously thinking of the fear before the despair of the next day.

And then I felt a sudden burst of fury, as if my brother were standing guilty before me. You have deserved it, my tearful anger hissed in me, what were you up to? what did you want? You've brought misery on us all, foolish man ! Why?

And then this was over too, it lasted only an instant, but it had me started.

From uphill, from the gypsies' quarter, the drum was beating deafeningly, with short pauses, and the zurna was wailing, incessantly, tirelessly, from early morning, from yesterday evening, from time out of mind, the terrible madness of St George's Day was rushing on to the town like a defiance, like a threat. I listened to it and trembled, the big kettle-drum was beating far away as if sounding an alarm, calling all those who were no more, all the dead brothers under the earth. Someone was left alive, and was calling.

He was calling in vain.

There was no thought in me, no tears, no direction. I should not

be going anywhere, but I was going, the footsteps of the dead
Harun could still be followed.

Under the small stone bridge my river was flowing, and on the
other bank there was waste ground. I had never crossed it except
with my eyes, the end of the town, of our community, of life,
was there, and the beginning of the short path leading to the
fortress.

My brother had gone that way and had never come back.

Ever since, in my thoughts, I had frequently walked from the
stone bridge to the heavy oak gate splitting the grey walls. And
during these imaginary visits I was sleepwalking, and the path was
always deserted, cleared for my painful journey, so that I could get
through more easily. The gate was the aim of everything, from
everywhere the path led only to it, it was the purpose of fate, the
triumphal arch of death. I could see it in my thoughts, in my
dreams, in my fears, I could sense its dark call and its insatiable hunger. I kept turning back and running away, but it looked at the nape
of my neck, baited me on, waited for me. Like an eclipse, like an
abyss, like a solution. Behind it was the secret, or nothing. There
questions began and ended, began for the living, ended for the dead.

I was in fact treading the street of my nightmares for the first
time in my mind, long since troubled about how I would face it.
And the street was deserted, as I thought and wished, then; it did
not matter now, I would even prefer it not to be so deserted, like a
graveyard. It was watching me – gloomy, frowning, malicious, as
if saying: so you've turned up at last! It is unnerving – this voyage into nothing, it kills even that little painful courage which is
called *indifference*. I wanted not to look, in order to calm the anxiety
and trembling of everything in me, but I could see it all, the hos-
tility of the deserted street, and the terrible gate before the secret,
and the eyes of the hidden sentry, in the small hole in the gate.
I had never seen these eyes in my imaginary journeys; at the time
when I was about to come, there was only the gate and the street
leading to it, the rope to the other bank.

'What do you want?' asked the sentry.

'Has anyone ever come here on his own?'

'You have. Have you got anyone in the fortress?'

'My brother. He is imprisoned.'

'What do you want?'

'Can I see him?'

'You'll see him when you get brought here.'

'Can I bring him some food?'

'Yes. I'll take it to him.'

I was madly turning back time, resurrecting the victim, he had not yet been killed, I had just heard that he was imprisoned and had come at once, to ask for him, it was human, brotherly, there was no fear, no shame, there was still hope, they would let him out soon, he would get what I brought him, and he would know that he wasn't alone and deserted, his own flesh and blood was in front of the gate. Neither the towers, nor the sentry, nor selfish considerations had kept him away, he had come, he had come, he was fifteen years younger than I, I had always taken care of him, I had brought him to town, oh, men, how could I leave him in his greatest trouble, his wretched heart would be lifted up when he heard that I had asked after him. He had no one but me of his kin, and should I also deceive him, why? and for what? You can all hold it against me, you can be angry with me, shake your heads, I don't mind, I am here, I am not giving up my nearest kinsman, you can crucify me, if you want, because of this love, can one fight against it? I've come, brother, you're not alone.

It was late. After all that had happened, and all that had not happened, I could only pray for the peace of his soul, hoping my prayers would reach him, and that he might need them, perhaps.

Bitter was this prayer, different from the prayers I read over the dead in the tabuts. It concerned only him and me.

Forgive me, brother, forgive me, sinner, for this belated love, I thought it was there while you needed it, but it is waking now that it cannot help anyone, not even myself. And I do not know whether this is love or coming back in vain. You had only me, except the graves in our village, now you and I have no one in the world, you lost me before I lost you, or perhaps you didn't, perhaps you thought that I was standing before this studded gate, as you would have stood for me, perhaps you hoped to the last that I was going to help you, and I wish you believed so much in me, you would not have been afraid of the last loneliness, when we are deserted by everybody. And if you knew the whole truth, may God have mercy on me.

'What are you whispering?' asked the man from behind the gate.

'I am praying for the dead.'

'Pray for the living, they are in greater trouble.'

'You have seen much, one should trust your judgement.'

'What do I care if you trust my judgement.'

'How many people have passed through this gate?'

'Many more going in than coming out. And no one's missing.'

'No one's missing?'

'Not if those in the graveyard count.'

'A twisted sense of humour you've got, my friend.'

'They've got a sense of humour. And you've got a sense of humour. And now clear off.'

'Have you got to be brutal because you're there?'

'Have you got to be stupid because you're there. Come on, step over the threshold – only a couple of feet – and you'll talk a different language.'

A couple of feet, that much, and everything would be different.

All people should be brought to see this couple of feet, to hate it. Or rather it should be hidden from every eye, nobody should come here before he is brought here, so that they wouldn't hide the thoughts they have, and make every word they say disgusting.

I went back with my eyes cast down, looking at the uneven cobbles, which were not overgrown by grass, looking for footsteps, for the place where he had stood for the last time outside the walls of the fortress. There was no trace of him in the world any longer. All that was left was in me.

At the nape of my neck I could feel the knife, coming out of the slots of a pair of eyes in the gate, thrusting forward, full of desire.

I was on the brink of death, at the gate of my destiny, not having learned anything. Only those who get in can learn something, but they cannot tell it to anyone.

Who knows, it might occur to them to make this the only gate of death, and let us all come, each in his turn, in droves – why wait for the accident and the fated hour?

But this crazy thought was only a defence against the unspeakable horror in me, an attempt to be blind to my own misery because of our common misery. I was looking for the last trace of the dead, and I was at his funeral, without him, without anyone, alone, without meaning to be there, unaware why it was necessary for me to come here and mention him who had died. Perhaps because this was the saddest place in the world, and the commemoration of the dead was most needed here. Because this was the most terrible place in the world, and one had to overcome fear oneself before one could commemorate those who were killed here. Or because this was the most disgusting place in the world, and the commemoration of what one used to be could become here a horrible eye-opener. I was not looking for it, but it happened; it was no use to me, but there was no other way.

At the entrance to the town a dozen people were standing, waiting as if I were coming back from another world. They were looking at me, motionless, their eyes quiet, but fixed on me, and I felt them like a burden, too many of them on my forehead, swarming there, I felt I might begin to stumble. I did not know why they had come there, I did not know why they had blocked the way, what they were expecting, I did not know what I should do.

I passed by, they moved aside to let me through. Everything was quiet for a while, I was walking on my own, but then I could hear the scraping of feet along the cobbles, they were following me. I quickened my pace, to get away, they followed me, hurrying, they did not mind the distance between us. It seemed that their numbers were growing.

Spring twilight; it was getting darker, the lanes were bluish, restlessly quiet.

I had not heard the muezzin, I did not know if this was the hour of prayer, but the mosque was open, only one candle burning in the tall candlestick.

I walked in and sat in my place at the front of the congregation. I heard, without turning back, people coming in and sitting behind me, without words, without noise. They had never been so quiet. And in their prayers they were quiet, and solemn, it seemed to me. I was moved by that solemn murmur behind my back.

While the service was in progress, I could feel it was strange, different from any previous service, hotter and more dangerous, a preparation for something to come. I knew it could not end in the way in which it always ended. *Amen* was a beginning, not an end: one could hear muffled, dense voices, everyone was waiting. What for? What was going to happen?

Their silence, their immobility, their intention not to leave although the prayers were over made clear to me what I did not want to know. They wanted to see me after I had learned about my misfortune, they wanted me to show what I was at that moment.

I did not know what I was, and I did not know what answer to give them.

Everything depended on me.

I could get up and leave, run away from myself and from them. This would have also been a kind of answer.

But if I were to do this, everything would have remained in me. Nothing would have reached anybody else. Even in front of the fortress gate I was afraid of the pain and the repentance of the morrow, I might be burned in fire, drowned in grief, muted forever by untold wrath and sorrow. I had to say it. Partly because of those who were waiting. I was a human being, at least now. But also because of him, undefended. Let it be the brother's sad prayer, the second one today, but the first one which people would hear.

Was I afraid? No, I was not. Not afraid of anything but the apprehension whether I would do well what I had to do. I even felt quietly ready for anything, the kind of readiness which comes with the inevitability of acting, and the deep agreement with it, stronger than revenge, stronger than justice. There was not anything I could do against myself.

I got up and lit all the candles, taking the light from one to the other, I wanted them all to see me, I wanted to see them all. So that I might remember them and they might remember me.

I turned back, slowly. No one was going to leave, not one of them. Sitting on their heels they looked at me, wrought up by my quiet movements, and the flames burning all along the front of the mosque and releasing a thick scent of wax.

'Sons of Adam!'

I had never called them sons of Adam before.

I did not know, not an instant before, what I was going to say. Everything was happening of its own accord. Grief and agitation found their own voice and their own word.

'Sons of Adam! I shall not preach a sermon, I could not even if I wanted to. But I believe you would hold it against me if I did not, at this moment, and I cannot recall a more difficult moment in my life, talk about myself. I have never cared more about what I was going to say, even though there is nothing I want to achieve by it. Nothing, but to see fellow-feeling in your eyes. I haven't called you my brethren – even though you are that to me more than you've ever been : I have called you sons of Adam recalling what we all have in common. We are men and we think in the same way, particularly in distress. You have been waiting, you have wanted to stand by my side, to be face to face with me, grieved because of the death of an innocent man, full of anxiety because of this crime. This crime concerns you, because you knew : whosoever killeth an innocent human being, it shall be as if he had killed all mankind. We have all been killed thousands of times, my brethren in death, but we are full of horror when the man we love best is struck down.

'Perhaps I should hate them, but I cannot. I haven't got two hearts, one for hatred, another for love. The one heart I have knows only grief at this moment. My prayer and my penance, my life and my death, all this belongs to God, the Creator of the world. But my grief belongs to me.

'Be careful of your duty to your kindred, is Allah's order.

'I have not been careful of mine, son of my mother. I have not been strong enough to avert misfortune from you and from me.

'Musa said : My Lord! Appoint for me a henchman from my folk, Harun, my brother, confirm my strength with him. Let my brother share my task.

'My brother Harun is no more, and I can only say : My God, confirm my strength with his death.

'With his death – not buried in the law of God, not seen or

kissed by his flesh and blood before the great journey without return.

'I am like Kabil; God sent him a raven scratching up the ground, to show him how to hide his brother's naked corpse. He said: "Woe unto me! Am I not able to be as this raven and so hide my brother's naked corpse?"

'I, miserable Kabil, more miserable than the black raven.

'I have not saved him alive, I have not seen him dead. Now I have no one but myself and Thou, my God, and my grief. Give me strength not to break under brotherly and human grief, not to poison myself with hatred. I repeat Nuho's words: "Distinguish between us, and judge aright between us."

'We live on earth for a day or some part of a day. Give me strength to pardon. For whosoever pardoneth and amendeth, his wage is the affair of Allah. And I know I cannot forget.

'And I beg you, my brethren, do not hold against me these words of mine, do not hold it against me if they have hurt and saddened you. And if they have uncovered my weakness. I am not ashamed of this weakness before you, I would be ashamed if it were lacking.

'And now go home and leave me alone with my misery. I am relieved now I have shared it with you.'

Left alone, alone in all the world, in the bright light of candles, in the blackest darkness, unrelieved (people have carried my words away with them), and my grief was left all to me, untouched, heavier because of the disappointed hope that it would be lighter, I beat my forehead against the floor, and knowing, alas, that it was in vain, in my despair I said the words of Surah 'The Cow':

Our Lord, we ask Thy forgiveness.

Our Lord! Condemn us not if we forget, or miss the mark.

Our Lord! Impose not on us that which we have not the strength to bear!

Our Lord! Do not bind us to that which we cannot bear and do! Pardon us, absolve us and have mercy on us.

Perhaps he has pardoned, perhaps he has had mercy on me, but he has not made me stronger.

Weak as I had never been before, I cried like a child. All that I had known and thought had no significance, the night was black and threatening outside the walls, the world terrible, and I small and weak. It would be best to go on kneeling like this, pouring myself out in tears, never getting up again. I knew we mustn't be weak and sorrowful if we were true believers, but I knew it in vain. I was weak, and sorrowful, and I did not think about whether I was a true believer or a man lost in the deaf loneliness of the world.

And then there was a voice of silence. A thundering noise was still sounding in me, but it came from farther and farther away, shrieks could still be heard, weaker and weaker. The storm had spent its rage and calmed down, of its own accord. Because of the tears, perhaps.

I was tired, I was a sick man just out of bed.

I put out the candles, taking their lives one by one, without the solemn feeling I had when lighting them. I was broken by grief, and I was alone.

I was going to stay in the darkness for a long time, I was frightened. Alone.

But when I choked the soul of the last candle, my shadow did not disappear. It rolled, heavy, against the wall, in the half-gloom.

I turned back.

Hassan, forgotten, stood by the door, with a living candle in his hands.

He was waiting for me, in silence.

. . .

It was a cloudy twilight, I remember well, I looked at the sky, like a peasant. I looked out of ancient habit which time had not worn out of me, even though I no longer needed it. And I could sense the change of weather many days in advance. But this time I was deceived by the cloud, it took me by surprise, I was too engrossed in myself. And yet, I had been looking forward to it, that cloud and bad weather; this was why, perhaps, I failed to notice it coming. I had hoped, unreasonably, that my father would not start his journey to town in rain.

The day was wearying, the sky was still red in the west. I remember seeing – against the background of the red in the sky – four horsemen at the beginning of the street. They were beautiful, as if embroidered on red silk, as if sewn on to the glaring background of the sky, it seemed that four lonely warriors were standing in a wide field, on the eve of the battle, holding back their horses by scarcely noticeable movements of their hands.

When I set off towards them, the horses sprang up, spurred on by blows which I did not see, and they rushed ahead in one line, closing the street from wall to wall.

They were running straight at me!

I was not a coward, once, I do not know what I am now, but in this situation neither courage nor cowardice could help me. I looked back, the gate was far away, ten steps behind me – but unattainable. I waved my hand at the horsemen: stop, you will ride me down! But their whips beat the horses' cruppers, hurrying them on, they were nearer and nearer, the earth thundering the most terrible thunder I had ever heard, and the four-headed dragon, whirled-up and bloodthirsty, was approaching with incredible speed. I tried to run away, or the thought only flashed through my mind, but my legs would not carry me, I could feel the horses' breath at my neck and, along my spine, the quiver of the blow which was about to cut into it, I was going to fall down, they would ride me down, I stood by the wall, stuck on to it, attenuated but still within their reach, I saw four equine jaws gaping above me, huge, red, full of blood and foam, four pairs of horses' legs whirling around my head, and four cruel Torbeš faces, four open Torbeš mouths, red and bloody like those of the horses, and four whips of bull's pizzle, four snakes hissing at me, twisting round my face, my neck, my breast, I felt no pain, I saw no blood, my eyes looked with horror at the crucified dragon with thousands of legs and thousands of heads. No! something voiceless shrieked in me, more fearful than fear, heavier than death, I failed to recall my God, or his name, there was only red, bloody, unfathomable horror.

Then they went away, and I saw them still in front of me, their imprint remained stamped in the bleeding cloth of the sky, stamped in me, under my eyelids, as if I had been looking at the sun.

I could not, I dared not move, I was afraid of sagging down on to

the cobbles, I did not know how I was standing, I had no sense of
my feet under me.

Then Mula Jusuf came to me, from somewhere, I did not know
from which side. He seemed frightened.

'Have they injured you?'

'No.'

'Oh, but they have.'

'It doesn't matter.'

His round, healthy face was pallid, shock and grief were in his
eyes. Was he grieved because of me?

It was my good luck that he was passing by, I would be cour-
ageous before him. I could not tell why, but I knew I had to. I
could show my fear before anyone else, but I mustn't show it before
him.

'Let's go into the tekke,' he said softly, and I recalled I was still
standing next to the wall, for no reason.

'I will be late for the mosque.'

'You cannot go to the mosque like that. I'll go instead of you,
if you like.'

'Is there blood on me?'

'Yes.'

I started for the tekke.

He held me by the arm, to help me.

'I can manage,' I freed my arm. 'Go to the mosque, people are
waiting.'

He stopped, as if ashamed of something, and gave me a sorrowful look.

'Don't go out of the tekke for a day or two.'

'You saw everything.'

'I did.'

'Why did they attack me?'

'I don't know.'

'I shall write an indictment against them.'

'Leave it alone, Sheik Ahmed.'

'I can't leave it alone. I would be ashamed of myself.'

'Leave it alone, forget it.'

He was not looking straight into my eyes, he was pleading, as if he knew something.

'Why do you say that?'

He was silent, his eyes looking aside, not knowing what to say – if he was afraid; or not wanting to say it – if he knew something; or repenting for letting on as much as he had; or remembering that it was none of his business. God, what we have turned him into.

For his sake I had hidden my fear and weakness, for his sake I wanted to go to the mosque with blood on me, for his sake I said I was going to write an indictment against them. I wanted to stand upright before this young man to whom I was tied by strange ties. He was sorry for me, for the first time. And I had thought that he hated me.

'Go,' I said, watching the colour quickly coming back into his cheeks. 'Go now.'

It would have been more natural if the incredible event had frightened me out of my wits, but – surprisingly – I got over the first moment without breaking down, and keeping it all to myself, I succeeded in pushing it aside, deep down, blotting it out for the time being. Terrible – said the voice of naïve recollection in me, but unable to make any of it live. I was rather proud of having hidden my fear, and I was still possessed by the fine sense of having braved it out – not a source of complete safety, but sufficient for the purpose of postponing the issue.

While Mustafa and Hafiz Muhamed were taking my clothes off and washing me, shocked and frightened, I tried in vain to stop the trembling of my arms and legs, but I was strong enough not to be ashamed and not to be afraid. The banked up fire in me seemed several times to be bursting into flames, the terrible thundering and the anxiety suddenly came back to life, but I succeeded in reducing everything to what had happened and was still not giving pain. It was over, I was saying to myself, nothing had happened which should make me too anxious, it could have been worse, only let this be all. And I listened eagerly to their rambling conversation, Mustafa's questions about what had happened because he could not understand anything, and Hafiz Muhamed's shocked gasping, alternating with clumsy attempts to cheer me up, with angry railing against Mustafa, and with threatening addressed to someone undefined, unknown who was called 'they'. His stammering protests gave support to the uncertain sense in me of having undergone a degradation, and when Mula Jusuf came back from the mosque and stood by the door, in silence, my desire to do something about it was firmer. I made use of it at once, afraid of the other desire – not to do anything. I wrote my indictment, addressed it to the governor's kadi and gave it to Jusuf to copy.

When I went to bed, I could not go to sleep. My indictment tormented me, it was still with me, I could not make up my mind whether to send it in or to tear it up. If I were to throw it away, that would be the end of it all. But then all that was hidden in me might come alive, the banked up fire might burst into flame. And I would hear again the thundering which freezes the blood in the veins. If I were to dispatch my indictment, I would keep the conviction that I could defend myself, that I could bring a charge. I was in need of that belief.

It seemed to me that I had not slept a wink, but I was awoken by the footfalls in the room – not at all circumspect – and by the light of a candle. A man with a flat face stood above me, the one who had informed me of the sheriff's threat. The other man, unknown to me, was holding the candle.

'What do you want?' I asked, frightened, startled from sleep, embarrassed by their impudence.

He was in no hurry to answer, he looked at me mockingly, curiously, like that other evening, in a slyly friendly way, as if only he and I knew of a joke which was a bond between us and gave us an opportunity of being merry without saying a word. The other was holding the light near my bed, as if examining an odalisque.

'He has not obeyed me,' said the man merrily. 'And I have warned him.'

He got hold of the candle and began to inspect the room, peering into my books. I thought he was going to throw them about nonchalantly, but he put everything back in its place carefully.

'What are you looking for?' I asked, flustered, eager to know. 'Who let you in? How dare you come into the tekke?'

My voice was very soft and very uncertain of itself.

He looked at me with surprise, without any answer.

He found the indictment and began to read it, shaking his head.

'What do you want this for?' he asked, surprised. And he answered his question:

'Your affair.'

And he put the indictment into his pocket.

And when I protested again and said that I was going to complain to the mufti, he looked at me compassionately and waved his hand, as if he found it not worth his while to argue with a naïve man.

'Your affair,' he repeated. 'Come on, get dressed.'

It seemed to me I had not heard him properly.

'Did you say "get dressed"?'

'I did. Of course, you can come along like this, if you want to. And hurry up, don't make trouble for yourself or me.'

'All right, I'm coming. But someone will pay for this.'

'That's the best way. And someone always pays for everything.'

'Where are you taking me?'

'Ah, where are we taking you!'

'What shall I say to the dervishes? When shall I be back?'

'You won't say anything. And you'll be back immediately. Or never.'

This was not a practical joke, it was only that he did not mince his words about real possibilities.

Hafiz Muhamed came into the room, flustered. Everything about him was white, his socks, his shirt, his face. He looked like a corpse, raised from his grave, unable to speak. It could be a bad omen. I was expecting something from him, and I knew it was unreasonable of me.

'They've come to take me with them,' I said pointing to the men who were waiting, inexorable. 'I will soon be back, I hope.'

'Who are they? Who are you?'

'Come on!' the man was hurrying me. 'Who are we? What fools there are in the world. Let us take you with us, and you'll learn who we are.'

'Take me!' shouted the corpse suddenly, because he was bewildered! 'Take us all. We're all as guilty as he is!'

'Foolish man,' concluded the guard reasonably. 'Don't come

before it's your turn, we can come to take you too.'

'He that takes pride in violence . . .'

He did not finish what might have finished him, just at the right time a sudden fit of coughing stopped him, it could hardly ever have been of greater service to him. He was bursting, as if all his blood had rushed into his throat, it was the excitement, I thought, without pitying him, for he was staying here. I watched him being torn to pieces by spasms, I stood and watched, alone, alarmed at this undesirable exit into the night. But I did not want to show my excitement.

I went up to him to help him. The guard stopped me.

'Poor man,' he said calmly, in abuse, or in contempt. And he gestured to me with his hand to go out.

In front of the tekke another man was waiting.

They went by my side, following me. I walked on, as if hemmed in, choking.

It was dark, there was no moon and no sky, a night in which nothing could be seen, a night with no life, only dogs barking in the courtyards, answering the distant barking of the dogs from the hills, near the sky; it was after midnight and ghosts were abroad in the world, the uncaught men sleeping, dreaming happy dreams, in darkness, and the houses were in darkness, and the town, and the world, this was the hour of reckoning, the hour of evil deeds, there were no human voices, no human faces, except the shadows in charge of mine. There was not a thing abroad, only my restless zeal lived in that dark landscape.

Here and there an occasional timid rushlight flared up – because someone was ill in the house, because an infant was awakened by my fears at the dead of night, because of an ominous sound; the thought of this quiet world filled me with horror and I tried to push it away so that I would not catch sight of myself wading through the darkness towards an unknown fate, wading through uncertainties, needlessly, nowhere, as if while wading on I was losing the sense of reality, it seemed to me I was no longer in this world, not awake, because of shapeless shadows, because I could not believe that this was myself, that this could be myself. I was someone else, I knew him, I looked at him, perhaps he was surprised, perhaps frightened. Or else I had lost my way, I did not know where I was, I must be somewhere, at some time or other of my life, treading the roads I was destined to tread, I had never been here before and I could not get out, but this minute someone would surely put the light on and call me into a safe shelter. But no one put the light on, no directions came from the voice I desired to hear, the night continued, in an unknown part of the country, in disbelief, it was all a bad dream, I would wake up and breathe again.

Why don't people shout when they are led to death, why don't they make themselves heard, why don't they ask for help? Why don't they run away? Even if there is no one to shout to, if there is no one to hear, if everyone is fast asleep, if there is nowhere to escape to, if all the houses are firmly locked. I was not saying this for my own sake, I was not sentenced to death, they would let me go, they would take me back soon, I would go back myself, along well-known roads, not along these which looked foreign and terrible, I would never listen again to the dogs barking, barking hopelessly, at death and waste, I would close the door, I would stop my ears with wax, I would not hear a thing. Did all who were being taken away hear the dogs? Was this barking their last farewell? Why didn't they shout? Why didn't they run away? I would shout if I knew what was awaiting me, I would run away. All the windows would open, all the doors would fly wide apart.

Oh, no, not one. This was why no one ran away, they knew it. Or they hoped. Hope is death's harlot, a more dangerous murderer than hatred. It dissembles, it knows how to win you, how to soothe you, how to lull you asleep, how to whisper in your ear what you want to hear, how to lead you under the knife.

They were taking me from one darkness to another, from one shapeless nowhere to another, because I could not see anything and I was engrossed in myself, engrossed in imagining things which deprived me even of what I might have recognized. We were changing darknesses, I knew because we were moving, and because time was passing, even though I was not aware of its passing.

They were met by someone, they whispered together, I was hemmed in again, I had become a valuable item which must not be lost, I no longer knew who was with me, as if that made any difference, they were all the same, they were all shadows, they were all on the night shift on my account. They could work in shifts, but no one could replace me.

When my forehead hit the low door-frame, I knew we had arrived. I had arrived, and they would go back. They would be replaced by walls.

'Give me light!' I shouted at the nail-studded door where I had come in, disbelieving that there was so much darkness anywhere in the world.

It was the last remnant of habit from outside, the last word which was left. No one heard it, or no one wanted to hear it, or no one could understand it. It might have sounded as if I were rambling in my speech.

Somebody's footfalls were going away along what was probably a corridor. And this was probably a prison. And this was probably me. Or it wasn't? It was, unfortunately. The thought was not lost in the dream-like fog, and I did not keep apart from this in order to look at myself from afar, as if at someone else, I was aware, awake, everything was uncomfortably clear in me, there was no delusion.

For a long time I did not move from the door and the sharp smell of rusting iron, this was the first place where I had stopped in the darkness, which was destined for me, known to me for all the duration of this moment, and therefore less dangerous. And then I walked in a circle, exploring, blind, trusting my fingers and feeling all round me the thick moisture of the uneven wall, as if I were under a well. The moisture was also below, I could feel it under my feet sticking foully in slime. I did not find anything, and I soon came back again to the door and to the sharp smell of iron, it seemed less unbearable than the stink of moisture.

I did not know if my wounds had been giving me pain before this and I had not been aware of it, or else they had shrunk back before matters of greater moment. I could feel them now, for either the time had come for pain, or my body had rebelled against oblivion and was reminding me of its existence. Unconsciously I accepted this unexpected help, and began kneading my wounds with my fingers, spreading the pain, laying it out, so that it should not all be in one place; I filled the gaps in order to stop the bleeding, I could feel the blood sticky on my hand. Yesterday evening they had washed my wounds in the tekke with camomile tea and clean cotton, and I was now thrusting all the dirt from the walls into the torn tissue, and I did not think of what was to come, I thought only of what was, and the pain was strong, it was burning in the darkness, I was living in it, my body was bringing me back to real life. I needed this pain, it was part of me alive, comprehensible, similar to the pain on this earth, a defence from the darkness and the vain search for an answer, an obstacle against remembering my brother, he might turn up on the black wall of my grave with a question to which I had no answer.

I fell asleep with my palm pressing a wound, as if guarding it so that it should not disappear while I was sitting by the damp wall; and I found it again under my hot palm, as if it had been in a nest. It was alive, it hurt. 'How did you sleep?' I wanted to ask it. I was not alone.

I was glad when I caught a glimpse of a small hole in the wall under the vault, the morning revealed it to me, and although the light of the day remained a desire and a foreboding, my darkness was no longer so complete. Dawn had come in that other world, and this brought a dawn to me too, even though my night went on. I stared at the dark grey spot above me, encouraged, as if observing the most beautiful rosy dawn coming up behind the wide hills of my childhood. Dawn, light, day, even a hint of this, but extant, not everything was lost. And when I turned my eyes from this poor sight, I was blind, and the darkness in my cave once again total.

Only when I got used to it did I realize that this was an eternal night in which, nevertheless, eyes were necessary. I looked round me, but I could recognize only what I had already felt with my fingers.

The square aperture in the door opened with a squeak, neither light nor air came in. Someone was peeping from that other darkness. I approached the aperture, and we were face to face, looking at each other. His face was hairy, featureless. There was nothing in it, no eyes, no mouth.

'What do you want?' I asked, afraid that he might not be able to answer. 'Who are you?'

'Džemal.'

'Where have they brought me? What is this place?'

'We hand out food once. Only once. In the morning.'

His voice was hoarse, dark.

'Has anyone inquired about me?'

'Will you have something to eat?'

Everything seemed to me dirty, slimy, rotten, I was sick even at the thought of eating.

'I don't want to eat.'

'Everyone's like that. The first day. Then they want it. Don't call me later on.'

'Has anyone asked after me?'

'No. No one.'

'My friends will come to ask for me. Come and tell me about it.'

'Who are you? What's your name?'

'Dervish, the sheik of the tekke. Ahmed Nurudin.'

He closed the peep-hole and opened it again.

'Do you know the prayer? Or the charm? Against gout.'

'No, I don't.'

'A pity, that. It'll be the end of me.'

'It's damp here. We'll all fall ill.'

'You're lucky. They let you out. Or they kill you. But I live like this. Forever.'

'Have you got a plank, or a mat. I can't lie down.'

'You'll get used to it. I haven't.'

Dervish Ahmed Nurudin, the light of faith, the sheik of the tekke. I had forgotten him, all night I had no name, no vocation. I remembered him, I brought him back to life to face this man. Ahmed Nurudin, preacher and scholar, the roof and the foundation of the tekke, the glory of the town, the master of the world. Now asking for a plank or a mat from this bat Džemal, to avoid lying down in the mud; he was waiting to be strangled and laid down dead in the mud in which he did not want to lie alive.

It was better without a name, with wounds and pain, with oblivion, with wounds and hope in the morning; but that dead morning without dawn woke Ahmed Nurudin and extinguished hope, pushing the wounds and the pain of the body away into nothing. They did not matter again because of the graver, more dangerous threat rising from within me, to destroy me.

I kept away from madness, anything but that. Once it got started, no one could stop it, it would burn, annihilate everything in me, only waste would be left, more horrible than death itself. And I could sense it wriggling, beginning to move, there was nothing my thought could get hold of – I looked back in panic, I searched for something, it was there, until the day before, until a moment ago, where is it, I searched in vain, no foothold; I have sunk into mud, it does not matter, it is all in vain, Sheik Nurudin.

But the wave that had risen stopped above me, it was not getting bigger. I waited, in surprise : silence.

I got up slowly, holding the wall, leaning with my palms against a clammy protuberance, I wanted to stand upright. I was still hoping, they would look for me, they would come, the day was just beginning, a moment of weakness would not kill me, and it was good I was ashamed of it.

And I waited, waited, during the march of long hours I kept the fire of hope burning, consoled myself by pain and fiery wounds, listened for footfalls and waited for the door to open, for a voice to reach me, and the night fell, I knew because I no longer had need of my eyes, I was sleeping in stinking slime, worn out, waking without the desire to be seated on the stone, and I ate Džemal's food in the morning, and waited again, days were passing, gloomy dawns followed one another, and I no longer knew whether I was waiting.

Then, weakened, in a daze of weary waiting, worn by the moisture which my bones had sucked in, in a fever which warmed me and brought me to the brink of my grave, it was then, I say, that I talked to my brother Harun.

We are equal now, brother Harun, I kept telling him who was motionless, silent. I could see only his eyes, distant, severe, lost in darkness, I followed them and placed them before me, or I moved following them. We are equal now, both miserable; if I have been guilty, there is no guilt now, I know how lonely you were, how you waited for someone to call you, you stood at the door, listening to the voices, footfalls, words, you thought they concerned you, over and over again. We have been left alone, both you and I, no one has come along, no one has asked after me, no one has remembered, there was nothing on my path any longer, no trace and no memory, if only I could have been spared seeing that! You waited for me, I waited for Hassan, nothing has come of our waiting, nothing ever comes of anyone's waiting, in the end everyone is left alone. We are equal, miserable! We are men, brother Harun.

I swear by time, which is the beginning and end of everything, that everyone is always the loser.

'Did anyone come?' I asked Džemal by habit, no longer hoping. 'No. No one.'

I wanted to hope, one could not live without waiting for something, but I had no strength. I left my sentry duty by the door, and sat down without choosing the place, quiet, defeated, quieter and quieter. I was losing the sense of living, the hard and fast line between waking and sleeping was disappearing, what I dreamt began to happen in reality, I walked free on the paths of my boyhood and childhood, never in the streets of this town; it seemed they could take me to prison even from my dreams, I lived with people I had met a long time ago, and it was wonderful because there was no waking, I was not aware of it. Even Džemal was a part of a dream, and so was the darkness around me, and the wet walls; and whenever I came to, I did not suffer too much. Strength is needed even for suffering.

I became aware of how man dies, and I saw that it was not difficult. Neither was it easy. It wasn't anything. One only lives less and less, one is less and less, one thinks, feels and knows less and less, the rich circulating of life goes dry, and the thin thread of uncertain consciousness remains, poorer and poorer, less and less important. And then nothing happens, nothing comes to pass, nothing *is*. And nothing matters – and it does not matter.

And once, in this withering away outside time, for the falling to pieces had not established itself as duration, when Džemal said

something through the peep-hole in the door, I could not understand what he was saying, but I knew it was important. I woke
and understood : my friends had brought me gifts.

I took the food, the dates, and the cherries, they were green
berries when I came here, they were pinky blossoms, I wanted their
painless blood to run through my veins so that I could blossom
painlessly every spring, as they do; this is how it used to be, a long
time ago, in the life which still had beauty. Perhaps life seemed
hard to me then, but when I think of it from this place, I would
like it to come back.

I was afraid that I might drop my bundle, my hands were hollow,
my hands were joyful, my hands were crazy and helpless, they
pressed hard to my breast – this proof that I was not dead. I knew
they would come, I knew it! I bent my head and breathed in the
fresh breath of early summer, eagerly, avidly, more and more,
mould would soon penetrate this transparent red smell of cherries,
my muddy fingers kept feeling their fine infant skin, in an instant,
in an hour, they would shrivel, grow old. Never mind, never mind.
This was a sign, a message from the other world. I was not alone,
there was hope. No tears flowed down my cheeks while I thought
that the end was near, but now they were gushing forth from the
revived springs of my eyes, surely leaving their trace on the film
of mud on my face. Let them flow, I had risen from the dead. The
smallest sign was sufficient, a sign that I had not been forgotten,
and my lost strength came back to me. My body was weak, but this
did not matter, I was warmed from within, and I did not think of
death, and things began to matter. It had come at the last moment,
to stop me on the slope down which I was sliding, to stop my
dying. It did begin, indeed! (I came to realize this time, and not
only this time, that the soul can often keep the body alive, but the
body can never keep the soul alive : the soul staggers and fades
away alone.)

Again I waited.

There was not a single ordinary thought in me, they were all
out of the world, out of the normal course of things. I listened for
the roar of my deliverance as I would listen for joy, I waited for the
thundering as vengeance for what I was drowning in me with fear,

as soon as it appeared even as a foreboding. There could be no ordinary ending to this waiting. Perhaps because of the grave in which I was shut, and the nearness of death I had breathed, perhaps because of the deep corridors and the strong gates which were never opened by a word or an appeal, perhaps because of the horror which had befallen me and which could be annihilated only by another, greater horror. I was waiting for some day of judgement and was sure it would come. The two of them had announced it to me.

On the next day I received gifts again, and I was back in time again, and again there were two of them, nameless, but I knew who they were, and waited for the earthquake.

'If there were an earthquake, a fire, or a rebellion?' I asked Džemal, surprised that he did not understand. Or perhaps he did understand. He asked me:

'You're a dervish. Do you know the words: "When the event befalleth?"'

Were we thinking the same?

'I know!'

'Come on. Here. Say it.'

'No, I won't.'

'A pity, that. You're not a good man.'

'What do you want it for?'

'I like it. I like to listen.'

'How do you know it?'

'From a prisoner. The one before you. A good man.'

'It's from the Koran. Surah "The Event".'

'Could be.'

' "When the event befalleth ..." '

'Not so loud. Come here.'

' "When the event befalleth, abasing some, exalting others. When the earth is shaken with a shock, ye will be three kinds." '

My chin leaned against the sharp edge of the iron framework, I could discern in grey darkness his shapeless face in the square peephole, quite near my eyes. He listened with surprise to what I was saying, with an interest which I could not understand.

'That's not it.'

'Perhaps it was "The Spider".'

'I don't know. It doesn't matter. What three kinds?'

'First those on the right hand, and then those on the left hand. And the foremost in the race, the foremost in the race: those are they who will be brought nigh in gardens of delight. A multitude of those old, and a few of those of later time. On lined couches, reclining therein face to face. There wait on them immortal youths with bowls and ewers and a cup from a pure spring wherefore they get no aching of the head nor any madness. And fruit that they prefer, and flesh of fowl that they desire. And there are fair ones with wide, lovely eyes, like unto hidden pearls. Reward for what they used to do. There hear they no vain speaking nor recrimination. Naught but the saying: "Peace, Peace!"'

'"And those on the right hand: what of those on the right hand? Among thornless lote-trees, and clustered plantains, and spreading shade, and water gushing, and fruit in plenty, neither out of reach nor yet forbidden, and raised couches."'

'Life's good for them too.'

His whisper was full of admiration, of envy.

'"And those on the left hand: what of those on the left hand? in scorching wind and scalding water, and shadow of black smoke, neither cool nor refreshing. – Ye verily will eat of a tree called Zaqqum; and thereon ye will drink of boiling water. Drinking even as the camel drinketh. We mete out death among you, and We are not to be outrun, that We may transfigure you and make you what ye know not."'

'What? Are they guilty?'

'God alone can know, Džemal.'

'Is there any more?'

'"On the day when the hypocritical men and the hypocritical women will say unto those who believe: Look on us that we may borrow from your light! It will be said: Go back and seek for light! Then there will separate them a wall where in is a gate, the inner side whereof containeth mercy, while the outer side thereof is toward the doom. They will cry unto them: Were we not with you?"'

'Oh, merciful God. Again. Without light.'

Then he was silent for a long time, his agitated brain was in torment. His breathing was heavy.

'And me? Where shall I be?'

'I do not know.'

'Shall I be on the right hand?'

'Perhaps.'

' "Glad news for you this day : Gardens underneath which rivers flow." This is what he used to say. The one before you. And about the sun. Where shall I be? This is for the deserving. And I? Am I deserving? For fifteen years like this. Here. But there – the sun. Rivers. Fruit. For the deserving.'

'What happened to that man?'

'He died. A good man. Quiet. He spoke to me. Like this. You shall go there, he said. There. And all good men. This is good. I said. Because of the sun. And because of the water. Clear. And because of the gout. My gout.'

'How did he die?'

'With difficulty. His soul was not willing. To quit the body. He struggled. I was there too. Well. I helped.'

'How did you help?'

'He was strangled.'

'And you helped to strangle him.'

'He tried to wrench himself away.'

'And you were not sorry for him.'

'I was sorry. Because of the sun. Of what he was saying to me.'

'What was his name? Was it Harun?'

'I don't know.'

'What was he guilty of?'

'I don't know.'

'Go away, Džemal.'

'I may get there too? On the other side. Of the wall.'

'Surely, Džemal.'

He asked me if I wanted to move to another cell, not so dark, not so damp as mine.

'It doesn't matter, Džemal.'

'Will you say it? Again? "When the event befalleth." Only

that. First. It is dark here too. And foul. For fifteen years. There would be no justice: the same again there.'

'Go away, Džemal.'

For a long time his butchered sentences stumbled about me, cramped, deformed, it seemed that the words could hardly stick to each other, but the wandering, beheaded pieces were formed into wholes, miraculously, and even expressed human longings.

My wits were wandering again.

And one day, later on, that day, or much later, or never, when the door of my cell opened, two opposite feelings splashed over me, the fear that he would strangle me, and the hope that he would release me. They rushed upon me simultaneously, these two feelings like two impatient, flustered creatures, pushing and overtaking each other. Or they were divided by such a small interval, that I could hardly separate them in time. Probably I waved off the first thought at once, because he was alone, and there was joy straightaway: deliverance! One thing could happen as well as the other: there had to be no reason for either. If they can kill you without guilt, perhaps they can release you without justification.

But neither was happening. I was supposed to move to another cell.

I was squatting, my forehead leaning against the rough wet wall, I was too weak to move away.

Someone stood above me.

He helped me to get up.

'You're free. Your friends are waiting.'

I kept reminding myself, by a distant bloodless thought, that I ought to be joyful, and I did not even try, I had no need.

An unknown man was waiting in the corridor. I had been brought here by three men, I was no longer important.

'Come on,' he said.

We went silently through the darkness, I kept bumping against the walls, the man held me up, we went on, I was running away, I wasn't there for a long time, and now I was coming back and thinking: who is waiting for me? And I did not care. And then we rolled on from a bigger darkness into a smaller one, I remembered it was night, transitory, everything is beautiful that does not last forever, the night and the rain, the summer rain, I wanted to hold out my hands in order to have the mud washed off, to put out the fire in me, but my hands were hanging helpless, unnecessary.

I went again to see Abdulah-Effendi, the sheik of the tekke of the 'mevlevije' order, and I begged him to help me to find my brother's tomb. I had come to him, I said humbly, because I dared not go myself and sue for mercy from those who had the power to grant or to refuse it, they would refuse me and then all the doors would be closed for me, therefore I was obliged to plead by proxy, and I would hope as long as I could find any. I had come to him first, trusting his goodness and hiding behind his reputation, for mine was no longer great, and God knows it was not my fault. I would be greatly indebted to him, because I wished to bury my brother as God had ordered, so that his soul should rest.

He did not refuse me, but it seemed to him that owing to my misfortune I had lost much of my knowledge and worth. He said:

'His soul is at rest. It is no longer tied to the body, it has passed to the other life, in which there is neither grief nor unrest, and no hatred.'

'But my soul is still tied to the body.'

'Are you doing it, then, for your own sake?'

'For my own sake too.'

'Is it grief or hatred? Beware of hatred – it can lead to sin against yourself and against others. Beware of grief – it can lead to sin against God.'

'I grieve as much as man must. I am on my guard against sin, Sheik Abdulah. All I have is in God's hands. And in yours.'

I had to listen quietly to his instruction and to humour him by my dependence. When people think that they are superior to you, they can be even noble-minded.

I was not strong enough to have the right to be impatient; neither was I weak enough to have any reason to resort to anger. I was using others, letting them feel stronger than I was. I had my mainstay and my sign-post, why should I be petty-minded?

He helped me, I was given a permit to enter the fortress grounds and find the grave. Hassan came with me. We took some men too, with an empty, lidless coffin and several shovels.

Someone led the way to the fortress graveyard – a sentry, a servant, a gravedigger; it was difficult to say what this silent man was, unused to talking, unused to looking other people in the eyes, timidly inquisitive, angry in his readiness to be of service, as if he were struggling all the time between the urge to help and the urge to drive us away.

'That's it,' he nodded in the direction of a solitary clearing further up from the fortress; there were the fresh ulcers of mounds and the wounds of ransacked graves, all over the clearing which was overgrown with weeds and thick brambles.

'Do you know where his grave is?'

He looked at us with half-closed eyes, without saying a word. This might mean:

'Of course I know, I buried him myself.'

But it might also mean:

'How should I know? Look how many there are, without any sign or name.'

He walked among the graves, strewn about in disorder, dug in haste and without respect, as potato-pits are dug. He would stop by a grave, look for a moment at the sunken earth and shake his head:

'Nikola. A bandit.'

Or:

'Bećir. Maša's grandson.'

Sometimes he was silent.

'Where's Harun?'

'There he is.'

I started off alone, among the covered pits to look for my dead brother. Perhaps my excitement will tell me, or my grief, or a sign, perhaps I will be warned by the sound of my blood flowing, by a tear, or a quivering, or by an unknown voice, surely we cannot be imprisoned forever in the helplessness of our senses. Isn't there a way in which the mystery of the same blood could speak up?

'Harun!' I called him silently, waiting for an answer from my inner voice. But there was no answer, no sign, nothing, no excitement, not even grief. I was like clay, the mystery remained deaf. I was only possessed by a sense of bitter emptiness, by a peace which was not mine, by a far-off sense of purpose, more important than anything that the living know.

Alone among the graves I forgot my hatred.

It came back when I approached other men.

They stood above a pit, the same as other pits.

'Is this it?' asked Hassan. 'For sure?'

'I don't care, take whichever you want. But this is him.'

'How do you know?'

'I know. He was buried in an old grave.'

And indeed, the men found two heaps of bones, they collected one in the coffin, covered it with a cloth and started down the slope.

Who is it we're carrying? I thought in horror. A murderer, an executioner, a victim? Whose bones had we disturbed? Many had been killed, Harun was not the only one who was put into another man's grave.

We followed the men who carried the coffin on their shoulders and the heap of bones covered with a green cloth.

Hassan kept jogging my elbow as if he were waking me up.

'Calm down.'

'Why?'

'There's something strange in your look.'

'Grief?'

'I wish it were grief.'

'In the graveyard, a moment ago, I expected, in vain, a kind of awareness when we got to Harun's grave.'

'You ask too much of yourself. You should be satisfied with your grief.'

His thought remained unclear for me, and I dared not ask what he meant. I was afraid he might guess what was going on in me. He must have had a reason to send me back to my grief.

Back in town, as we were walking in the streets, people gathered around us, I could sense more and more feet following us, their footfalls were duller and duller, the human wattle was thicker and thicker, I had not expected so many, I was doing this for my sake, not for theirs, but what was mine was being snatched away from me and becoming theirs. I never looked back to see them, but I was excited and felt the crowd carrying me on like a wave, and I was growing with it, becoming more important and stronger, they were the same as me, enlarged. There was grief, condemnation, hatred in their presence, in their silence.

This funeral was a vindication of my hatred.

Hassan said something softly.

'What was that?'

'Don't say anything. Do not speak when they lay the coffin down.'

I shook my head. I was not going to speak. It had been different then, in the mosque. They had followed me on my way back from the gate of death, and we did not know, neither I nor they, what ought to happen. Now we knew. They were not waiting for a word from me, for condemnation, it had matured in their own minds, now they knew everything. It was good I was doing this, we were not burying him, who had once been a man, just in order to justify his innocence, we were going to do more than that : we would sow his bones as the seed of a memorable injustice. And let them grow into whatever they want and whatever God decrees.

So my hatred became nobler and deeper.

In front of the mosque the men laid the coffin covered with the green cloth on the stone. I made my lustrations, stood in front of the coffin and began to pray. And then I asked, not merely doing my duty, as always before, but with a note of challenge and triumph :

'Tell me, men, what kind of a man was the dead?'

'Good !' a hundred voices answered with conviction.

'Do you forgive everything he did?'

'We forgive.'

'Are you his witnesses before God?'

'We are.'

Never had the witnessing for a dead man before his last journey been more sincere and more challenging. I could have asked them ten times, they would have answered louder and louder. We might begin to shout, threatening, in fury, with foam all over our mouths.

Then they carried this man, long dead, on their shoulders, one group taking the coffin from another, rendering him the last honours, in loving kindness, and in defiance.

We buried him by the wall of the tekke, where the street opened towards the town. So as to be between me and the townsmen, a shield and a warning.

I had not forgotten that Moslems used to bury their dead in a common graveyard, equal beyond death. They began to separate when they became unequal in life. And I had separated my brother from the others, so that he would not be mixed with them. He died because he opposed; let him still wage war in death.

When I was left alone, when everyone had gone away, having thrown a handful of earth into the grave, I knelt by the swollen mound, someone's eternal abode, and a memorial to Harun.

'Harun!' I whispered to the earth, his home, to the mound, his guardian. 'Harun, my brother, now we are more than brothers, you have given birth to me, such as I am today, to live and remember; I have given birth to you, separated in your grave, to stand as a milestone. You will meet me every day, in the morning and in the evening. I will think of you more than I did while you were alive. And let everyone forget, for human memory is short, I will not forget either you or them, I swear by this world and by the next, my brother Harun.'

Ali-Hodja was waiting for me in the street, he hung back respectfully while I conversed with the shadow of the dead. I would have liked to avoid meeting him, particularly now, agitated as I was after the burial, but it was not possible. Fortunately he was serious, and kind, even though strange – as always. He expressed his sympathy and advised patience, for me and for everyone, because of the loss, and it was everybody's loss, even though it was also a gain, for the dead may sometimes be more useful than the living, and they are such as we need them, they do not grow old, they do not quarrel, they do not have their own opinion, they agree to be our silent soldiers, they will not betray us, until they are called under another flag.

'Do you see me?' I asked him. 'Do you know me?'

'I see you and I know you. Who does not know Sheik Nurudin?'

He did not despise me, I was no longer like air for him.

What did he expect from me, considering his admission that I existed?

Hassan and Sinahudin, the jeweller, paid for a tombstone to be put above the coffin, and for a beautiful iron fence around it.

Coming back after the evening prayers, on the first Friday after the burial, I saw in the darkness a candle burning on Harun's tomb. Someone was standing by it.

I came nearer and recognized Mula Jusuf, he was reading the prayer.

'Did you light the candle?'

'No, I didn't. It was burning when I came.'

It had been put there and lit by a pair of human hands, for the peace and for the memory of the slain.

Ever since, on the eve of every holy day candles have burned on the tombstone.

I always stopped in the darkness and looked at the small quavering lights, agitated, touched at first, and later proud of them. This was my ex-brother, it was his pure soul glittering, it was his shadow bringing unknown people here, to light these tender fires to keep his memory alive.

He became the memory of the town after his death. While he was alive, hardly anyone knew him.

To me he was a blessed memory. In his lifetime he had only been my brother.

Translated by Svetozar Koljević

Gregor Strniša

THE VIKINGS

1 THE COMING

The ships came sailing through the grey-red morning.
The sea was dark, sails heavy in the wind.
Shadowy figures leapt over the gunwales
and swam and paddled to the distant strand.

A great cloud covered the eastern sky.
There was a heavy stench in the air of salt.
Each shadow held a sword in front of it,
sliding the flat blade through the turbid water.

Like the shadow of a wave that rises and falls back,
they quickly walked up the unknown strand.
The morning world was calm and very wide,
the sea dark, sails heavy in the wind.

2 THE CASTLE

The castle, laden with weapons and pale faces,
with bolts and chains down in deep cells,
with gold in the tower. The castle with flag flying,
gold needles gripped in maidens' childlike palms.

Like the shadow of a wave that rises and falls back,
amid the clangour of swords they have passed on.
The sky is very high, with a lone cloud
and a small green sun.

The cloud changes shape, now half a man,
now wings without bird, now an empty mitten.
Tiny ships go rowing, slowly, over the sea.
No wind. Beyond the horizon a storm whispers.

3 THE SHIP

From a cold country of ice and moss,
From a country of night and snow,
see how she comes, she comes,
the long ship over the grey sea.

One day the sea turns blue.
She sails by an island where cuckoos call in the woods.
On the far horizon a piled white cumulus glows,
along the shore stand high mountains, cities and towers.

How slowly she sails, how she comes
along the long green shore.
The blackened dragon's head high on the prow
glitters with gold in the southern sun.

4 THE LION

A southern city with carved and gilded bars. Behind them
whispers, the rustle of heavy gowns, a lion's cage in a palace garden.
There he lies, like a desert in the dusk, the lion with heavy eyes,
as if the rest of the world's eyes were brimming inside them.

Like the shadow of a wave that rises and falls back,
amid the clangour of swords they have passed through the city
    streets
A cloud in the night sky spins in the wind and changes,
the uncaged lion slowly paces the streets.

The dark ships dwindle, disappear in the glint of the sea.
A big, yellow shadow moves noiselessly through the gloom.
High in the sky a flying cloud is engaged in a duel
with the tiny, quicksilver moon.

5 GOLD

Far south they sailed in search of fiery gold.
Their homeland was empty and cold.
Ravens perched on the roofs of the huts,
wolves came up to their doors at night.

Many gave their lives for the gold,
their homeland was empty and cold.
Shores, islands, woods where the cuckoos sing –
deep down on the sea bed the long ship lies.

Dark ships on the sea bed, keeled on their sides,
like the shades of warriors from countries of snow and night,
sliding deeper and deeper in their search for fiery gold –
down to the world's mighty heart.

BROBDINGNAG

I

Bright sun over Lilliput,
winter gloom over Brobdingnag.
Gentle sea before Lilliput,
before Brobdingnag a stone tower.

Fortresses, mills, giants.
Thunder and lightning in the sky.
Between the mountains over Brobdingnag
hangs the iron sickle of the moon.

Sometimes the mountain rumbles like a shield.
The eyes of children see horrors.
Their dreams are guarded by a magic sign
carved on their cradles.

II

In a border fortress on a high cliff
is a young giant with three eyes.
When the spring snow melts
he stares into the valley below.

Sun and shadows on the mountain slopes.
No man or beast in sight.
Now and again his iron-hooped chest
gives out a quiet ping.

He steps forward and stands firm
on the steep and topmost parapet.
The plain's glitter in the distance,
the humming of bees down below.

III

The glowing fires of Brobdingnag
beneath the moon with red eyes.
The ring of steel in smithies,
smoke rising to peaks of white.

In Brobdingnag they have cast a bell
that echoes the heart of the world.
It hangs in a snow-filled valley.
Not a single man is there.

A whispering comes from out of the bell.
And when the bell's bronze quietly sings
fiery dreams in the heart of the world
are recalling an ancient sun.

IV

A wide cobbled road
Winding among the fortresses.
Higher and higher it climbs
but never comes to an end.

Thundering from mountain fortresses
comes the sound of drums and pipes.
Eagles perch upon precipices
and fly at dusk to the other side.

Below the road, in a muttering gorge,
a gigantic mill like a black dragon.
Beneath the mill, in a deep cellar
is all that world's golden treasure.

V

Unknown people of Brobdingnag,
triple-eyed, with triple heads,
and a big black god like the earth
with a name as long as a thousand days.

Five valleys, says the legend,
somewhere meet to form a sign of magic,
and there between five mountains
is the heart of Brobdingnag.

Is there there a lake of blue
or a glacier green perhaps?
All is known about Lilliput,
never a thing about Brobdingnag.

Translated by Veno Taufer and Michael Scammell

Miodrag Pavlović

WARRIORS' TALES

With our shields we flattened the walls
with our hooves the graves
in the afternoon we paved the fields
with red marble,
and when we heaved the palace into the abyss
the sea re-echoed blackly.
We were real heroes.

The homeward journey was long
we subdued the slave girls along the milky way,
at last we reached home
to flatten the walls with our shields
and our memories with our hooves.
We were real heroes.

Again we returned to the red marble
to seek younger slave girls.
A lofty city had arisen,
our shields buckled in;
they gave us bread and water
and killed us in the night like beggars.
Of course we came back in the morning
and sounded our trumpets beneath the walls.
We were real heroes.

THE DOGS MUSTER IN CNOSSOS

They yapped and howled round the walls
people like enraged hounds,
and we with our voices served as cover
to those who were making a getaway.
In the tumult they stopped locking the rooms
we chased each other over the royal beds
licked the oxen's horns
while the snakes hung over the bolts.
We had nothing to lose
We could scarcely wait to be owned again
otherwise the masters would eat us.
When the Dorians burst through the gates
they saw one of us on the throne
and their jaws dropped in amazement.
He had a long snout
and its shadow fell across their faces.

They plundered but gave us no meat
and we were demanding great freedom,
but we got only the king's corpse, in mockery
Should we eat it?
Why not,
we had even sat on his throne !
His flesh was as tough as old boots,
and his liver shrunken
Afterwards they came for us carrying chains
and threw us out to bay at the moon,
but the snakes fared even worse;
they grilled them on skewers
We had hoped for a better life
under the new masters.

THE STATUES' TESTIMONY

It's not easy for us to last either.
From the abyss of the skull of stone
we have passed into trembling webs of appearance;
in us the created crossbreeds, pain sears.

From night to night the stone quarries
call us like wolves to return
to the adamantine pack.

In the morning men drag us by the heels
from the temple frieze to come down into flesh
like distant relations helping in time of need.

But for us the transformations are completed;
Above the contrary confluences of being
we stand with unmoving eyes,
and the sun, before it opens its eyes
always touches our forms
to recall to itself the true face
of that world on which it bestows light.

A SLAVONIC SINGER BENEATH PARNASSUS

I wait for a new robe to be brought me.
My tribe came from afar, shepherds of fire,
and we offered up a torch on the funeral pyre of that people
turned to stone in the fire
and doused in the water of the flood.
Now we take the belts from the waists of the stone
and from its ashes we make pillows
but under our tongues a new warmth arises.

To the warmth of speech the enchanted rock opens
in which the hand finds out honey :
letter by letter returns to my memory
to clothe me in verse, word by word.
Sad are the temples, see, and the eyes of heaven,
they are thinking still of the courts and the courtiers of yore,
and those around me tell me to take off my surplice,
for divinity is no more, in vain I speak.

Come, then, tell me, was anyone at the gods' funeral?
Who saw eternity in its last agony, who?
Was it you, O night? Wait for the dawn on my shoulder !
Though the statues are broken,
You will see their shape on the hill
All shimmering in the light and sound.

I am already devising new names
for the immortals to take when they come down from the mountain,
and a young singer takes the primeval word in his hands
and lifts it to his forehead.

SVENTOVID SPEAKS

Still my empty necks itch
and my four severed heads
on the sea bed speak
Slavonic words.

Alas, I fell in the conspiracy
that was hatched
from Bethlehem to the Baltic
I am the victim of the migrant faith
that flew from the south on wings
to descend on the north with swords.

I was a divinity
and now I am a monster –
I was caught out of step in the transformation
between man and stone
and my fairhaired children
now sing hymns of praise to another.

See, even flowers last longer
than garlanded gods,
and man has hope after death
but for me there is no more hope.
Neither in slavery nor in battle
will anyone call for help
on a vanquished idol.

Bitter is the fate of gods
bitter the dependence on the race of men
which changes its smell and its faith together

Only the beemasters are left
to make honey in the trunks of tongues

BOGOMIL SONG

They're after my head.

Anything that looks like a head
they fling on heaps in the meadows
and trample with horses by night.
They sink shafts in the earth
and take out the veins of silver
which resemble a prophet's head,
and hang them on the oak trees.
Even the man-shaped clouds
they drag down with hooks and pierce with spears.

They're after my head
and they haven't even heard my word.
Like a viper without venom in my head
I lie in the impenetrable forests
unable to change my skin.
Oh you drunken princes
who spy on me from the ramparts
do you really think my speech
will go no further than the pools of my blood?
I am close to the earth,
who remembers words better than blood;
embracing the elder trees I will speak into her breast
all that I know of love.
Your sword is too small
to cut off the whole earth's head.

LAMENT FOR SMEDEREVO

We are left with no fortress and no law
the fortress has fallen.

We know not where our land begins,
but its end is everywhere.

The stronghold has fallen with our names,
the river has swept them away.

Armies and travellers pass over us,
but no one comes to us.

No more will there be fine fortresses
in our land.

Long nights we wish for, and deep forests,
where the sight is created before the eyes.

Let us sing and remember ourselves,
others have forgotten us.

And may the law of a constant heart reign
by the devastated fortress.

Translated by Anne Pennington

Bogomil Djuzel

MEAD

1

Mirages of blood above the sun's noontide grave
the liberated space begs for victims,
empty rattling-headed night, mules'
halters from the stars.
Now comes the high priest of our follies;
axis of life!
turn – let the dead rest in peace.
My head will be burnt by the sun,
my vigour and my body blackened;
with blood like this we shall reach sanctity.
The saint is drunk, invisible
we shall get to hell
with these devils of blood on our back.

2

There is no beginning of the heart;
a thousand dewy bodies shall we sacrifice to its altar;
time keeps silent, sand shifts,
rains will bring back my birth.
Neither buried beauty
which all the world has nourished
nor the sun in the bloodstream of birds, endures.
I put them aside.
These are your last mementoes of the world, martyrs.

O I am dead for those white daybreaks
of summers exhausted
in heavy chained tankards;

we wait for
the true drops from the sky
to fall on our skulls.

3

our fire burns low,
twice we bind them;
three lilies go out
three lilies, three soldiers
armed with lime and fog;
flare up stronger, pain;
our fire burns low,
slender pine trees do not hear our thunder.
Alas, it is late, late
even for death with open well-springs.

4

We shall fly on white steeds up to Istanbul
you can't help but escape;
madness stands before three hundred doors,
the first is fire, the second wind, the third
a blue silence which dashes us with waves.
Now the peasants come to run us down;
there's no escape for us,
save some strange wind;
will it come to human conflagrations?

Already there are no flowers for dying.
On the beach light feasts;
toys and people of rags –
but the heart has golden scabbards,
scabbards of dead kings.

I shall rise to the surface
like a gun with four throats.

TROY

The gates of the city flew open
and in came the wind – like someone
who has long kept the siege, like
an empty lost soul of a victor
who after the victory expects nothing;
senseless idle gust, sauntering
along the streets and worn
away by the corners; beggar's breath
looking for warmth and crusts of bread.
Only the cobbles moaned
and the palaces shivered.

Then the wind brought people
who have thrown away their ploughs
to rust; let them till the sky, alone
and reap the harvest of the summer night,
with fat grains of early rising stars
and let them leave it unwinnowed.
Instead the people started with their swords
the deep seasonal ploughing in bodies
with the unmistakable furrow to the heart
plucking it out like a rooted stump,
bursting the gall-bladder, and with the liver
feeding vultures roosting on their shoulders;
rolling at last the skulls like stones
usable only for building, but for that,
as always, never enough time.

Mothers parted from their children
until the milk and the cry dry up;
streets watered by pipes
of torn-out arteries still pulsing,
and hastily slain sacrifices

with the hope of nothing better
but to turn the temples into sties
with the inevitable familiar stench.

The wind untied the bells and the flags
and with its whirling tail
passed like a broom through the city
and bumped into the gong of the sun.

Translated by Bogomil Djuzel and Howard Erskine-Hill

Ivan V. Lalić

INSCRIPTION IN THE SEA'S SILVER

And yet we were once so close
Beside our birthplace,
                              just on the other side
Of the arrested air; we used to listen
To swift-winged words, sense perceived
In lightning's crude translation;
Frightened we fled into time's
Illusion, into false equilibrium –
The truest pictures recalled are at waking:
Wild fig and chestnut tree, the slow flame
In the ruins;
                  all we call memory
Shines on the tip of a long bright needle
Where the taste of fire is mixed with the silence
In the air up above the shortlived silver
Of the sea between storms.

THE DARK PROVINCE

A rustling like crumbling shingle
In a long tunnel,
                      the clatter of broken hooves,
We clutch at voices, at shoulders
In the dark of the ultimate world;
                              drops of light break through,
The wick is fed by the thin oil of memory, others,
We ride under roots, under years,

We share our portion of bitter poppy with hungry shadows,
Our faces frighten us, far off, at the exit;

Here somewhere all roads cross
Somewhere before the final parting, and beasts' tracks mingle
With tracks of angels at the centre's awesome stillness:
He who stops here will repent his choice,
He who goes on will repent his choice.

MADMAN-PROPHET

The years of anger are coming,
The drops of fire are singing
Born on the wind of storm,

The measure of time runs out
And the sand of the world's deserts
Slips down to the lower abyss,

The bird remembers the wave
Whence its movement began,
Form remembers formlessness,

The tongue remembers voices
Mingled with pollen hovering
Over the first shoreline,

And ice remembers the flame
Where it dwelt mixed
with rose, eye and rains,

And lovers start in their sleep
touching each other with fingers
of the same memory,

For in it is parting
And the fine measure of ash
Which will never mingle;

And all this hums and murmurs
Under this firm cupola
Where echoes assemble together,

In this festering hearing,
In this doomed head,
In this overfull flesh,

For I am destined to see
The springs of this memory
Which returns all things to their source

Like seas taking the heavenly path
Like a name falling asunder
In a swarm of innocent voices :

Born on the wind of storm
The drops of fire are singing,
The years of anger are coming.

SMEDEREVO

We raised up a town, Ivoje, a city of stone
And we moistened the shadows of square-sided towers
In the wide grey river. Now the town's on the right bank
The wind's on the left. Autumn has come
And behind us the rain has rusted the woods.
The people are guards at night at the gates
Under arms, and dark in armour like scarabs,
Warming their frozen hands at the red-glowing fires,

We wait, and with us the twenty-four towers
Exposed to time, as to rain, we here
Think we shall not be forgotten, ever,
We in the last town on the river's right bank,
Though we shall not turn to stone neath its towers,
Sufficient that we are those who wait, listening,
To the echo of thousands of hooves, which grows in the night
Beneath the indifferent stars. Our Lord the Despot
Drinks wine that is gold like the carp in the river,
But his beard has grown grey like his ancestors' glory;
May God grant him a most glorious ending.
We are the last. If we sleep neath these towers
Who will awake us? The fires burn low.
The town on the right bank, the wind on the left.

THE STONEMASONS

DUBROVNIK

In the stone is measure and the language of earth
Fragmented in the voices of chisels searching
For themselves in an echo of dust, like children's voices
Amidst the raindrops; sometimes we caught
A cry or a word, we cut it short
And planted it upright in air. We found the measure of walls,
The lament of battlements, laughter and vines,
The movement of beasts which emerged from the stone
Like a star from the sea; guiltless, washed clean –

We measured the stone with a yardstick of iron,
With our imperfect adoration;
                              we rendered
That unknown tongue into known forms,
And proclaimed that most silent concord
With the firmer measure of substance;

Then the earth trembled –
Somewhere there was an error,
which was not clear
In the glimmer of dust settling, and a language fusing
With its beginnings like water;

When the blood had dried
We began to try again.

IN PRAISE OF DUBROVNIK

The ash of a tongue in a dead mouth
Is honey in the tree to the chronicler's lips,
History dies without stone –

So the sea has sung around the town
In the south wind, the wind of winter fruit
In the spear-shaped leaves, it sings in the foam
Beneath the towers' fundaments:
but the falseness begins

In the first stone word of the translation
Of that speech into your speech, town,
Beauty with no comparative dictionary,
The uncreatable created.

Handful of pure cinders,
The flame reforms you in a new mouth;
That which is lost without measure
Returns as a measure
To repose in your name like honey in the comb.

Translated by Ivan V. Lalić and Bernard Johnson

Danilo Kiš

GARDEN, ASHES

In this new setting, my father's behaviour altered somewhat. I say
somewhat, for the change was due rather to the surroundings, the
scene, than to any profound modification of his character. It
simply was that, up till that time, I had had no chance of observing
my father; my curiosity in that respect had been completely handi-
capped by his continual absences, by what I would call his conscious sabotaging of my Oedipean inquisitiveness. For who would
say that my father did not purposely evade any kind of revelation
of himself, that he did not intentionally hide his personality behind
a mask, appearing from time to time as a writer, a chess-player, an
apostle, a flat-foot? To tell the truth, he played an unworthy part
before me, and lacked the courage to show his real face, but was
always changing his mask, hiding in one role or another, always
a histrionic one, and, lost in the labyrinth of the city, mixing in the
crowds of felt-hats and bowlers, he was, thanks to this mimicry,
quite screened from my gaze.

When he came into the country, my father could no longer conceal himself. Suddenly, one day in spring, in the course of one of
his sprees, I beheld him in his true dimensions: he was walking
along the dike beside the swollen river, returning quite unexpectedly, after six days' absence, when we were already thinking he
had come to grief in Baron's Wood or had run away again after his
star. In that moment, as he walked along the dike in his black
frock-coat, swinging his stick high in the air, rolling in his gait like
the mast of a ship, with his yellowed celluloid collar and his steel-
rimmed spectacles, gazing into space – in that moment, my father
fitted into the landscape as into a picture-frame, and quite lost his
air of mystery. Not wishing to be noticed – for he must have seen
me from some distance – he hid his hard-brimmed hat under his
arm and tried to slip past me without being seen. He was indeed a

sorry sight : without his hat, that dignified hieratic headgear, his ash-grey hair parted in the middle, stumbling along, a stocky, flat-footed figure, he seemed diminished in stature, unremarkable. I didn't venture to call out to him. The river was swollen with the spring torrents and I was afraid I might rouse him from his som-nambulist-like trance, real or feigned, and cause him to fall into the stream. I thought it better to step to one side and let him pass me. He literally brushed me with the flying skirts of his frock-coat, almost overpowering me with the smell of tobacco, alcohol and urine, but his face remained perfectly blank. In those bare natural surroundings like a frame of new, untrimmed boards, his face showed up clearly, his magnificent nose covered like a piece of old blotting-paper with a network of tiny red and purple veins. Re-moved from the baroque frame of town gateways and the lighted entrances of pretentious middle-class hotels, he now appeared no more than life-size, and quite lost his power of mimicry. For it would have been too great an effort for him – the chess-champion, the writer, the world-traveller, the apostle – to start playing the part of a peasant or a wood-cutter. Of course, it was not only pride which prevented him (as he liked to persuade himself), but really complete physical exhaustion and weakness; otherwise, who knows, he might have donned peasant dress and continued to hide behind yet another mask. Recently officially deprived of his status, that of a pensioned railway head-inspector, a loss which also entailed financial consequences, he had found a perfect excuse for his sprees; he gave himself up completely to drink, and went spreading an-archistic ideas round the countryside and sometimes singing the Internationale. Soon he became known throughout the district as a dangerous revolutionary anarchist, a poet and a crackpot, but he was still respected in certain circles on account of his clothes, his frock-coat, walking-stick and hat, and on account of his rhapsodic monologues, full of fine phrases, and his impressive booming voice. He was particularly admired by the landladies of village inns, whose very appearance inspired him, and drew out of him the golden strains of his lyrical inventiveness and sense of gallantry. Thanks to these Muses, whose eyes sparkled at him from behind the bar-counter, though they understood neither his words nor his songs, he managed to preserve his integrity and indeed his skin, for it was they, those plump bucolic Muses of his oratorical flights, who saved him from the police, let him out by secret doors, and defended him from the village brawlers whose glory as drinkers and singers he quite eclipsed. Standing on a table, high above them all, like a monument to some great orator and demagogue, he would take a sip of wine from someone else's glass, spit it out at once on the floor, then, half-closing his eyes, as if recollecting something, he would tell the year of the wine, its alcoholic strength, the species of vine and its exposure to the sun, direct or indirect, and the district from which it came. The effect was always prodigious. Suspecting the possibility of an understanding between my father and his Calliopes and Euterpes, the peasants would bring bottles of wine in their pockets, to try to show him up and discredit him. But he would spit out the wine even quicker than usual, with an expression of god-like indignation on his face, like a conjuror if someone should peep into his sleeve just as he was plunging the sharp steel blade into his heart. 'Gentlemen,' he would say, 'a mere novice wouldn't be taken in by your tricks. You try to cheat me, gentlemen, with faked Tokay from Lendava, as you might a raw youth with forged banknotes. The presence of that lady' – here my father bowed towards Madame Clara, who the moment he entered the tavern had taken up her position on the Captain's bridge, gripping the lever of the beer-engine like the spoke of the helm of a ship, which raises the waves' foam – 'the presence of that lady, I say, alone restrains me from spitting out this wine in the face of your suspicions and renouncing my claim to be an authority, in protest against your insinuations, and so dispersing this fairground atmosphere and the banally rational suspiciousness with which you would degrade everything which is of superior quality. . . . But I'll proceed more indirectly, to expose your base doubts still further, and show up your ignorance even more in that moment, in that great and shameful moment when I tell you what this wine is made of, what gives it its false sparkle, its twopenny-halfpenny imitation of excellence, when I unfold under your noses the artificial rose of its bouquet, the flimsy tinsel of its ruby shade, the false rouge of its complexion, which I have just touched with my lips, – remaining, gentlemen, astounded at the degree of refined cunning with which these people attempt to counterfeit the intoxicating fragrance and virginal fire of true Tokay . . .'

This was only the first act of the comedy which my father put on of an evening in the village inns; or rather, only one item of his full programme, into which he put all the fire of his delirious inspiration, all his genius, all his turbulent eloquence and his vast and varied erudition. He would take to singing only when provoked, and one had the impression that he only sang in order to put the village brawlers out of countenance. He would burst out all of a sudden, with such force that the glasses rattled on the bar-counter and in the cupboards; other singers were all silenced, not even venturing to hum an accompaniment lest they should appear ridiculous in the eyes of the ladies and the rest of the company. My father had a large repertoire of sentimental love-songs, old ballads and barcarolles, popular songs, jigs and czardasi, arias from operas and musical comedies, which he would sometimes follow with dramatic recitatives, but in his interpretations the sentimentality of the words and melodies seemed to acquire the brightness of a major key, and their saccharine content would crystallize in the silver chalice of his voice, becoming crisp and bell-like. He introduced new subtleties into the tearful tremolo singing of the *fin-de-siècle*, clearing it of its false Biedermayer sensibility and prudery; he sang without *glissandi*, with all his lungs, manfully, but not without warmth. Undoubtedly this was due in the first place to the quality of his voice, its timbre, which did not permit of trivial melodic grace-notes, but surged forth in great waves, breaking slightly, like the sound of a horn.

The third act of Father's long performances, which lasted for days and even weeks, like an Elizabethan pageant, always ended pitiably, like some tragic farce. He would wake up in a ditch, mottled with bruises he could not account for, covered with mud, his trousers wet and splashed with vomit, without a farthing in his pocket or a single cigarette, and with a devilish thirst in his belly and an insatiable impulse to commit suicide in his soul. Like some ageing harlequin, he picked up his pitiful properties from the mud, his stick, his hat, his spectacles, fumbled in his pocket in the hope of finding at least a cigarette-end, the last in his life, and then began to try to reckon up the sorry account of his evenings and of his life, adding up from the bottom. As he could not recall even how and when he got the bruises which he found on himself, he tried to decipher the figures noted down in his own handwriting on the empty box of Symphonies. The thick column of figures, suffering the fate of all fundamental reckonings, now rose before him like an excavated Egyptian obelisk covered with the hiero-glyphs of his own writing – figures whose meaning he had completely forgotten.

And now at last my father was outside the frame of that drama or farce of which he himself was the author, producer and chief actor; now he was stripped of every mask, an ordinary mortal, a famous singer without the organ-pipe of his voice, without his dramatic gestures, a genius in the hour when he is forgotten by his Muses and goddesses, a clown without his make-up and his false nose; his frock-coat and his famous properties lay thrown across a chair – the hard celluloid collar, now as yellow as an old domino, the black tie, like a head-waiter's, with its large artist's bow. The room stank of drink, defecation and tobacco. On a chair by the bed stood a large enamel ashtray advertising SYMPHONY. A tarnished silver cigarette-case. Matches. A large clumsy watch with an old-fashioned dial and Roman numerals ticked some mythical time, communicating its vibrations to the wooden seat. Behind his frock-coat thrown over the chair, behind that black curtain which hid the inglorious relics of the famous artist, rose a line of blue smoke, first straight, then spiralling like a corkscrew. Although he looked as though he had been dead a long time, his Symphony was still burning on the ashtray. The column of ash was slowly crumbling.

And where, if you please, was his famous hat?

In his hat, which stood on the table like a black vase, there lay decomposing a kilogram of beef which he had bought six days before at Bakša and carried in his hat from tavern to tavern pressed under his arm. This was the sixth day. And the meat was covered, like a corpse, with a swarm of flies and a bumblebee, whose buzzing sounded like distant, very distant, bells ringing.

Lying there, with his chin pointing upwards, half-dead, his jaws relaxed, his lips loose, his Adam's apple emitting some half-strangled guttural consonants, thick and aspirated, my father evoked compassion. Without the emblems of his dignity, the walking-stick which was his sceptre and the bowler-hat his crown, without his glasses and severe expression of serious meditation, his face revealed its anatomy of skin and veins, the blackheads on his prominent manly nose, the relief-map of his wrinkles which until then I had believed were only the mask of the martyr and apostle. It was, however, a hard, rough crust, pockmarked and sticky as though smeared with grease-paint, and threaded with tiny purple veins. There were great bags under his eyes like blisters full of lymph. His arm, like a mummy's, lay alongside him on the bed, the guardian of his body, a sleeping sentinel, the fist clenched in a gesture of defiance – the last insult my father could think of – to shake his fist in the face of the world and of the dreams in which he no longer believed.

The next day, coming to himself, but still muzzy, and tortured by an infernal thirst which he tried to quench with water like a house on fire, he would attempt to recover his dignity, putting on his tie in front of the mirror hastily, as one puts in false teeth. He would go off without a word to us, taking up his inspired monologue once more, and return late in the evening, without our knowing where he had been. Later the peasants and shepherds would tell us that they had seen him in the heart of Baron's Wood, ten kilometres or so from the village, or perhaps even in more distant, 'foreign' parts. He only came home to shave, change his collar and have a sleep, and he spoke to nobody and refused to eat anything, fearing that we should poison him. He fed on fungi in the woods, sorrel and wild apples, and sucked birds' eggs, which he extracted from the nests with the crook of his stick. Later, in the course of the summer, we used to come upon him here or there in the fields, unexpectedly; his black bowler would emerge from the ripe corn, the sun would glint on his spectacles. He would stride through the fields, deep in meditation, swinging his stick high, walking like a somnambulist, following his star, which he would lose among the sunflowers and find again at the end of the cornfield – on his own greasy black frock-coat.

My father's lonely wanderings inevitably aroused the suspicions of the peasants and the local authorities. By arrangement with the local gendarmerie and with the collusion of the Mayor and the church dignitaries, the national civil defence corps and the village (Fascist) youth organizations took upon themselves the painful task of investigating my father's secret mission, the reason for his wanderings and changes of role. They began to follow him, to listen secretly to his soliloquies and send in reports on them, often very much travestied and malicious, put together from the somnambulistic fragments which fell from my father's lips and, carried by the wind and air currents, reached the ears of the eavesdroppers torn from their context and quite bereft of any probability. For without doubt my father's soliloquies were as inspired as the prophetic books, they were apocalyptic parables, full of pessimism, an endless song of songs, a torrential, eloquent, rhapsodic and unrepeatable Jeremiad, the fruit of his many years' experience, of his insomnia and meditation, the heavy, over-ripe fruit of his inspired, mystically illumined spirit at the height of its powers. The prayers and vows of a Titan opposing the Gods mingled with pantheistic psalms (based undoubtedly on the philosophy of Spinoza, the source of my father's ethics and aesthetics), but it must not be supposed that in his oral flights of creation, which had their origins in far-distant history, in the Biblical era of the Semitic tribes, there were no lyrical cadences, and that it was all, as might at first appear, limited to a dry Spinozan variant of Semitic philosophy. Not at all. In direct contact with nature, among the lacework of the ferns and the needles of the fir trees, surrounded by resinous scents and the songs of blackbirds and chaffinches, my father's philosophy underwent a remarkable transformation. Especially as compared with the principles and style set forth in the so-called 'Railway Guide' of 1939, which remains, alas, the chief and indeed the only printed manual for the study of his pantheism. (His philosophy began to lose its cold rationalism, its arguments were more and more reduced to lyrical proofs, no less powerful, and indeed more acceptable, shrewder and more certain. The ballast of difficult erudite matter fell away; the learned process of thesis and antithesis, from thesis to proof, became easy, almost imperceptible, when accompanied by the resinous fragrance of the fir trees, and *quod erat demonstrandum* fell into its right place at the right moment, like an acorn from the tree, while false and unproved assertions withered like branches and fell with a crash, like warnings, witnesses to reason and measure.) Fundamentally, my father was a modern variant of the pantheistic hermits and wandering philosophers, a personality similar to Zoroaster, but conscious every moment of the demands of the times, located in space with absolute certainty, never for a moment losing his bearings: hence his clinging to his frock-coat and bowler-hat: the time of hermits in rags had gone for ever. For the same reason he was so attached to his watch with its Roman numerals on the dial – it showed him the *right time*, wiping out the difference between the natural and the calendar year and even serving as an example and a warning lest he should involve himself in some super-temporal or non-temporal philosophical excursus which disregarded the burning problems of the day.

Contrary to all expectations, it was the Church which regarded my father with most suspicion. The civil authorities took down in shorthand the reports of their spies and stored them in Father's already thick dossier with a certain contemptuous indifference, being quite uninterested, for on the top of the whole confused and voluminous file lay a doctor's certificate that my father was of unsound mind, which released them from all immediate responsibility. Nevertheless, the authorities were waiting for some outbreak of his which would definitely compromise him and give them an occasion to get rid of him without unpleasantness. The Church, however, already had firm evidence of his destructive and blasphemous activities. The fact that he was a mystic, a visionary and, quite simply, mad, was for the Church only a proof of his lucidity, of his trafficking with the dark powers, for in the opinion of the clergy, he was nothing but a sinner, an unclean spirit, through whose lips spoke Satan himself as through a medium. It was said, and even declared from the pulpit, that the touch of his stick with its iron ferrule had magic power, that wherever he passed in Baron's Wood the trees withered like grass, that his spittle produced a deadly poisonous fungus – *Ithyphallus Impudicus* – which borrowed the appearance of the homely edible mushroom. Soon the whole business of spying on my father was taken over by the 'Sisters of the Third Order', half-crazy village devotees who in reward for their services wore a rope round their waists with three huge knots; they were bigoted widows who quenched the lusts of the flesh with prayers and fasting, sickly and hysterical females in whom sexual desire found expression in religious trance and superstition. By agreement with the village curate, they trailed in my father's steps, following him at a discreet distance. He, naturally, noticed nothing, and recited his psalms with his usual fervour, gazing unseeingly at the ferns and birds' nests. Louisa, my father's most devoted sleuth, sometimes took down his words, sentences and fragmentary phrases, clumsily, licking the bit of copying-pencil till her lips were as purple as blackberries. With the diligence of a demented fanatic, a 'Sister of the Third Order' and a war widow, she followed my father's every movement, copied down in her notebook the 'mysterious signs' which he described in the air with his stick, marked the trees against which he made water, to find them next day 'black and withered, as if struck by lightning from heaven'. Filling his mouth with sorrel and setting his tie straight, my father would push his stick into the soft earth, balance his hat on his stick, like a pagan setting up an idol, then turn to the west and, lifting up his hands, recite his hymn to the setting sun, second of gods in the hierarchy of my father's religion (the first being the Sun First-Created, the Sun-Elohim, He who appears in the east in the morning, and who is a divinity of the first order, at once Father and Son); then he would draw himself up and begin to sing, to chant, lucid and inspired, a pantheistic genius whose language became the divine word, a song of songs, and in the distance the woods would soon begin to crackle and to blaze with fire ...

The evidence against my father continued to pile up. The civil authorities, under pressure from the Church, had at last to do something about it. But as they had no actual *corpus delicti*, they contented themselves with giving the Christian Youth of the village a free hand. The authorities had decided to wash their hands of all the dirty work, and to appear only when my father was already nailed to the cross. The intervention of the authorities would be confined to a formal report and, perhaps, if necessary, to the interrogation of a few witnesses, and in the last resort to a very short imprisonment of one of those who had taken part in the lynching. They had already found a volunteer for this purpose, one Tot, who would consent to spend a week in jail, on condition that they didn't arrest him till ten days after the event, for in the meantime he had to plough his field. From the accounts of Father's watchers and spies, the conspirators knew more or less his exact timetable, they were acquainted with all his habits, even with what might be called his personal, private life, if such an expression were not in contradiction to his very unselfish mission and altruistic intentions and proceedings. But the fact was that they knew that my father had not given up any of his habits, and that he tried not to lose the attributes of a modern man, lest he should become a philosopher-Bohemian or a village hermit. In the details of his dress, in his regular taking of food three times a day at certain fixed hours, in his afternoon siestas and so on, he endeavoured to conform to the modern European way of life, to remain faithful to the demands of the times, without regard for the hard conditions of wartime and his own isolation. So it came about that they surprised him in his sleep, among the bracken, just when he was beginning to snore magnificently, which convinced them that he was sound asleep, and that therefore his magic, demonic powers were asleep also. He lay on his back, his arms stretched wide, as if he were crucified; his tie was loosened and there were ants crawling about his forehead and flies sipping sweet wild almond and spurge-wort juices at the corners of his mouth. Beside him, within reach, his magic stick was stuck into the ground, hardly showing above the tall bracken, and on it balanced his hard-brimmed black hat, a little to one side like the helmet on the Unknown Warrior's gun, or a scarecrow in the maize.

'Who disturbs the sleep of the righteous?' exclaimed my father rhetorically as he sat up.

He was perfectly calm, at any rate in appearance, when he felt a double-barrelled gun pressing against the small of his back in the shape of a horizontal figure eight. The peasants, armed with stout sticks, breathless and dirty, came creeping up through the bracken. Louisa stood nearest to my father, her eyes blazing, crossing herself busily. Under her feet lay Father's stick, trampled on like a poisonous snake. Father looked perfectly calm and his voice never trembled for an instant. He bent down to pick up his hat, and looked round for his stick. Then all at once he began to fidget, to shift his weight awkwardly from one foot to the other, like a duck, and his hands started trembling like a drunkard's. He began carefully stroking his hat, to hide the panic agitation which was coming over him as he saw that he had been disarmed, then he fumbled in his pocket for a Symphony.

'Look out, Tot, he may have a gun,' cried someone.

But my father had already taken his hand from his pocket, and they could all see the bit of newspaper he put to his nose to wipe it. (All excitement caused great disturbances in his metabolism and a plentiful secretion of fluids. I knew that, if he came out of this alive, the first thing he would do would be to go and make water behind a bush, breaking wind vigorously as he did so.) A woodpecker was drumming somewhere overhead, unseen: tap-tap-tap, tip-tip-tip, tap-tap-tap, tiptiptiptip, and perhaps it sounded like a bad omen. I saw that my father heard it, for he almost imperceptibly turned his head to that side, as if to decipher the Morse-code message. My father, after his bankruptcy, had begun to work as a railway clerk at Šid, so Morse held no secrets for him. He was easily able to take in the ciphered message of the Morse-woodpecker and translate it for himself more or less accurately, – not literally, but rather like a love-letter in illegible handwriting. And that, I think, except for what he took down at Šid railway-station long before I was born, was the only message he ever received in cipher. And all they told about my father's having a radio receiver-transmitter with which he sent messages in cipher to the Allied planes that flew over the village, was most probably nonsense. And it was only my desire to see him in a heroic light, and not only in the role of a saint and martyr, which gave my imagination a faint hope: that he had sat there, flat-footed as a goose, but a great actor, hero and martyr, there in the heart of Baron's Wood, in a cave, with ear-phones on his ears and his fingers on the keyboard : ti, ti-ti-ti-ti, ti ti titititi, suddenly all-powerful, holding in his hands the fate of humanity, directing with his messages squadrons of Allied bombers which at one signal of his could wipe out whole villages and towns, leaving not a stone standing, turning all into dust and ashes. Unfortunately, all this was not so much the result of my suspicions of my father's possible heroism, as of sheer fantasy. (For I have inherited from my father an inclination for the unreal : I have lived, as he did, on the moon. But he was also a fanatic – he believed in the possibility of realizing his fantasies and fought passionately for them. I have lain in the shed at Farmer Molnar's, where I minded the cows, lain on the fragrant, new-mown hay, and felt the Middle Ages on my senses. The rattle of armour, the scent of lilies and half-naked slave-girls – all very bookish. The fluttering of green muslin on the head of the fair betrothed – Julia – her hands heavy with rings. The trumpet call, the creaking of the hinges and chains of the castle drawbridge. I would keep my eyes closed another two or three seconds, and then I should be standing in front of Farmer Molnar, my employer, white-faced in my short green hempen pants : 'Yes, Mr Molnar, I got you. Chop the mangolds up fine and tie up the calf.' And I would be thinking : 'Nay, Your Majesty, I accept not such conditions. They are servile. We shall fight with sabres !')

My father was beginning to lose his self-possession. He was looking more and more pitiable.

I saw that the whole force of his body and mind was concentrated in a mighty effort to hold back his diarrhoea. He pressed his lips, and looked in the direction of the bushes, helplessly, fearing the worst. As he had recognized, in spite of the false beard the man was wearing, the mayor of the village, who had come in disguise to this compromising place where a serious crime was likely to take place, my father turned to him, and to him alone, looking on the others with contempt and completely ignoring them, and began explaining to him in outline, though actually very confusedly, his pantheistic principles, with which all such feeble inventions as Morse's had absolutely no connexion. 'If these gentlemen had accused me,' he began, trembling on the verge of distraction and addressing the feigned commercial traveller, who was trying to hide behind the crowd, unmasked and shamed – 'if they had accused me of collaborating with the birds of heaven, of ill-intentioned and tendentious meddling in the life of Nature and her mysteries, even with the purest pantheistic intentions of winning her and forcing her into an alliance with Man, who indeed is not worthy of her friendship – I should understand their accusations. But the gentlemen are wrong! For what possible connexion have I with their senseless accusations and with these perjurors who attribute to me such human, alas! all too human, acts of mischief? None at all, gentlemen! (Turning at last to the crowd): I am only preaching in my temple, in the woods, my religion, which, unfortunately, has as yet no followers, but which will one day appear again among men and its temple will be raised here (pointing with his finger), just here, where you are preparing to commit a hideous crime. Therefore, gentlemen, carry out quickly what is in your minds, found the new powerful faith, the religion above all others, enthrone by your acts the first saint and martyr of the Religion of the Future. My tortured and helpless body is at your disposal, and my spirit, philosophically speaking, is ready for crucifixion. Carry out, I repeat, what is in your minds, and the consequences will be far-reaching. A crowd of pilgrims from all over the world will tread with their bare feet the paths to this temple which already shines out in my mind and will be raised over my grave. Tourism, gentlemen, will flourish like tares in the cornfields. Therefore, proceed, if you have proofs in your hands and clear consciences before the One who sees all. (After a short pause): As I see that you hesitate, and that my personal fate has touched you, the fate of a husband and the father of two helpless children – (his wild gaze sought me in the crowd) – let us settle this misunderstanding, gentlemen, like gentlemen. ...' His eloquence and demagogic passion did not desert him even in that critical moment. At first the peasants impatiently and timidly waved their sticks in his face, interrupting his speech with curses and oaths, but his rhetoric overwhelmed them, and they soon began to listen, without understanding anything, except the fact that it was a genius who was speaking to them, a holy idiot, and they, especially on account of the puzzling presence of the 'commercial traveller' (in whom they had themselves recognized the representative of the authorities and who had finally removed his false beard so as to be less compromised), agreed to Father's conditions: that if they should find the radio-station in the bush indicated by the 'Sister of the Third Order', they might hang him on the nearest tree or crucify him like Jesus or one of the thieves, but if they did not find it, they should leave him in God's peace, and give him back his stick so that he might go 'after his star'. The representative of the authorities, flattered by the fact that my father addressed especially to him the flowers of his rhetoric and invited him in particular to conclude the gentlemen's agreement, nodded, and all approached the incriminating bush. It was a beautiful flowering hawthorn, and it hid an old fox's lair. First they beat the tree with sticks, and the petals began to rain down like a snowstorm. Then they pulled out an old rusty stove-pipe, or the curved joint of one: the rust had already corroded the ribbing. ('There,' I thought in myself, 'that's how your father sent his Morse-code messages.') Tot pulled a cartridge-case out of his gun-barrel and stuffed it in his trousers pocket. He struck the stove-pipe with his stick as one strikes a snake on the neck. Its ribbing broke up with a crackling sound, not like the sound of metal.

'I'm not lying,' said the Sister of the Third Order, turning up her skirt to show the rope with its three knots tied round her waist. 'The Lord is my witness.'

At that moment the woodpecker again began sending his ciphered messages and the peasants hid their ropes under their coats. My father shifted from one foot to the other, and his troubled gaze searched the trampled fern like a hawk's. Suddenly he bent down and triumphantly retrieved his stick, straightened himself up, once more tall and strong, his physical balance regained, and tightened the knot of his tie (his stick hung on his arm); then with the ferrule of his stick he poked the rusty broken bend of the stove-pipe as one pokes a toadstool. Next, taking a scrap of newspaper from his pocket, he blew his nose violently, holding his head up like a cock about to crow, then carefully folded the newspaper into four, into eight, as though it held gold-dust, or aspirin. You'd think:

he's going to put it in his waistcoat pocket, beside his watch. Suddenly, however, he flung it far from him, to one side. The paper fluttered like a bird, struggling for a minute against the force of gravity, then dropped like a stone, and disappeared in the flowering hawthorn ...

My father had a habit of blowing his nose into bits of newspaper. He would cut up the pages of the *Neues Tageblatt* into four and keep them folded in the outside pocket of his coat. Then he would stand still in the middle of a field or somewhere in the wood, hang his stick on his left arm, and blow his nose like a hunting-horn. First vigorously, then twice more, more gently. You could hear him, especially in the wood, in the evening, a full mile away. Then he would fold up the piece of rather heretical newspaper and throw it away to the right, into the grass, among the flowers. And so sometimes, when I was minding Farmer Molnar's cows, far enough away from Baron's Wood, in places where I thought no man's foot ever trod, I would come across a yellowed bit of *Neues Tageblatt* and would think to myself in surprise: It's not long since my father came wandering in this direction too.

Two whole years after his departure, when it was clear to us that he would never come back, I found in a glade deep in Baron's Wood, among the grasses and gentian flowers, a piece of faded newspaper and I said to my sister Anna: 'Look, that's all that's left of our father.'

Translated by Mary Stansfield-Popović

Živko Čingo

FROM'S DAUGHTER

So here is Uncle From, all alone again. The Local Organization decided to take his daughter, Etja, away from him. They were afraid lest Uncle From's strange spirit should take root in her young heart.

Perhaps there have been braver and stronger men than Uncle From in our valley, yet in the whole of Paskvelija nobody is more deeply respected. This is certainly because he has never been heard to utter a false word. He has always spoken his mind and was never afraid of anyone. Of all the members of the Local Organization, he was the first to say exactly what he thought of the sacred Party conferences. 'I'd like to kick their guts in,' said Uncle From, 'I'd like to kick their guts in and shove them up their mother's ...' he kept on saying this and was not at all frightened. That was why people were wary of him, since it was not a time when one could speak one's mind openly. Only Uncle From could get away with it and he did just that. But then he was left all alone and it was hard to hear his voice any more. It seemed that he had lived in silence for days, weeks, even months. And like this he would leave his home towards evening and walk up and down along the ploughed fields. He could be seen, tall and gloomy like a tree, walking beside the fields for hours on end.

This was towards the end of February, at the very beginning of spring. Spring had not yet come to the village. First the warm south wind began to blow across the fields, making its noisy, untidy arrival heard for a whole day and a whole night. Its breath thawed out the trees into little bluish flames and it seemed that the orchards had begun to blossom, but that was only a momentary illusion for the little flames quickly detached themselves from the branches and rushed murderously towards the ground like meteors. All around the snow was shaken by their fiery explosions. The earth was unbuttoning its breast: spring was on its way. Perhaps that was why Uncle From came to the fields so often.

That spring a new life began in Paskvelija. First we took down the smaller barriers and then we cleared away the lattice fences. The river was declared collective property, we dug up boundaries and smashed the boundary stones, and brought in the first tractor to plough up the small and crowded plots. Everything became common and collective property. But the old men, our fathers and grandfathers, did not come to the fields the whole of that spring. They could not bear to hear the fences groaning. 'Let the young men get on with it,' they murmured. 'It's their job, we've lived our lives.' That is what they said, but of course in secret they cursed the collective and with it their foolish younger generation. But we mercilessly tore down the fences and even accompanied our work with resounding songs and slogans on our lips.

It was in those days that Uncle From used to visit us from time to time. Whenever he came, as if by mutual consent no one ventured to sing songs or utter slogans. He looked at us with his eager, brilliant eyes – you could not bear Uncle From's eyes on you for long. Their brilliance made us lower our heads and we wanted to hide from his gaze, and to run away from it like the worst kind of criminals. But he would keep on looking at us with his reddened eyes. Then we would hear his voice.

'Hey, lads, where's my Etja,' Uncle From used to say: 'Hey, lads, what's happened to my girl?' he kept asking. 'Where have you sent her, aren't you ever going to tell me?'

We went on pulling up the deeply entrenched boundary stakes in silence with our hands stuck in the ground as though held prisoner in the snow. The cold pierced right up into our veins.

'Hey there, lads, hey, my good lads,' Uncle From kept repeating, 'will you leave me on my own like this all my life?' Nobody spoke, nobody turned his head and even Comrade Lako looked completely lost, although he had no right to in his capacity as Secretary. But by now we were all troubled; we all kept silent. Uncle From stood a moment longer, and then, having received no reply, went off along the fields with that same gait, stooping and alone. He went off as if being carried along by the wind, as if being rolled along.

'Where's my Etja?' his voice came from all sides of the fields. But we knew nothing about Etja either. They took her away the very same day that Uncle From was expelled from all the Party organizations. That must have been how it happened because after that they all agreed to everything and were allowed to go home. It was the seventh evening that they had been locked up in the school-building. Those tired, haggard human faces looked like logs of wood. Their eyes, dull and yellowed, had begun to look wild; no one uttered a word nor moved from their seat. Seven days. And during those entire seven days there was only that weary but implacable voice of the man at the table, only that voice asking who knows how many times: 'Who will voluntarily apply to join the collective?' He went on asking and asking, yawning out loud.

In the school-room everything was covered in smoke and the bitter smell burned people's eyes. It was because of the raw walnut leaves everyone was smoking. At night they could hardly recognize each other, all that could be made out were those dark, human faces with the bitter walnut glow in their mouths. They smoked and kept silent.

It was as quiet as at a funeral. Only now and then the table of those presiding creaked, coldly and ominously. One of them cleaned his revolver with evident satisfaction. That was on the seventh day. It was the seventh day when Uncle From saw that lout with the revolver in his hands and could stand it no longer. Uncle From could never stand someone doing something like that. Then he became the real From. He got up from his seat, taller than ever before and said in that deep, clear voice of his: 'This is no good, comrades. It's better for everybody to just take care of their own work. It'll come about by itself.' That was what Uncle From said and they all raised their heads and nodded their agreement. But the men at the table jumped up sharply and vigorously.

'What's that, From,' said Antonie Aštalko, Secretary of the Regional Committee, 'You're suggesting are you From, that we should dissolve the collective? Is that what you want, my good comrade?'

'There's nothing to dissolve,' said Uncle From, and I think he even smiled; Uncle From was always ready to smile, that was his way of speaking. 'There's nothing to dissolve since we haven't yet organized anything,' he said, 'and nothing can be done by force. Not as long as people don't want it,' said Uncle From, and then he added: 'You can't just force people,' and he slowly sat down in his seat.

'From,' said Antonie Aštalko sternly: 'Do you realize what you're saying? It's a filthy slander, it's treachery, it's a blasphemy against our People's Government and our glorious Party. That's treason, From.'

Uncle From again rose from his seat and unhurriedly went up to those seated at the table. 'You, Comrade Aštalko,' he said in a slightly different tone, 'you, Antonie Aštalko, you can't speak to me like that. That's all I have to say to you.' Comrade Aštalko could not restrain himself, there was a derisive smile on his yellow, puffy, melon-like face and with mockery in his voice, scratching his thin, bristling moustache he asked: 'Do you want us to forgive you, From?' 'No,' said Uncle From, 'there's nothing to forgive.'

'You've turned traitor, From,' said the Secretary then, thrusting his face forwards, towards the people in front of him. 'You've turned traitor to the people. You've betrayed our Party by your action.' 'Don't take that tone with me,' repeated Uncle From. 'You can't speak to me like that,' and he wanted to add: 'You dirty bastard, Antonie Aštalko, I know you well, I've known you ever since Klenoec. I know very well how you shot yourself in the foot to get out of the fighting; we all knew that very well and you'd have been done for for sure if so many of our comrades hadn't been killed at Klenoec. You stayed somewhere in one of the villages. I know all that. And you've always been like that.' 'An accident,' Uncle From could still remember how Antonie Aštalko had tried to clear himself before the other comrades. 'It was an accident,' he kept saying with faked tears. 'I've known all about you for a long time, Antonie Aštalko.' But From did not say all that; he merely said in a hushed voice: 'Don't remind me of the war, Antonie Aštalko, don't smear the Party for me,' and looked the Secretary straight in the eyes. 'You have betrayed it,' said Antonie Aštalko in a similarly hushed tone. But then his power as Secretary re-asserted itself in his voice, he started to shout out one word after the other; 'You have betrayed it, you have trampled upon it,' he said, 'it will punish you as it punishes everyone who dares to set himself up against it. It will punish you without mercy.'

Uncle From went even closer up to the table and, looking steadily into the Secretary's eyes; 'The Party can't punish me, it knows what kind of person I am. You, Comrade Secretary,' said Uncle From to Antonie Aštalko, 'You, Comrade Secretary, speak much too arrogantly,' and he stood there in front of him, straight, tall and unperturbed.

That same evening Uncle From was expelled from the Party, excluded from all its organizations and Etja was taken away from him. It was terrible to see his face while the Secretary was reading out the resolution. He could not control himself. He shouted: 'People, comrades, brothers, fellow communists, you can't do this. The Party can't punish me like this. Look here, I carry the Party here!' Uncle From tore his shirt open all the way down to his heart. 'People, comrades, communists,' he repeated, 'sooner kill me, trample me to death, than take away from me the dearest thing I have in life.'

There was silence in the school-room, an unholy silence, and everyone stayed silent, like unripe dough. In vain did Uncle From look hopefully for a word or a glance from them. No one turned his head or said anything.

'Speak up, say something,' he said more quietly, 'say something, comrades, tell me what I've done. Who are you attacking? What do I have in life beside the struggle and Etja?'

'From, that's enough, you must leave us now,' said Antonie Aštalko. 'There's nothing more to discuss. Party discipline is sacred, – and Etja isn't even your daughter.'

'Oh yes, she is,' said Uncle From, 'and if you try to take her away, I'll not let her go. You can bring out the whole militia and all the secretaries you like. I shan't let her go. She's my daughter.'

But Etja was not in fact From's daughter, although she could not have belonged to anyone else except Uncle From. And Uncle From had nobody but her. When he came back from the war, he no

longer had wife, children, or anyone of his family left. It was then
that he found Etja. In that first year after the Revolution when a
great blizzard had covered all the fields, Uncle From was the
people's guard commander and he found her in the snow. 'She'll
be a daughter for me,' Uncle From said to them, 'she'll be my
child.' And so Etja stayed with Uncle From and became his daughter. But afterwards she was separated from him and sent off·to some
course in the city. For quite a long time no one knew anything of
Etja. Perhaps we would have forgotten her if Uncle From had not
kept coming to the fields all that spring and asking us endlessly:
'Hey, lads, what's happened to my girl, aren't you ever going to tell
me where my Etja has got to?'

Spring came into the valley, with greater urgency now, and
greater force. It was the time of the heaviest preparations for the
spring sowing. We had just finished off the slogans; we had painted
them on the walls with red mud. They were beautiful and enthusiastic and we all thawed out with happiness. But one morning that
spring we found that all those slogans on sowing and the collective
had been daubed over with blue paint and in the same paint was
written: FROM IS MY FATHER. It was written on all the house
walls. And on the Commune Centre house. People went from wall
to wall reading: FROM IS MY FATHER. And when they came to
the school building they saw Etja, so small and tiny, reaching up
on her tiptoes to write as high as she could FROM IS MY FATHER.

'Etja, hey, Etja,' Comrade Lako's voice startled her. But she did
not even look up at him. 'Hey, Etja,' he said, 'that old good-for-
nothing must have put you up to this.' Then Etja turned towards
the Secretary and raised her small, round face; she did not look the
least little bit like Uncle From but in his very same voice she said:
'No, no one put me up to it. It's simply that I know that From is my
father. Just so as you should know, Comrade Lako,' Etja added,
looking at the Secretary. While Etja was saying all this, her face
began to smile, that familiar smile which Uncle From always had
on his face. 'And so,' Etja's insistent voice made itself heard again,
'I'm going to stay with Uncle From. I want everyone in the world
to know.' She was defending herself with all her insignificant, be-
draggled, undergrown, diminutive being. 'I shall stay with him all

my life and be his daughter.' Her eyes shone like the morning sunlight and she herself seemed a piece of that sunlight, echoing over the valley like a huge bell ringing out for a festive occasion.

'She's the devil's own,' they said as they looked at her. 'She really is From's. ... Heaven preserve her, she's From himself . . .'

The red paint of the slogans and the blue paint of Etja's handiwork all mixed together on the wall gave birth in the morning to some unknown flower. The villagers thought it might be a flower that springs up along the field boundaries amongst the weeds . . .

Translated by Michael Samilov

Antun Šoljan

RAIN

I had stood by the window for a long while, waiting for the clock
to strike the hour. Looking through the window into the rain, and
at the wet roofs and façades of the neighbouring houses, I felt myself filled with a feeling of freedom, a freedom into which I would
soon plunge to allow it to carry me along with it. Of course this
was a special type of freedom. Every Saturday I was certain that
this freedom had something in store for me. Freedom is always full
of hidden possibilities. I didn't know what it could be that was
waiting for me but coming down the stairs I was almost certain
that maybe right here, just beyond the door, two steps further, on
the corner of the Funicular, or just a little further at the bus stop,
this very day something was waiting for me, for me only. Every
Saturday.

Looking at the rain, I had been trying to imagine what it was
that was waiting for me. (Just as at night, half-dreaming, one makes
up long complicated stories.) I am already too old to dream about
winning a lottery, or an inheritance, or about rich women. Whatever is waiting for me is something of a completely different kind,
it belongs to me alone, and it can satisfy no one but me. The rain
was falling incessantly in fine, invisible drops. The sky was completely uniform. It looked as if this was one of those early autumn
rains, still warm and pleasant for walking.

It was still raining when I came down the stairs and went out
through the office door. I opened my umbrella and felt smugly
self-satisfied that I had remembered to bring the umbrella in the
morning when there had not been the slightest sign of rain. For a
moment, I thought of the pleasure of walking in the rain, protected by the umbrella, looking out at that other world from the
dark dome of space beneath it. But as soon as I reached the first
corner, it was already Ilica, I felt the cold, wet wind coming down

the street and the drops stinging my face. I couldn't manage to protect myself completely with the umbrella. At first I held it slanted to the right, then to the left, and then quite level. Each time the wind blew more sharply, I had to hold the umbrella straight. Then the wind became steady, and I held the umbrella upright all the time, but my arm began to hurt and I had to change its position. The hand which I put in my pocket was wet. The rain was cold and unpleasant. And it had begun to rain harder and harder. People were hurrying to find shelter.

In Ilica, there was a large shop window, set back a little, so that it could serve as protection from the rain. I stopped in a doorway a bit further on, not in the shop window, because there were already too many people there. I thought they wouldn't like me, an intruder, to push in. I stopped there and shut the umbrella. Now it was hanging down along my arm like a huge dead black bat. Men carry only long umbrellas and only black umbrellas, which look like dead bats when shut. Women carry all kinds of umbrellas. I'm not even sure if I could tell what a dead bat looks like. But women too don't know what they look like, and they still carry different umbrellas. Perhaps bats don't die at all. It was raining harder and harder. A multitude of large black umbrellas was swinging along down the street. A separate world of umbrellas above people's heads, a world on a separate plane, as it were. Perhaps one of them is as lonely and purposeless as I am on this lower, lowest one. I swung my umbrella, not knowing what to do, where to go.

Looking for some solution among the passers-by, I noticed a woman I knew. She was dressed in a tight autumn suit. She was as good-looking as ever. Just as she had been good-looking three, no, four years ago, when I had seen her for the last time. She was walking along on the other side of the street, looking at the shop windows, without noticing me, and I could almost feel her lips, her scent, her arms, her voice, her hips. It all came to me across the street from out of the distant past. I was about to open my mouth to call out to her; I lifted my arm to wave, so that she would notice me when she turned around, and then I would say to her. ... But she was on the other side of the street, and the trams passed between us, clanging madly, they had already passed along four years of glistening rails in the drizzling autumn rain, rain that covered us all, isolated us, made us insignificant and separated us with curtains of streets. I know that if I went towards her, everything would become very complicated. We would shake hands warmly, and ask our questions, not daring to think about all those unpleasant occasions, the memory of which time does nothing at all to heal. I stood there, watching her as she walked away, along past the shop windows that were beginning to be lit up, into that curtain of grey, brown rain.

I couldn't do it, just as for a long time now I hadn't been able to find enough courage to go to Marija and tell her, that it's all over between us. It's been all over between us for a long time, but I ought to have told her in so many words, she'll never be able to realize it on her own. She won't want to realize. I'll just have to find a good, not too hurtful way, of putting it. Whenever I should have gone to Marija I was always too busy. Or too tired. Or in too good a mood. Just a wet rag.

No, I didn't feel like going to see Marija. Nor did I feel like going home. To my empty home, just an uncomfortable place to sleep. I didn't feel like going to the cinema, I didn't feel like going to the Hall. I mean the basket-ball club; for a long time I have been playing basket-ball which I don't like, in a club which I don't like, with people I don't like. Altogether I do far too many things which I don't like in the least. I could go to the 'Silver Stag'. The 'Silver Stag' is a pub at the end of Gaj Street. At least that's what it used to be called. Maybe there's something else written on the name plate now, but everyone still calls it the 'Silver Stag'. Boys of my mob always used to meet at the 'Silver Stag'; we used to drink white wine or plum brandy but this was a long time ago. Nowadays there are too many people in the 'Stag' who I don't know and don't like. I might say that the two things go together rather. At the time, when I used to drink with the boys from the mob, we used to like strangers and people we didn't know because we did not need them. But now we work only with strangers, who we need, who we don't like, who mean nothing to us as we mean nothing to them. I don't know where we'll end up if things carry on like this.

No, I couldn't go on to the 'Stag' on a day like this, to be melancholy about the past.

With my wet hand I took out a cigarette and made it too wet. I changed it into my dry hand but it was already too late. I stopped a passer-by and asked for a light. Out of habit I cupped my cigarette in my hand while lighting it. The man was in a hurry and went off quickly. I didn't have time to glance at him. He might have been that very messenger I was waiting for, and I hadn't even succeeded in guessing at the message from his face. I did not have the feeling that the cigarette was lit, until I had smoked to the end, in spite of the thick white smoke that formed in the cold air. Why hadn't I looked at the man? But this was not the problem that really bothered me. What was I going to do? What was I going to do – that was the real problem.

I stood there, smoking and staring at the pavement over which shoes were walking, trying to avoid the puddles. As I stared at the same spot I had the feeling that the shoes were walking on their own. Shoes too live in their own little world. There were all kinds of shoes. Some old, some new. About some there was nothing in particular to be said. But of course more of them were walking on their own. In every single one there lived a tyrant, an overlord, who made them miserable, lonely, with no purpose of their own. I looked at my shoes. Poor lonely shoes. They were of yellow leather and water was dripping from the umbrella on to their lonely toes.

I did not feel like doing anything. Going home. Going to the cinema. These things are too old, there's nothing more to be said about them. At home it's cold, I can only lie in bed, and read or sleep. For a long time now I have been bored with reading, but I can't sleep. I go to bed and turn off the light and can't get to sleep. I don't think about anything, but I can't get to sleep. In the cinema I've had enough of both good films and bad ones. I can still enjoy a western, but there are so few of these lately. I don't feel like going to a café, because I don't drink, and it's just as good for me to be here as at the café. What shall I do? WHAT SHALL I DO? That is the problem. This is the problem, not the cigarette, and not the cinema, and not Marija, and not home, no, none of these things. To find something to do, that is the problem.

There were other places where I could probably go. If you think
that I've no friends, you are mistaken. I've a very large number of
friends. They're very nice friends, and I like them all very much,
and I know that they like me more or less in the same way, and
there are a few more people I like very much but you don't know
them and there is no point in telling you about them now. But
they're all very pleasant people and we could play chess, or organize
a game of preference, or listen to new records that somebody has
just brought from abroad. We could all go somewhere together to
some place where the waiters know their job and where nobody
would throw us out before eleven o'clock; we could do all this if it
were all true. But I've dreamt it all up, because we don't really exist.
I only imagine us all like this. We're not together. I am here and
they are somewhere else. We do exist but we're not together. That's
why we're so pleasant. That's why we are such good friends. It
only seems we can do all this. It would be very pleasing for me to
expect something like that from us. I tried to draw something on
the pavement with the tip of my umbrella. But the rain went on
incessantly. It fell incessantly from on high, and everything around
was soaking wet. Even my hands were wet and I had the feeling
that they were unclean. And the idiotic feeling, that I could go
somewhere. That is, that I could really go somewhere, but that
there was just one thing which I had to decide before I went, where
I was going to go. Perhaps I could still go to a dance. To a really
good dance with a first-class jazz band. With very exclusive women.
With a trumpet. I could go, and I knew that there would be some
people there. That something was waiting for me there as well. But
I say again, this is only a pretence. I can only pretend that I could
move from this spot where I am fenced off by the iron bars of the
rain, fixed to the ground by the black nail of the umbrella. It's only
a pretence. To make this clear to you I should have started the
whole story in a completely different way, and thinking about it,
I am inclined to believe that everything should have been begun
in a different way. Something somewhere a long way back, from
the very beginning and so on. For to go to a dance was the same as
going nowhere. To go to Marija was like going nowhere. Anywhere I went was like going nowhere. It was just as good to stay

here, where we are and wait for the rain to stop. This too was going nowhere. Nowhere is everywhere, where there is emptiness, boredom, loneliness, rain and cold. Nowhere is everywhere, because each place is very much like this. Sometimes, we must add sometimes. Sometimes is everywhere. Sometimes is nowhere. Now is nowhere, and yesterday. This is how you realize, you're getting old.

The rain was still coming down, as if fish were falling, as if small, fine fish were falling, with silver bellies, odourless. I was standing in front of a shop window, tall, dark and straight, and I had the feeling that I was hung up by the collar, and my feet were not touching the ground. I was hanging like an enormous dead black bat. I was hanging like an umbrella. Nowhere was everywhere around me, nowhere was across the street, at the other shop window, nowhere was everywhere where it was raining, and where it wasn't raining. Nowhere was endless. I could be standing in the same way in any other place, not in front of the shop window, I could be doing something else instead of nothing, I could be. But you must understand, all this was just a pretence. Wherever I was like this, I would be nowhere. But this too did not change the irrefutable fact of my standing here.

The rain was still coming down, from nowhere into nowhere, and I was hanging like a dead bat, and women were afraid of me. It's as if I were remembering myself in similar situations. The rain is still falling. I am standing here and don't go away. I am not going to leave. At least, not at once. Maybe not tomorrow. Maybe not the day after. Maybe not at all this week.

Translated by Mirjana Pospielovsky

Notes on Authors

MATIJA BEČKOVIĆ: born 1939, Senta. Bečković is one of the young satirical generation. He studied Yugoslav literature in Belgrade and was involved in a number of student periodicals. His first published poetry was personal and lyrical – *Vera Pavladoljska*, 1961, and *Metak lutalica* (The Wandering Bullet), 1963 – but he subsequently made a name for himself in newspapers, journals and literary society with his incredibly witty political and social satire. His latest book of verse, *Tako je govorio Matija* (Thus spake Mathias), is typical of this style. Bečković's pen is so sharp that many writers are often as interested in his reaction to their works as that of the more accepted critics, but his own reputation as a poet is not yet fully established.

MIODRAG BULATOVIĆ: born 1930, Bijelo Polje. Probably the best known in the West of the younger Yugoslav writers, Bulatović combines a powerful feeling for his native Montenegran traditions with a technique of anarchy and chaos in his writing akin to Joyce and Beckett. His main works are *Djavoli dolaze* (The Devils are Coming), 1955, and the novels *Vuk i zvono* (The Wolf and the Bell), 1958, *Crveni petao leti prema nebu* (The Red Cockerel), 1959, and *Heroj na magarcu* (Hero on a Donkey), 1964. The last two have been translated into most European languages, including English. Bulatović used to live in Belgrade as a professional writer, but has now moved to Slovenia.

ŽIVKO ČINGO: born 1936, Velgošti, Ohrid. The most promising Macedonian prose writer, Čingo graduated at Skopje after studying Yugoslav literature and now works for Skopje Television. His main works are *Paskvelija*, 1963, and *Nova Paskvelija* (New Paskvelija), 1965, both collections of stories.

BORA ĆOSIĆ: born 1932, Zagreb. Ćosić began publishing as early as 1949 in Belgrade, where he has lived since before the war, and has written poetry, critical essays and prose, as well as film scripts and translations, notably of Mayakovsky. He has been connected with a number of journals and was one of the editors of the avant-garde review *Danas* from 1961 to 1963. He is a realist writer who has recently turned to satire; his novels include *Kuća lopova* (House of Thieves), 1956, *Vsi smrtni* (All Are Mortal), 1958, *Andjeo je došao po svoje* (The Angel Came for His Own), 1959, and *Priča o zanatima* (Tale of the Trades), 1967.

DOBRICA ĆOSIĆ: born 1921, Velika Drenova, near Kruševac. A political commissar with the partisans during the war and a politician for some time after it, Ćosić achieved fame with his first novel, *Daleko je sunce* (Far is the Sun), in 1951, and this work has remained a classic of the occupation and resistance movement. His other novels, *Koreni* (Roots), 1954, and *Deobe* (Divisions), 1961–3, are basically vividly drawn, realist novels, but Ćosić also gives indications of a more modernist approach, and his latest work, *Bajka* (A Fable), 1966, shows him ready to experiment with satire and parody. He is an excellent writer by any standards and his work has been translated into most European languages.

VLADAN DESNICA: born 1905, Zadar. A law graduate, Desnica studied in Zagreb and Paris, fought with the partisans, and practised law until 1950 when he began to devote himself exclusively to literature. He has published stories and a number of novels and is characterized by his satire, together with his psychological insight into his protagonists' motives. His best-known collections of stories are *Olupine na suncu* (Junk in the Sun), 1952, *Tu, odmah pored nas* (Here, Right Beside Us), 1956, and *Fratar sa zelenom bradom* (The Monk with the Green Beard), 1959, and his best-known novels, *Zimsko ljetovanje* (A Winter's Summer), 1950, and *Proljeća Ivana Galeba* (The Springs of Ivan Galeb), 1957. Desnica has also written for the theatre, and has written some poetry.

BOGOMIL DJUZEL: born 1939, Čačak. A graduate of English from Skopje, Djuzel is a young Macedonian poet of exceptional promise. He has translated from English and French and now works for television and the theatre. His books of verse are *Medovina* (Mead), 1962, *Alhemiska ruža* (Alchemist Rose), 1963, *Nebo, zemlja i sunce* (Sky, Land and Sun), 1963, and *Mironosci* (The Peacebringers), 1965.

DANIJEL DRAGOJEVIĆ: born 1934, Vela Luka, Korčula. A Croatian from Dalmatia, Dragojević studied history of art at Zagreb and has published several monographs in this field. He began with poetry in short prose pictures but now writes lyrical verse with strong religious undertones and an often elliptical style which derives something from painting techniques. His books of verse are: *Kornjača i drugi predjeli* (Tortoise and Other Landscapes), 1961, *U svom stvarnom tijelu* (In Your Real Body), 1964, *Svjetiljka i spavač* (Lantern and Sleeper), 1965, and *Nevrijeme i drugo* (Bad Weather and Others), 1968.

VLADO GOTOVAC: born 1930, Imotski. A philosophy graduate from Zagreb, Gotovac is the Croatian poet of his generation who most closely corresponds to the pattern of pure poetry of ideas. He writes prose as well as verse and copious critical studies, mainly concerned with poetry. He works for Zagreb Television and his books of verse include: *Pesme od uvijek* (Poems from Always), 1956, *Opasni prostor* (Dangerous Space), 1961, *Osjećanje mjesta* (Sense of Places), 1964, *Čujem oblake* (I Hear the Clouds), 1965, *Zastire se zemlja* (The Land is Covered), 1967, and *Čarobna špilja* (Enchanted Cave), 1969.

JOVAN HRISTIĆ: born 1933, Belgrade. A philosophy graduate, poet, critic and dramatist, and a one-time editor of *Književnost* and the avantgarde review *Danas*, Hristić now works as an editor with Nolit, and writes mainly for the stage. He has translated Bertrand Russell, T. S. Eliot, Henri Michaux and C. P. Cavafy, and his books of verse are *Dnevnik o Ulisu* (Ulysses' Diary), 1954, *Pesme 1952–56* (Poems 1952–56), 1959, and *Aleksandrijska škola* (Alexandrian School), 1963. He is also the author of a number of critical works on poetry.

ANTONIJE ISAKOVIĆ: born 1923, Belgrade. A partisan during the war, Isaković held several political posts before dedicating himself fulltime to literature when he became director of Nin in 1952. His first book of stories, *Velika deca* (Big Children), came out in 1953 and was followed by *Paprat i vatra* (Fern and Fire) in 1962, a collected edition of his stories in 1964 and *Prazni bregovi* (Empty Shores) in 1969. His stories have been adapted for radio, television and the cinema, and translated into several European languages. In the main they deal with war, the occupation and the resistance movement. Isaković is now director of the Belgrade publishing house Prosveta.

JURE KAŠTELAN: born 1919, near Omiš. A Slavist and a lecturer in Yugoslav literature at Zagreb, Kaštelan spent the war with the partisans and his early poetry was full of his dedication to the Revolution and the new regime. More recently, he has turned to a very personal and slightly exotic lyricism, which is often tinged with deep melancholy. He has published several books of poetry, of which the best are *Malo kamena i puno snova* (A Few Stones and a Lot of Dreams), 1957, and *Čudo i smrt* (Miracle and Death), 1964, and he has also published some prose, a number of serious academic studies on literature, and translations from Macedonian, French, Russian and Spanish.

DANILO KIŠ: born 1935, Subotica. A graduate in comparative literature at Belgrade, Kiš is a former editor of the student journal *Vidici*. His prose is lyrical, almost mystical, but none the less powerful in its often unexpected impact. His works to date are the novels *Mansarda* (The Attic), 1962, *Psalam 44* (Psalm 44), 1963, and *Bašta, pepeo* (Garden, Ashes), 1965. Kiš has also translated from French and written for the stage.

ERIH KOŠ: born 1913, Sarajevo. A Bosnian Serb, Koš is a well-established short story writer and novelist. He graduated from the Law Faculty in Belgrade in 1935, fought with the partisans in the war and spent some time in England immediately afterwards as a diplomat. His stories are concerned with his early Bosnian background and with the war, and his best novels, among which are *Veliki Mak* (Big Mac), 1956, *Il Tifo* (Typhoid), 1958, and *Imena* (Names), 1964, are satirical.

MIRKO KOVAČ: born 1938, Petrovići, near Bileća. Kovač began publishing while still a student in Belgrade in the student journals *Student*, *Vidici* and *Mladost*. He earns his living by writing, and his two novels, *Gubilište* (The Scaffold), 1962, and *Moja sestra Elida* (My Sister Elida), 1965, show considerable talent and promise.

LOJZE KOVAČIĆ: born 1928, Basle, Switzerland. Kovačič's family returned to Yugoslavia just before the war and he himself grew up in Slovenia during the war. He is closely associated with the Puppet Theatre in Ljubljana and writes drama (mainly for puppet plays) and prose, both novels and short stories. These include: *Novele treh* (Stories of Three Authors), 1954, *Ključi mesta* (The Keys of the Town), 1964, and the novel, *Deček in smrt* (The Boy and Death), 1968, as well as several books for children. Selections of his work have been translated from Slovene into Serbo-Croat, French, German and Danish.

KAJETAN KOVIČ: born 1931, Maribor. A member of the Slovene *Beseda* and *Perspektive* group, Kovač graduated in Comparative Literature at Ljubljana. He has translated such diverse figures as Rilke, Pasternak and Eluard. He began publishing poetry in 1953, in a book together with Zlobec, Pavcek and Menart, and has since written : *Prezgodnji dan* (Too Early Day), 1956, *Korenine vetra* (Roots of the Wind), 1961, *Improvizacije* (Improvisations), 1963, and *Ogenjvoda* (Fire-Water), 1965, and the novel *Ne bog ne žival* (Neither God nor Animal), 1965.

IVAN V. LALIĆ: born 1931, Belgrade. A graduate of the Law Faculty in Zagreb, where he worked for radio for some time before moving to Belgrade, Ivan Lalić is a former secretary of the Yugoslav Writers' Union. He now works as an editor with the publishing house Jugoslavija. Influenced by both Serbian and Croatian streams and highly conversant with all the modern European currents (he has translated from contemporary German, French, English and American poetry with excellent results), Lalić's own poetry has developed consistently over the years he has been publishing. He has close affinities with the poetry of Popa and Pavlović, but tends to confine his fluent and musical verse to more classical forms. His books of verse are *Bivši dečak* (Grown-Up Child), 1955, *Vetrovito proleće* (Windy Spring), 1956, *Velika vrata mora* (The Sea's Great Doors), 1958, *Melisa*, 1959, *Argonauti i druge pesme* (The Argonauts and Other Poems), 1961, *Vreme, vatre, vrtovi* (Time, Fires, Gardens), 1961, *Čin* (Act), 1963, *Krug* (Circle), 1968, and *Izbrane i nove pesme* (Selected and New Poetry), 1969.

RANKO MARINKOVIĆ: born 1913, Vis. Marinković is a Dalmatian Croat and a novelist, satirist, short story writer and dramatist. His collections of stories, *Proze* (Prose), 1948, *Pod balkonima* (Under the Balconies), 1953, *Ruke* (Hands), 1954, *Poniženje Sokrata* (The Humiliation of Socrates), 1959, and *Karneval i druge pripovijetke* (Carnival), 1964, were followed by his novel, *Kiklop* (The Cyclops), 1965. A former director of the National Theatre in Zagreb, Marinković now lectures in drama and writes theatre and literary criticism. His stories are witty and satirical and many of them are set in his native Dalmatia, showing the typical outlook and attitude of mind of the island and coastal people. *Kiklop* is a study of the revolt of an individual against the stifling atmosphere of a large town just before the war. Its modern baroque style is characteristic of Marinković's manner of writing.

DRAGOSLAV MIHAJLOVIĆ: born 1930, Ćuprija. Mihajlović is one of the newer generation of prose writers who came to the fore in the late sixties. His book of stories, *Frede, Laku noć* (Goodnight, Fred), was published in 1967, and his novel *Kad su cvetale tikve* (When the Pumpkins Blossomed), in 1969. His writing is set in the violent atmosphere of teenage gangland in Belgrade in the late forties and early fifties, and relies greatly on Mihajlović's personal experiences as a young man. (He himself was a boxer and later a political detainee after the break with Moscow). The novel *Kad su cvetale tikve* was adapted for the stage, and the adaptation made plainer many of the more indirect political references. It survived some ten performances and was then singled out for criticism by Tito himself.

SLAVKO MIHALIĆ: born 1928, Karlovac. After working for some time as a newspaperman in Belgrade and Zagreb, Mihalić launched the journal *Tribina* in 1952. Since then he has been involved as editor of a number of Croatian journals, and contributes regularly to many more. Secretary general of the Yugoslav Writers' Union, he is fundamentally a poet and critic but has also published novellas. His main collections of poetry are: *Komorna musika* (Chamber Music), 1954, *Put u nepostojanje* (Way into Unbeing), 1956, *Početak zaborava* (Beginning of Forgetting), 1957, *Godišnja doba* (Time of Year), 1961, *Ljubav za stvarnu zemlju* (Love for the Real Land), 1964, and *Prognana Balada* (Exiled Ballad), 1965. He now works as an editor for the Lykos publishing house.

BRANKO MILJKOVIĆ: 1934–61, Niš. Miljković studied philosophy at Belgrade and began publishing poetry in *Delo* and *Mladost* in 1955. His brilliant, eloquent verse with its startling images received immediate acclaim and his reputation went from strength to strength in the late fifties. His books of poetry include *Uzalud je budim* (I Wake Her in Vain), 1959, *Smrću protiv smrti* (Death against Death), with *Branimir Šćepanović*, 1959, *Poreklo nade* (The Origin of Hope), 1960, *Vatra i ništa* (Fire and Nothing), 1960, and *Krv koja svetli* (Blood Which Shines), 1961. He died by his own hand in Zagreb in February 1961. A posthumous edition of his collected verse was published in 1965. As well as his own poetry and some critical writing, Miljković translated widely, in particular from the French symbolists and the Russian poet, Osip Mandelstam. His death deprived Serbian letters of one of the most original poetic talents of the second post-war generation.

MIODRAG PAVLOVIĆ: born 1928, Novi Sad. Pavlović studied medicine in Belgrade and practised as a doctor for some time before becoming a professional writer. He now works as an editor for Prosveta. He first made his mark in the early fifties and has continued to publish poetry regularly to the present time. His books have been translated into most European languages and have made considerable impact in French and German, although he has not yet been translated at length into English. Pavlović also writes for the theatre and has a number of important critical works to his name. His books of poetry are 87 *pesama* (87 Poems), 1952, *Stub sećanja* (Pillar of Memory), 1953, *Oktave* (Octaves), 1957, *Mleko iskoni* (The Milk of Yore), 1963, *Velika skitija* (Great Scythia), 1969 and *Svetli i tamni praznici* (Light and Dark Spaces), 1970. He is also the compiler of the very important *Antologija srpskog pesništva* (Anthology of Serbian Poetry), 1964.

ŽIVOJIN PAVLOVIĆ: born 1933, Šabac. Zivojin Pavlović is a graduate of the Belgrade Academy of Applied Art and has become a very successful film producer. He writes film scripts, stories and novels, of which the best are the collections *Krivudava reka* (The Crooked River), 1963, and *Dve večeri u jesen* (Two Evenings towards Autumn), 1967, and the novels *Lutke* (Puppets), 1965, and *Dnevnik nepoznatog* (Diary of a Stranger), 1965.

RADOVAN PAVLOVSKI: born 1937, Niš. Pavlovski graduated in law at Skopje, and is one of the younger group of Macedonian poets whose writing has begun to transcend purely regional concepts. His books of poetry are *Suša, svadba i selidba* (Drought, Wedding and Moving), 1961, *Suša* (Drought), 1963, *Korabija* (Boat), 1964, and *Visoko podne* (High Noon), 1966.

BORISLAV PEKIĆ: born 1930, Titograd. One of the younger generation of prose writers, Pekić graduated in psychology at Belgrade and now works as a script writer in the film industry. So far he has produced a satirical novel, *Vreme Čuda* (Time of Miracles), 1965, and the first volume of a multi-volume novel with a Durrell-esque structure, *Graditelji* (The Builders); his immaculate prose style and modern approach show great promise for the future.

VASKO POPA: born 1922, Grebenac, near Bela Crkva. Perhaps the most significant Yugoslav poet of the post-war period, Popa studied in Bucharest, Vienna and Belgrade. His books of poems are *Kora* (Bark),

1953, *Nepočin-polje* (Unrest-Field), 1956, *Pesme* (Poems), 1965, and *Sporedno nebo* (Secondary Heaven), 1968, and he has been translated into most European languages. A selection of his poems, translated into English by Anne Pennington, was published in the Penguin Modern European Poets series in 1969. His poetry is concentrated and precise, trimmed of all externals, concerned with the development of ideas but full of the most striking metaphors and not without a profound visionary quality.

STEVAN RAIČKOVIĆ: born 1928. Nesresnica. On graduating from the Philosophy of Faculty at Belgrade, Raičković worked for a time with Radio Belgrade but is now a full-time editor with Prosveta. A lyrical, philosophical poet, his best books are *Pesma tišine* (Song of Silence), 1952, *Tisa*, 1961, *Kamena uspavanka* (Stone Lullaby), 1963, and *Prolazi rekom ladja* (Boat on the River), 1967. He has translated from French and English, notably Shakespeare's sonnets, and also writes books for children.

TOMAŽ ŠALAMUN: born 1941 Zagreb. Šalamun studied history of art at Ljubljana and is now a freelance writer there. He began publishing poetry in *Perspektive* in 1963, and thereafter in *Problemi* when *Perspektive* was banned. His two books of poetry are *Poker* (Poker), 1966, and *Namen pelerine* (Cloak's Purpose), 1968.

MEŠA SELIMOVIĆ: born 1910. Tuzla. Selimović graduated at Belgrade and for a long time worked in his home town of Tuzla as a teacher. During the war he was with the partisans and became a member of the committee investigating war crimes in Belgrade immediately afterwards. Later he became vice-president of the governmental Committee for Culture. After 1947 he returned to Sarajevo and worked as lecturer at the University, director of the National Theatre and chief editor of the Svetlost publishing house. He is also a former president of the Yugoslav Writers' Union. He began publishing with a book of war stories called *Prva četa* (The First Company), in 1951; the novel *Tišine* (Silences) followed in 1961, a book of novellas, *Tudja zemlja* (Alien Land), in 1962, and another book of stories, *Magla i mjesečina* (Mist and Moonlight), in 1965. By far his greatest work is the novel *Derviš i smrt* (Death and the Dervish) which came out in 1966. Selimović's fundamental talent is for psychological character analysis and *Derviš i smrt* is an admirable account of a strong man obsessed with vengeance and power, against the background of the Turkish administration in decline in Sarajevo.

LJUBOMIR SIMOVIĆ: born 1935, Titovo Užice. Simović studied Yugoslav literature at Belgrade before becoming a television programme director. He began publishing poetry as a student and has published *Slovenske elegije* (Slavonic Elegies), 1952, *Veseli grobovi* (Gay Tombs), 1961, *Poslednja zemlja* (The Last Land), 1964, and *Šlemovi* (Helmets), 1967. He has used humorous and direct poetry as well as satire, but more recently his poetry has become experimental and philosophical, and he has begun to show a deeper interest in his country's past history.

IVAN SLAMNIG: born 1930, Metković. A professional academic, Slamnig lectures in comparative literature at Zagreb University. He writes both prose and poetry, has translated from Russian, French and English, and his poetry has clearly been influenced by the directness and clarity of expression of the current of Anglo-Saxon poetry of the fifties. His book of verse are *Odran* (Early Morning), 1956, *Aleja posle svečanosti* (Avenue after Festivities), 1956, *Naronska siesta* (Naron Siesta), 1963, *Monografije* (Monographs), 1965 and *Limb* (Limbo), 1968, and his prose *Neprijatelj* (Enemy), 1959.

ANTUN ŠOLJAN: born 1932, Belgrade. One of the foremost Croatian figures of the younger generation, Šoljan graduated in English and German at Zagreb and has translated widely from these languages and from Russian (Eliot, Hemingway, Faulkner, Dos Passos, Steinbeck, Rilke, Blok). He is a professional writer and has appeared in print in most genres of literature – prose, poetry, the drama, criticism and essay. His main books of prose are the stories *Specijalni izaslanici* (Special Envoys), 1957, *Devet priča za moju generaciju* (Nine Tales for my Generation), 1966, and the novels *Izdajice* (The Traitors), 1963, and *Kratki izlet* (Outing), 1965. His books of poetry include *Na rubu svijeta* (On the Edge of the World), 1956, and *Izvan fokusa* (Out of Focus), 1957.

GREGOR STRNIŠA: born 1930, Ljubljana. Strniša studied English and German at Ljubljana and later became a member of the *'Beseda'*, *Revija 57* and *Perspektive* group which included Zajc, Taufer, Kovič and Šeligo. He is a freelance writer and writes for the stage as well as poetry. He is perhaps the most exotic of the Slovene group, but his poetry is sensitive, extremely musical and noteworthy for its highly developed use of historical and allegorical parallels with the present day. His main books of verse are *Mozaiki* (Mosaics), 1959, *Odisej* (Odysseus), 1963, *Samorog* (Unicorn), 1966 and *Brobdingnag*, 1968.

VENO TAUFER: born 1935, Ljubljana. A Slovene poet, Taufer graduated in comparative literature from Ljubljana. He published in *Beseda* and *Perspektive* and was chief editor of *Revija 57*. He spent three years in England – 1966–9 – working for the BBC and has now returned to Ljubljana to work in the drama section of Slovenian television. He has translated, notably from Macedonian and from English, and his main books of verse are *Svinčene Zvezde* (Leaden Stars), 1958, *Jetnik prostosti* (Prisoner of Freedom), 1963, *Vaje in naloge* (Exercises and Homework), 1969. He has also written for the theatre.

ALEKSANDAR TIŠMA: born 1924, Horgoš. Tišma graduated from Belgrade University in philosophy and spent some time working for a newspaper. He is now the director of the Matica Srpska publishing house in Novi Sad and an editor of the journal *Letopis matice srpske*. His prose is concerned with the problems of the post-war generation and the psychology of violence. His books include *Krivice* (Guilt), 1961, *Nasilje* (Violence), 1965, and the novel *Za crnom devojkom* (In Search of the Dark Girl), 1969.

DANE ZAJC: born 1929, Žgornja Javorščica. One of the Slovenian poets connected with *Revija 57* and *Perspektive*, Zajc has published several books of verse, including *Požgama trava* (Burnt Grass), 1958, *Jezik iz zemlje* (A Tongue from Earth), 1961, and *Ubijavci kač* (Snake Killers), 1969. His poetry is hermetic and makes use of symbolism to a large extent, and his latest collection shows a certain similarity in approach to the concise, metaphorical style of Vasko Popa.

Some other books published by Penguins
are listed on the following pages

The Writing Today Series

An interesting venture by Penguins which aims to inform the English-speaking reader of new developments in the literature of other countries.

The following volumes are available

Australian Writing Today
Writers in the New Cuba
England Today : The Last Fifteen Years
New Writing in Czechoslovakia
Italian Writing Today
French Writing Today
South African Writing Today
Polish Writing Today
Latin American Writing Today
South African Writing Today
German Writing Today
Canadian Writing Today

PENGUIN MODERN EUROPEAN POETS

Vasko Popa

This is the first collection of poems by Vasko Popa, the
leading Yugoslavian poet, to appear in English translation.
A rich poetic imagination and extreme concentration of
language lend special fibre to the 'new epic' construction of
Popa's poems, which are arranged in cycles. Vasko Popa
was recently awarded the Austrian Lenau Prize.

PENGUIN MODERN EUROPEAN POETS

Zbigniew Herbert

Few countries have suffered more of the brutalities of
Communism and Fascism than Poland. Yet Zbigniew
Herbert, the most classical of its poets, is neither nationalist
nor Catholic. He speaks for no party. *Avant-garde* in
manner, but controlled, precise, and honest in thought, he
stands aside from the chaos all round him, ironically bent
on survival. His is the voice of sanity.

PENGUIN MODERN EUROPEAN POETS

Four Greek Poets

CAVAFY
ELYTIS
GATSOS
SEFERIS

Of the four Greek authors represented in this volume,
Cavafy and Seferis are poets with international reputations
and Seferis has won a Nobel Prize. Elytis and Gatsos, who
belong to a younger generation, are fully established in
Greece and now winning recognition abroad.

Not for sale in the U.S.A.

PENGUIN MODERN EUROPEAN POETS

Three Czech Poets

VÍTĚZSLAV NEZVAL
ANTONÍN BARTUŠEK
JOSEF HANZLÍK

This volume represents three generations of Czech poetry.
Vítězslav Nezval (born in 1900) adopted surrealism to
express the paradoxes of experience, above all in his briefer
impressions of Prague. Antonín Bartušek (1921), like Eliot
(whose influence he admits), is a master of suggestion :
there are hints of greatness in his language and rhythms, in
his concern with life and death. With Josef Hanzlík (1938)
we enter the contemporary world : here is a poet who,
freshly and fluently, records his response to a world of
political violence.

MILOVAN DJILAS

Conversations with Stalin

'By any test this is an extraordinary and absorbing book – a classic contribution to the great controversies about Socialism and freedom' – Michael Foot in *Tribune*

Milovan Djilas was for years Tito's closest associate. As Vice-President of Yugoslavia he sat in the inner cabinet and led three important missions to Moscow prior to Tito's break with Stalin. This book records the creeping disenchantment of a sincere revolutionary with the effects of socialism in practice and with Russia's cynical imperialism. Djilas's opinions, courageously voiced in *The New Class*, in newspaper interviews, and in his championship of the Hungarians in 1956, resulted in his ostracism and repeated imprisonment.

'Here, for the first time, a man who was a senior Communist politician, who has talked as a Communist with Stalin and his creatures, relaxed, behind drawn blinds, writes of what he saw and heard as a human being writing about human beings' – Edward Crankshaw in the *Observer*

Not for sale in the U.S.A. or Canada

A

Ar
cei
of
do
rai
Me
wh
me
Sta